THE AMERICAN MEDICAL ASSOCIATION
CHILDREN: HOW TO UNDERSTAND THEIR SYMPTOMS

Editors-in-chief Charles B. Clayman, MD
Jeffrey R. M. Kunz, MD

**RANDOM HOUSE
NEW YORK**

Library of Congress Cataloging-in-Publication Data

Main entry under title:

Children, how to understand their symptoms.

Includes index.
1. Children – Diseases – Diagnosis – Charts,
   diagrams, etc.
2. Symptomatology – Charts, diagrams, etc.
I. American Medical Association.

RJ50.A44   1986   618.92'0075   85-25681
ISBN 0-394-74046-7

Manufactured in the United States of America

2 4 6 8 9 7 5 3

First American Edition

Preface

Few events can be more alarming or make a parent feel more helpless than the sudden illness of a child. Especially with children too young to describe their symptoms clearly, the parent is often in a quandary about what to do, yet hesitant to call the child's pediatrician for fear of feeling foolish later if the problem turns out to be minor.

No one, of course, can make an instant diagnosis, and this book does not pretend to do that. But it does deal with the common childhood health problems and discusses those that most frequently cause parental anxiety. It provides the answers most physicians give to the questions most parents ask.

By following the easy-to-read decision charts in this book, you can learn to tell the difference between minor problems and conditions that need attention urgently. The charts tell you when you should call the pediatrician; they identify the signs (such as rapid or noisy breathing) of a potentially dangerous illness; they tell you what you ought to do in an emergency. As a matter of fact, this book contains illustrated sections on emergency and first-aid treatment.

But this is more than a book on infant care. It contains charts on normal growth and development. It addresses the problems of children into their late teens. Whether you have a baby, a child or an adolescent, this book will make you a more effective parent. Its purpose is to help you play a more *informed* role in the healthy development of your son or daughter.

These self-help charts have been developed under medical supervision, tested on patients under real conditions and reviewed by American medical authorities. We are pleased to add this book to the American Medical Association Home Health Library, a series of books aimed at improving the health education of the American public.

James H. Sammons, M.D.
Executive Vice President
American Medical Association

The American Medical Association Home Health Library

Contents

Introduction

The symptoms

1 Babies under one

page 27

2 Children of all ages

page 43

3 Adolescents

page 115

From babyhood to adolescence

A child's primary physical characteristics are determined from conception. The embryo is the mass of rapidly dividing cells that forms the basis of the new life. Each cell of the embryo contains genetic information carried in the chromosomes. The chromosomes are composed of chains of smaller units (genes). Certain single genes control a specific aspect of the baby's development (such as color of hair). Height is determined by several groups of genes, making this trait complex. While we know that smoking and drinking during pregnancy has an adverse effect on the fetus, a child's potential for good health is to a large extent determined before the pregnancy. The care a baby receives both in the uterus and during childhood cannot change the fundamental characteristics of inheritance. However, correct nutrition, good health care and a secure home environment may modify the good or bad effects.

You can affect your child's development in many ways. Most children, in the absence of a serious inherited disease or birth defect, will grow and develop physical and mental skills within a healthy, stimulating and safe environment. A varied diet of fresh foods will encourage growth, and immunization against infection will prevent diseases during childhood and later in life. Fresh air and exercise encourage the development of a healthy heart and healthy lungs and the growth of strong bones and muscles. Rapid acquisition of mental skills and physical coordination, whatever your child's level of ability, can be promoted during childhood through play and school activities. While young children need protection from external dangers (such as traffic), older children and adolescents should be taught about the risks of unhealthy habits such as smoking, drinking and drug-taking (see also *Keeping your child healthy,* p.13). Be alert to the possibility of illness and take action to prevent a treatable disease from causing long-term damage.

You are the best person to observe and monitor your child's growth and development. You can use the tables on pp.122-125 to record weight and height and make comparisons with average rates of growth. And you can note whether your child's progress through the milestones of physical and mental development roughly matches the pattern described. In addition, day-to-day contact with your child will give you a special sense of what is normal and will allow you to notice any abnormal development. Reference to the diagnostic charts (see *How to use the charts,* p.22) will help you to decide on the best course if your child seems to be sick. Discuss any concerns with your pediatrician.

Conception and fetal growth

If an egg is penetrated by a sperm in the fallopian tube shortly after ovulation, it becomes fertilized. It takes only one of the millions of sperm ejaculated during intercourse to fertilize an egg. As soon as the sperm's nucleus joins with the egg's nucleus, a process known as cell division begins.

week 7, the limbs are beginning to develop as buds and the intestines are almost completely formed. All internal organs are in place by week 8. By week 10, the embryo looks recognizably human. During these early weeks the embryo is most vulnerable to damage from alcohol, tobacco, drugs and infection.

The path of the fertilized egg
The cells, which contain chromosomal information from the father and mother, divide every few hours as the fertilized egg travels along the fallopian tube toward the uterus. The ball of cells embeds itself in the uterine wall about a week after fertilization.

Fertilization by one sperm usually occurs about a third of the way along the tube.

The fertilized egg subdivides to form a ball of cells.

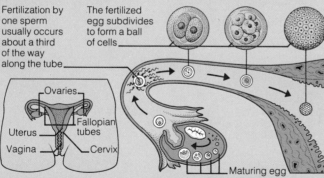

Ovaries
Uterus
Fallopian tubes
Vagina
Cervix
Maturing egg

The developing embryo
The developing baby is called an embryo until about the 12th week of pregnancy. Between weeks 5 and 7, the embryo, though small, has begun to develop rapidly. By

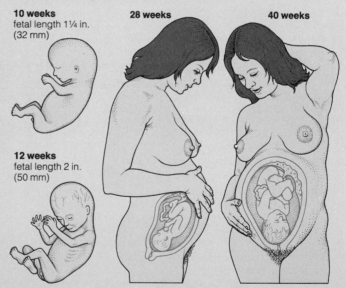

10 weeks
fetal length 1¼ in. (32 mm)

28 weeks

40 weeks

12 weeks
fetal length 2 in. (50 mm)

The fetus
From week 13 the fetus is completely formed. In the uterus, the fetus swims at the end of its umbilical cord. By the fourth month the genital organ develops into a penis or clitoris, an event that was decided when sperm met egg. By mid-pregnancy the inner ear is completely developed and the fetus responds to a variety of sounds (such as loud music) by moving. About six inches long at four months, the fetus is working its hands and feet, exploring its surroundings. Nevertheless, the brain of the fetus is very immature, and it is unlikely that he or she has the ability to think. However, the fetus does respond to external stimuli.

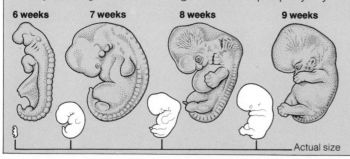

6 weeks **7 weeks** **8 weeks** **9 weeks**

Actual size

The placenta

A healthy placenta is the most important factor in the successful growth and development of your baby. It provides the link between the mother's body and the fetus.

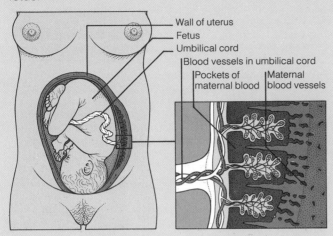

Wall of uterus
Fetus
Umbilical cord
Blood vessels in umbilical cord
Pockets of maternal blood | Maternal blood vessels

The fetus is attached to the placenta by the umbilical cord – three intertwined blood vessels. Blood flows from the fetus to the placenta, where it absorbs oxygen, nutrients and protective antibodies from the mother's blood. The placenta itself is firmly rooted to the wall of the uterus throughout pregnancy. After delivery of the baby, what is commonly called the afterbirth becomes separated and is expelled.

The newborn baby

At birth, the placenta stops supplying the baby with oxygen and food, and stops taking away waste products. A baby is born with instincts and reflexes that help him or her survive the first few days of life. For example, during breast-feeding, a baby will naturally latch on to the mother's nipple and suck. The bladder of the infant empties automatically.

A small baby or a premature one may require special treatment at birth. Some of the body's systems, particularly the respiratory system, may be immature. A premature baby may have difficulty breathing, feeding and maintaining his or her body temperature. In an incubator, the baby's signs can be carefully monitored and he or she can be protected from infection and certain disorders related to fetal maturity until the systems become fully developed. A premature baby also may have difficulty grasping, have very little fat, and may seem "floppy" (a term that indicates that the infant's neuromuscular development is immature).

Appearance of the newborn
The head: Pressure on the head during birth and bone movement in the skull for the protection of the brain commonly lead to temporary changes in the head's shape. It will seem proportionally large in comparison to the rest of the body.

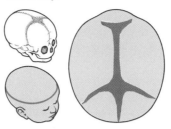

The fontanelles
At birth, the skull bones are made up of areas of cartilage with spaces between them. The larger ones are known as the fontanelles. During birth the areas of cartilage interlock to protect the brain from damage. A baby has two main "soft spots," or fontanelles, one at the front and one at the back of the head.

The skin: The skin is rarely perfect. A baby who has been undernourished in the uterus or a baby of a long pregnancy is likely to have exceptionally wrinkled skin. Red or blue patches, jaundice and small, white spots are also common. The skin usually clears by the end of the first month. Vernix, a white, waxy substance, and lanugo, fine body hair, often cover parts of the body. Vernix is absorbed by the skin and lanugo will rub off after 1 to 2 weeks.

Blood tests on the newborn
A blood test is usually carried out on every baby one week after birth to test for phenylketonuria, a disorder in which the body is unable to break down certain proteins. The blood is usually taken from the heel. Additional blood tests may be carried out to check on the level of the chemical bilirubin in the body if the baby is jaundiced, or to check for any known hereditary biochemical disorder.

Examination of the newborn
The following tests are carried out, usually before one week of age, to detect any congenital defects.
- **backbone** – checked for a swelling or ulcer that may indicate spina bifida
- **navel** – checked for a swelling typical of an umbilical hernia
- **face** – checked for a hare lip and cleft palate
- **face** – checked for features of Down's syndrome (upward-slanting eyes and puffy eyelids)
- **anus** – checked for imperforate anus
- **genitals** – checked for doubtful sex
- **feet** – checked for club foot
- **hips** – checked for dislocation of the hip
- **eyes** – checked for discharge and physical defects

The Apgar scale

At birth, 5 simple tests are carried out to assess the general well-being (particularly the breathing) of a newborn baby. A score between 0 and 2 is given for the following and the total is known as the Apgar score:

A score of 4 or less indicates severe breathing difficulties (asphyxia). Most babies score between 7 and 10. The test is repeated after 5 minutes, by which time the score has usually improved.

What is tested	Points given		
	2	1	0
Color	Pink all over	Blue extremities	Blue all over
Breathing	Regular	Irregular	Absent
Heart rate	More than 100 beats a minute	Less than 100 beats a minute	Absent
Movement	Active	Some movement	Little or no movement
Reflex response	Cries	Whimpers	Absent

The growing child

At the moment of conception, one complete cell is formed that contains the genetic information (inherited from each parent) that not only determines the sex of the new child, but also many of his or her characteristics. Different genes define physical traits (such as height) and the rate at which a child develops. For example, a child whose parents were relatively late to walk may follow a similar pattern of development. A child's potential for good health is also genetically determined – a child may inherit a susceptibility to some diseases at conception.

A growing body requires both nutrients and exercise. A child who is happy, eats a well-balanced diet (see *Keeping your child healthy,* p.13) and who regularly plays or participates in sports will develop normally and establish a basis for long-term good health.

Although the fundamental characteristics of a child cannot change, the effects of inherited physiological traits can be modified. For example, if a child has a susceptibility to ear infections, prompt treatment each time the symptoms occur should alleviate permanent damage to the ear mechanism. Poor or good quality teeth are inherited. If a parent has poor quality teeth, he or she can help safeguard the teeth of the young child by seeing that the child brushes with a fluoride toothpaste and has regular checkups.

Emotional development

From birth a child has individual needs that, in infancy, are reflected in the baby's feeding and sleeping patterns. The infant is entirely dependent on his or her parents. Gradually, the child begins to assert his or her individuality and broaden relationships to include those outside the family. The environment in which a child grows affects his or her emotional development. If the home environment is loving and secure, a child is usually able to adjust to emotional change relatively easily.

As a child develops certain skills (see *Milestones,* opposite), his or her personality begins to mature. For example, between the first and third years a child is often "difficult" as he or she practices and builds on newfound skills (see *The terrible twos,* p.66). During nursery and school years, a child's environment is widened and children begin to form new relationships independent of those formed at home. The time of greatest emotional development is during adolescence. The physical development of puberty is accompanied by increased hormonal activity that affects the adolescent's feelings about him- or herself. Adolescence is usually a time of experimentation. For example, smoking, drinking and sexual relationships are often experienced for the first time. See also chart 51, *Adolescent behavior problems.*

Hyperactivity

Some children are constantly physically and emotionally restless. They are known as *hyperactive,* a type of behavior that is at one end of the spectrum of "normal" development. Hyperactive children demand a great deal of patience and understanding. Occasionally, help from outside the family is necessary. Hyperactive children often need relatively little sleep.

Changing proportions and features

There are 2 "growth spurts" in the development of a child, one during the first year of life and the other during puberty. In the years between, the rate of growth declines gradually each year, reaching its lowest point immediately before the dramatic development of puberty begins.

At birth, a baby's head is a quarter of his or her body length, and as wide as the shoulders. The legs account for ⅜ of body length at birth. Gradually, these proportions change so that, by adulthood, the head is less than ⅛ and the legs are ½ of the total body length.

During puberty, differences between the male and the female become notable. On average, the male grows taller: during adolescence the male's height generally increases by 11 in. (28 cm) and the female's by 8 in. (20 cm). Change begins in the legs and progresses to the trunk, where most of the growth occurs. Muscle bulk, particularly in the male, increases as chest, shoulders and arms become noticeably muscular. Facial muscles develop, again more noticeably in the male. The forehead becomes more prominent and the jaw and chin lengthen so the "chubby" look of the young child is lost. During adolescence, the diameter of the head grows and the skull thickens by 15 percent. In the adolescent female, the pelvis broadens and layers of fat are laid down on the hips, making them wider than the male's. Breast development occurs as the first sign of puberty in two thirds of girls. In one third, the first sign is pubic hair. See also chart 50, *Delayed puberty,* and *The reproductive system,* p.12.

Newborn	2 years	5 years	8 years	Adolescents

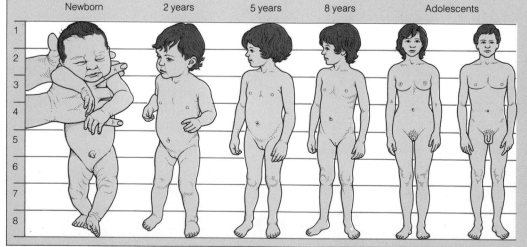

During the first eighteen years of life the body is constantly growing and changing. In this time it undergoes radical change – in total body length, weight, proportions and shape. The features of the face gradually become more defined. At birth the weight of a baby equals 5 percent of its young adult weight. In the first year alone a baby's growth rate triples. In the second year, while growth is still rapid it is slower – the baby now weighs four times the birth weight. By the age of ten, 50 percent of young adult weight has been attained. Between infancy and adolescence the legs change from ⅜ of the total body length to ½, and the head from ¼ to ⅛.

Developing skills

Immediately after birth a baby is unable to walk or speak. The development of these and many other skills – physical, mental and social – is a gradual process, the speed of which varies from child to child. At birth, the nervous system, which controls all conscious and unconscious movement and thought, is immature. A child becomes capable of developing certain skills only as his or her nervous system matures. In most children, development begins with control of the head and progresses down the body to control of the arms, trunk and legs. This control allows the child to develop new skills known as *milestones* (see right), which are useful as a means of assessing a child's overall development.

Factors affecting the rate of development

There is a wide variation in the rate at which each child progresses, although there is a predictable age by which most children have developed certain skills. The variation is due to several factors, particularly the rate at which the nervous system develops (see above), but also the rate of development that has been determined (inherited) at conception (see *From babyhood to adolescence,* p.6). The home environment plays an important part in developing the child's potential for certain skills. Speaking to and playing with the child is essential for language development and to encourage him or her to practice new physical skills. Introducing the child to other children at the age of 2 to 3 years will provide him or her with plenty of stimulation. Girls often begin to walk and/or talk at an earlier age than boys. The premature child has missed out on some growing time in the uterus and the time he or she takes to progress should be calculated from the full-term pregnancy date, not the actual date of birth. Sight and hearing are particularly crucial to a child's progression, for it is through the senses that a child can watch, learn and imitate. Any defect will therefore affect development (see chart 27, *Eye problems;* chart 28, *Disturbed or impaired vision;* chart 29, *Painful or irritated ear;* and chart 30, *Deafness*). A child's level of intelligence will also affect development in certain areas, such as the use of muscles and bones in a coordinated way.

How a child develops skills

For the first 2 to 3 months after birth a baby will move involuntarily in response to sound, touch and movement. For example, he or she will grasp the parent's finger placed in the palm. These reflex actions gradually give way as the child's muscles strengthen (see *Muscles,* p.10). Often, the baby's actions progress from seemingly unconnected movements to the ability to control part of his or her body. Walking is achieved in numerous stages, from lying with head raised, to sitting unsupported, to crawling, to tottering, to standing and, finally, to walking unaided. A baby begins to develop hand-eye coordination from birth. He or she watches objects, learns to focus and judge distances, and develops the connection of seeing and doing by watching his or her hands. Both hand-eye and body-limb coordination can be encouraged in the child (for example, through practicing ball games). At birth, a child is able to communicate his or her needs by crying. After vision and hearing are sufficiently developed, a child will watch the parent's mouth intently to learn how to smile and will listen to the parents speaking before attempting to imitate sounds. A child is able to concentrate on learning only one skill at a time, often forgetting a recently mastered skill that will appear again at a later time. (For example, some children will start learning to walk, then suddenly become more interested in learning to talk, and so put their attempts at learning to walk "on hold" for a while.)

Milestones

The dates below are the average ages at which children develop skills. Remember that each child develops at a different rate.

6 weeks
- Smile

10 weeks
- Roll over from a sideways position onto the back

4 to 6 months
- Raise head and shoulders from a face-down position
- Sit up unsupported

7 months
- Pass a toy from one hand to the other

8 months
- Try to feed him- or herself with a spoon

9 months
- Rise to a sitting position

12 months
- Understand simple commands
- Stand unsupported for a second or two

18 months
- Walk unaided

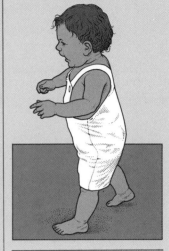

20 months
- Achieve bowel control

2 years
- Stay dry during the day

3 years
- Talk in simple sentences
- Stay dry during the night

4 years
- Get dressed and undressed (with a little help)

5 years
- Draw a figure with separate body and limbs

Your child's body

The skeleton

The skeleton is a rigid structure that supports and protects the body and its organs. At birth, the skeleton consists mostly of cartilage, a soft, fibrous, flexible tissue. During childhood, bone forms within this tissue at certain developmental stages until, during adolescence, the skeleton matures.

Ossification

Bone is an active and living (but hard) tissue that grows, develops and renews itself. Old bone cells are constantly reabsorbed and new ones are formed. In childhood, the growth of bones involves a process of constant remodeling known as ossification. Most growth of the long bones takes place in one region – the epiphysis, or the "growing" end of the bone. Injury to this region may impair growth. Both exercise and adequate supplies of vitamins (particularly vitamin D), minerals (particularly calcium) and protein in the diet encourage the growth of healthy bones (see also *Keeping your child healthy*, p.13).

Structure of the bone
The cells in the hard part of the bone are arranged in thousands of cylinders that help distribute the forces acting on the bones. The larger bones are hollow, giving strength with the minimum of weight. The marrow, the fatty center of the bone, produces most of the body's white cells and all of its red cells. In a young child, all bone contains blood-producing marrow (the marrow remains active [blood-forming] only in the bones of the trunk of an adult). Each bone contains many blood vessels.

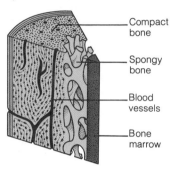

- Compact bone
- Spongy bone
- Blood vessels
- Bone marrow

Bones

- Skull
- Collarbone (clavicle)
- Shoulder blade (scapula)
- Breastbone (sternum)
- Humerus
- 12 pairs of ribs
- Radius
- Ulna
- Pelvic bone
- Sacrum
- Thighbone (femur)
- Kneecap (patella)
- Shinbone (tibia)
- Fibula

Muscles

- Pectoralis major (moves shoulder)
- Serratus anterior (supports shoulder)
- Biceps (bends arm)
- Flexor digitorum superficialis (bends fingers)
- External oblique (part of abdominal wall)
- Rectus abdominis (strengthens abdominal wall)
- Sartorius (bends leg)
- Quadriceps (straightens leg)
- Tibialis anterior (aids walking)

Symptoms

The most common problems in childhood include fracture of the bones, dislocation of joints, and muscle strains. Conditions such as bone infections and tumors are rare. Occasionally, the spine tends to curve sideways, a condition known as scoliosis that requires early recognition for satisfactory treatment. An injured child who lies still or who refuses to move the damaged limb has probably suffered a serious injury, while a child who uses an injured arm or hand freely during play is unlikely to have done much damage.

See also the following diagnostic charts: **45** Painful arm or leg **46** Painful joints **47** Foot problems

Muscles

All movement of the body and its internal organs is carried out by the muscles. Muscles are made up of thousands of muscle fibers that contract to produce movement. The voluntary muscles control body movements and the involuntary muscles are responsible for movement within the body. For example, involuntary muscles in the digestive tract contract rhythmically to propel food through the gut. Muscles thrive on work. Exercise improves the circulation of blood in the muscles, increases their bulk and improves their chemical efficiency. At birth, babies are unable to move purposefully but, gradually, the young child achieves control over the body and the central nervous system and muscles develop. At birth, the baby has certain instinctive reactions known as reflex movements. These gradually become less prominent as the baby's range of voluntary movement develops.

The heart and circulatory system

The heart is the center of the body's circulatory system. Blood, which carries nutrients and oxygen and takes away waste products, is pumped through the body by the heart, first to the lungs where oxygen is added and carbon dioxide eliminated, and then back to the heart for distribution to the brain and other major organs. Arteries carry blood away from the heart, and veins return the blood to it. In the fetus, two temporary paths (which close shortly after birth) allow the blood to bypass the nonfunctioning lungs. Oxygenation of the blood takes place in the placenta.

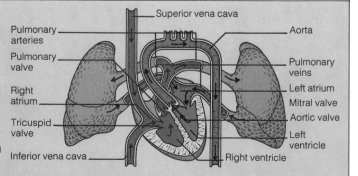

- Pulmonary arteries
- Pulmonary valve
- Right atrium
- Tricuspid valve
- Inferior vena cava
- Superior vena cava
- Aorta
- Pulmonary veins
- Left atrium
- Mitral valve
- Aortic valve
- Left ventricle
- Right ventricle

Symptoms

If there is any congenital heart disease, it is discovered during tests at birth or shortly thereafter. Rapid breathing and difficulty eating in an infant, and poor physical development in a child, are occasionally symptoms of a heart disorder. Serious heart disorders in children are rare, but congenital heart disease accounts for almost half the major physical defects present at birth.

Structure of the heart
The heart is a muscular organ made up of two pumps. Each pump is divided into two compartments linked by valves: the main pumping chambers are the left and right ventricles. Blood that has been freshly oxygenated by the lungs enters the left atrium, passes through the mitral valve into the left ventricle and is pumped throughout the body via an arterial trunk known as the aorta. The blood then returns to the heart, entering the right atrium, passing through the tricuspid valve to the right ventricle, which pumps it to the lungs to receive oxygen.

Respiratory system

Respiration, the process of inhaling and exhaling, allows a child's body to absorb the oxygen it needs to enable the body's cells to produce energy and to discharge carbon dioxide, a waste product of that process. The respiratory system consists of the lungs and the tubes through which air passes on its way to and from the lungs. In the uterus, the fetus receives oxygen from the mother via the placenta.

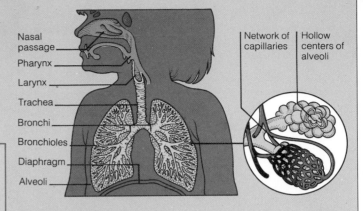

Nasal passage
Pharynx
Larynx
Trachea
Bronchi
Bronchioles
Diaphragm
Alveoli
Network of capillaries
Hollow centers of alveoli

Symptoms

The most common breathing problems in childhood are due to infections and asthma. Young children are particularly susceptible to viruses until they have developed immunity to the common ones. Sore throat, runny nose, coughing and raised temperature often accompany a cold. With asthma, the child has attacks in which the small airways in the lungs become narrow and, thus, make breathing difficult.

Asthmatic attacks tend to become less frequent as the child grows. Fast, noisy and difficult breathing is symptomatic of a breathing disorder.

See also the following diagnostic charts: **3** Fever in babies **9** Feeling sick **14** Fever in children **18** Headache **31** Runny or stuffed-up nose **32** Sore throat **33** Coughing **34** Fast breathing **35** Noisy breathing

The respiratory tract

The respiratory tract consists of the lungs and the tubes through which air passes on its way to and from the lungs. Air breathed in through the nose and mouth passes down the trachea (windpipe) and enters the lungs through a branching tree of tubes (the bronchi and bronchioles).

The lungs themselves are sponge-like organs made up of millions of air sacs (alveoli). The thin linings of these sacs bring the blood into close contact with the breathed-in air, allowing oxygen to pass into the bloodstream, and carbon dioxide to pass out to be exhaled into the atmosphere.

Brain and nervous system

Your child's ability to develop both physical and mental skills is largely determined by the gradual development of the nervous system. This system is made up of the brain, spinal cord, nerves, ganglia, and parts of the receptor organs. The nervous system controls all conscious activities and is also responsible for unconscious movement of the stomach and intestines.

Development of the nervous system

The nervous system is made up of nerve cells that receive information from inside and outside your child's body. At birth, the connections between these cells are immature and the brain is not fully developed. As your baby grows, he or she acquires better control over his or her internal organs and muscles. Your child also becomes capable of intellectual tasks (such as speech). These abilities arrive at predictable ages (see *Milestones,* p.9).

The brain

The brain is a complex organ nourished by a dense network of blood vessels. It is connected to the spinal cord by the brain stem and has three main parts. The two cerebral hemispheres control functions including speech, memory and intelligence. The cerebellum is responsible for coordinating movement and balance. The brain stem contains nerve centers which control "automatic" functions.

Nerves

The peripheral nerves run from the spinal cord to all other parts of the body. Most large nerves serve to convey information to the brain and instruct muscles to respond to that information. Other nerves have one or the other of these functions. An artery and vein usually accompany the nerves found throughout the body.

Symptoms

The most common childhood disorder of the nervous system is fainting. Convulsions are more common in infancy than in later childhood. They must always be investigated. Delay in reaching milestones (see *Milestones,* p.9)

may indicate an underlying problem.

See also the following diagnostic charts: **17** Fainting, dizzy spells and seizures **18** Headache **20** Confusion **21** Speech difficulties

The special senses

Sight and hearing provide your child with the most information. Your child builds up a visual vocabulary from birth, learning how to focus and coordinate movement with sight. Hearing involves the conversion of sound waves into electric impulses for transmission by nerves to the brain (see *The structure of the ear,* p.81).

Structure of the eye

The eyeball is a complex structure consisting of three layers: the sclera, visible as the white of the eye; the choroid layer, rich in blood vessels that supply the sensitive inner lining of the eyeball; and the retina, which contains the light-sensitive nerve cells that pick up images and transmit the information through the optic nerve to the brain.

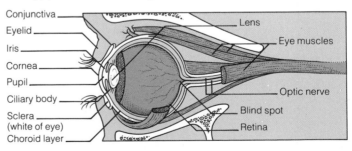

Conjunctiva
Eyelid
Iris
Cornea
Pupil
Ciliary body
Sclera (white of eye)
Choroid layer
Lens
Eye muscles
Optic nerve
Blind spot
Retina

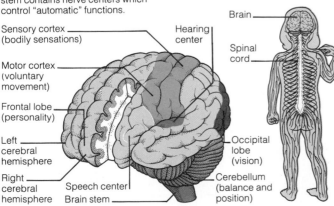

Sensory cortex (bodily sensations)
Motor cortex (voluntary movement)
Frontal lobe (personality)
Left cerebral hemisphere
Right cerebral hemisphere
Speech center
Brain stem
Brain
Hearing center
Spinal cord
Occipital lobe (vision)
Cerebellum (balance and position)

Symptoms

The most common ear problem is infection. Symptoms include earache, itching, a raised temperature and discharge from the ear. In a baby, symptoms of loss of hearing are failure to respond to sounds, and, in an older child, difficulty hearing. Common childhood eye problems are infections and irritations that

cause pain, itchiness, redness and discharge. Loss of sight is rare but a neglected squint could eventually lead to impaired vision.

See also the following diagnostic charts: **27** Eye problems **28** Disturbed or impaired vision **29** Painful or irritated ear **30** Deafness

The digestive system

The series of organs extending from the mouth to the anus responsible for carrying out the digestive process is known as the digestive tract. The digestive tract is made up of a tube in which food is broken down so that minerals, vitamins, carbohydrates, fats and proteins can be absorbed into the body and the waste products can be excreted.

The mouth

Digestion begins in the mouth when, as food is chewed, enzymes in the saliva break down certain carbohydrates. The tongue and the muscles of the pharynx then propel the mixture of food and saliva, known as the bolus, into the esophagus and down into the stomach.

Salivary glands

Esophagus

Duodenum

Stomach and duodenum

Food may spend several hours in the stomach being churned and partially digested by acid and more enzymes until the food becomes a semiliquid consistency called chyme. The chyme passes into the duodenum, where it is further broken down by digestive juices from the liver (via the gallbladder) and pancreas.

Liver

Pancreas

Small intestine

The final stage of digestion is completed in the small intestine, where the nutrients are split into chemical units small enough to pass through the wall of the intestine into the network of blood vessels and lymphatics.

Large intestine (colon)

Undigested material is passed into the large intestine (the colon), where water is absorbed, and then into the rectum, from which the undigested matter is expelled from the body.

Rectum

Symptoms

Gastroenteritis, infection of the digestive tract, is the most common digestive disorder of childhood. Symptoms include vomiting, diarrhea and abdominal pain. Vomiting and diarrhea can cause dangerous loss of body fluids. If this fluid is not replaced, a child may become seriously dehydrated.

See also the following diagnostic charts: **7** Vomiting in babies **8** Diarrhea in babies **37** Vomiting in children **38** Abdominal pain **39** Loss of appetite **40** Diarrhea in children **41** Constipation **42** Abnormal-looking bowel movements **43** Urinary problems

The urinary system

A baby's reflexes automatically expel urine from the bladder. Your child will master control of bladder and bowels when he or she is physiologically and mentally ready to do so. A child urinates more frequently than an adult because he or she has a smaller bladder (see *Structure of the urinary tract,* p.103).

Symptoms

Infection in the urethra or bladder, causing pain when your child passes urine, is the most common disorder of the urinary system. Pain, or a change in urine color or the number of times your child passes urine in a day, may indicate an underlying disorder.

See also the following diagnostic charts: **8** Diarrhea in babies **40** Diarrhea in children **41** Constipation **42** Abnormal-looking bowel movements **43** Urinary problems **44** Toilet-training problems

The endocrine system

The endocrine glands manufacture hormones and distribute them to all parts of the body via the bloodstream. These hormones regulate the body's internal chemistry, its responses to hunger, stress, infection and disease, and its preparation for physical activity.

The pituitary gland stimulates and coordinates the activities of the other endocrine glands and manufactures growth hormone which regulates body growth during childhood. **The thyroid gland** produces the hormones that control the conversion of food into energy and regulate body temperature. **The parathyroid glands** produce a hormone that controls the level of calcium – essential for healthy bones and for the nerves and muscles to work efficiently. Hormones produced by **the adrenal glands** influence the shape and distribution of body hair, regulate the amounts of sugar, salt and water in the body, and increase the flow of blood to the muscles, heart and lungs to deal with excitement, or physical and mental threats. **The pancreas** produces the hormones insulin and glucagon, which play an important part in regulating the glucose level in the blood. **The ovaries** in the adolescent female and **the testes** in the adolescent male produce the hormones responsible for the onset of puberty and the development of female or male characteristics.

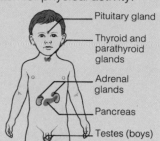

Pituitary gland

Thyroid and parathyroid glands

Adrenal glands

Pancreas

Testes (boys)

Symptoms

Disorders usually occur when the level of a particular hormone increases or decreases. Delay in the onset of puberty may be the result of a hormonal disorder and should be investigated. Symptoms of diabetes mellitus, an upset in the level of insulin, include thirst, weight loss and abnormally frequent urination.

See also the following diagnostic charts: **10** Slow growth **40** Diarrhea in children **43** Urinary problems **50** Delayed puberty **51** Adolescent behavior problems

The reproductive system

Boys

The male reproductive system consists of the external genitalia (the penis and the two testes in the scrotum) and a series of internal organs (the prostate gland, two seminal vesicles, and two tubes known as the vas deferens). In the fetus, the testes lie in the abdomen and descend into the scrotum shortly before birth. The male's reproductive system usually matures between the ages of 12 and 15. The penis enlarges and the ability to ejaculate sperm develops. Sperm are produced in the testes and carried to the seminal vesicle by the vas deferens.

Girls

The female genital system includes the vagina, the ovaries, the uterus and the fallopian tubes. Menstruation and ovulation, the releasing of an egg each month from one of the ovaries, usually begin between the ages of 11 and 14. Development of breasts and growth of hair in the armpit and genital areas are usually the first signs of puberty in a girl. The breasts are glands that develop as a result of the activity of the female hormones.

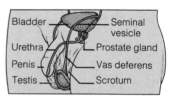

Bladder

Urethra

Penis

Testis

Seminal vesicle

Prostate gland

Vas deferens

Scrotum

Symptoms

Boys: One of the most common problems affecting the genitals is a urinary tract infection. The organs of the reproductive and urinary systems are closely linked in the male. Injury to the groin can result in internal damage.

The usual symptoms of a genital problem are pain, swelling and inflammation. Persistent pain and swelling should always receive medical attention. A delay in the onset of puberty is not unusual but should be investigated.

Girls: The most common genital problem in girls is inflammation and irritation of the external genital area. Pain when urinating and greater frequency in urinating are common symptoms of a genital disorder.

See also the following diagnostic charts: **43** Urinary problems **48** Genital problems in boys **49** Genital problems in girls **50** Delayed puberty

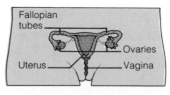

Fallopian tubes

Ovaries

Uterus

Vagina

Keeping your child healthy

Children are surprisingly resilient. They are usually able to remain healthy and strong if you give them a basic framework of care and encourage healthy activities. This framework should consist of the following: good diet, exercise, safety rules inside and outside the home, and good medical care. Following the advice given on this page will not ensure that your child avoids disease or other health problems, but doing so will help provide a foundation for good health. It may also establish a pattern of healthy living that will continue as your child grows. Habits developed in childhood tend to persist throughout our adult lives.

Eating a healthy diet

A child who eats a diet containing sufficient quantities of all the essential nutrients (see *Components of a healthy diet,* p.97) is likely to grow and develop at least at the expected rate. He or she will have better resistance and will be less susceptible to, and more likely to recover quickly from, many of the minor complaints of childhood. Also, good eating habits started in childhood are likely to be continued in adulthood. Avoiding refined sugars and saturated fats, and enjoying raw fruits and vegetables, is best begun in childhood.

Your main concern is to provide your child with all the nutrients the body needs for healthy growth and day-to-day functioning. You can start by breast-feeding (see *Breast and bottle feeding,* p.39). As your child grows older, ensure that he or she receives a balanced diet containing a variety of nutritious foods including meat, fish, dairy products, whole-grain products, fresh fruit and vegetables, and a minimum of processed foods. In particular, it is wise to limit your child's consumption of sugary foods such as cakes, cookies and candy, which can lead to obesity and tooth decay. Processed "junk-foods," too, contain little nourishment and many calories.

A balanced day's eating

Breakfast
Whole-grain cereal (high fiber and vitamins) with milk (high protein and vitamins); glass of natural orange juice (high vitamins); whole-grain toast spread with low-fat margarine, with scrambled egg (high protein, high carbohydrate and fiber). Alternatively, serve toast with jam (medium protein, high carbohydrate, fiber).

Lunch
Peanut butter sandwiches made with whole-grain bread (high fiber, medium carbohydrate and protein); tomato (fiber and vitamins); oatmeal cookies (high carbohydrate, fiber); milk (high protein and vitamins).

Dinner
Potato baked in skin with grated cheese (high protein, high carbohydrate, medium fiber and vitamins); fish sticks (high protein, medium carbohydrate); broccoli (high fiber and vitamins); bananas and milk (medium carbo-hydrate, fat and fiber); fresh fruit (high fiber and vitamins); natural fruit juice (high vitamins).

Snacks
Fresh fruit and raw vegetables (high fiber and vitamins); dried fruit (high fiber, carbohydrate and vitamins); nuts (high protein, high carbohydrate and vitamins).

Getting enough exercise

Exercise is important for children. It will encourage a healthy appetite and will help develop muscle power and a healthy heart and lungs. Exercise can be encouraged from an early age. Babies should be out of the buggy or stroller and free on the floor as often as possible. A young child can be encouraged to walk and perhaps push the buggy some of the way on an outing. Older children should be encouraged to participate in strenuous physical activities in the form of sports and informal play.

Preventive medical care

Your physician has an important role to play in your child's health. Regular visits (well-baby visits) will give you the opportunity to discuss your child's progress and to receive advice on your child's development. Well-baby visits will ensure that minor problems are noticed and treated before they become more serious. The most important element in your child's preventive medical care is immunization against a range of infectious diseases (see *Immunization,* p.75). Regular immunizations will become part of your child's health care program.

Preventing accidents

Accidents are a common cause of death in children and account for a high proportion of visits to the emergency room. The majority of accidents can be avoided by ensuring that your home is safe and by making an effort to reduce the risk of accidents outside the home. Here is a checklist of the basic precautions you should take:

- keep all medicine and dangerous chemicals out of reach
- use back burners on stoves and teach the meaning of "hot"
- put child-proof plastic plugs on all exposed electric sockets
- put a safety gate at the bottom and top of the stairs
- make sure that there are no electrical cords dangling from appliances
- place decals on any clear glass at child's eye level
- keep garden tools locked away
- teach your child safety rules for crossing the street
- check your child's bicycle to ensure that brakes, tires and lights are in good condition
- teach your child to swim
- provide safety equipment for all sporting activities.

Nursing a sick child

A child who is ill is likely to be more anxious than usual and in need of comfort, even if the disease is not painful or serious. The reassurance of your presence is an important part of nursing your child whether he or she is at home or in a hospital (see *Children in the hospital* and *Treating the most common symptoms and disorders at home,* opposite). Advice on dealing with specific disorders is given in the diagnostic charts (see *How to use the charts,* pp.22-23). On these pages you will find general advice on nursing a sick child at home.

How to tell when your child is sick
Most parents know quickly that their child is sick. Apart from obvious signs such as a rash, vomiting or pain, there are likely to be less specific indicators that all is not well, including loss of appetite (particularly in young babies), irritability and crying, or unusual lethargy. If you suspect that your baby or child is sick, consult the appropriate diagnostic chart in this book (see *How to find the correct chart,* pp.24-25) to discover the possible cause and to find out whether your physician's advice is needed. If your child's symptoms are vague, try starting with chart 9, *Feeling sick.*

Bed rest
For most illnesses, it is not essential that your child stay in bed all day. If your child feels well enough to get up and play in the house, it is usually safe to allow this. However, if your child does not feel like getting out of bed or if your physician has advised rest, try to prevent boredom by providing plenty of amusements. Sick children may not be able to concentrate for as long as usual and will not want to play games that are too demanding. Your child is likely to want extra attention from you and you may have to spend more time than usual to keep him or her amused. Often, a child will be happier resting in a bed made up on the sofa, where he or she can feel closely involved with other members of the family, rather than in an out-of-the-way bedroom. This will also allow you to supervise your child more closely. Don't force your child to sleep if he or she doesn't feel like it.

Keeping a sick child occupied
Keeping your child amused will help raise the spirits. If your child needs or wants to stay in bed, a variety of activities such as drawing or sticking pictures in a scrapbook may entertain him or her. Your child may be happier in a bed made up on a sofa in a room with other people.

Lowering your child's temperature
You can safely try to reduce your child's high temperature in the following way:
- Remove as much clothing as possible.
- Keep the room temperature at about 60°F (15°C).
- Sponge your child repeatedly with cool water, or put your child into a cool bath.
- Give the recommended dose of an aspirin substitute.
- Make sure your child drinks at least 1½ pints of fluid daily.

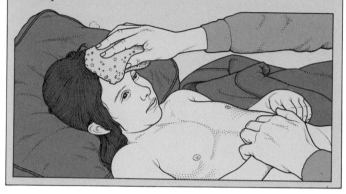

Diet and drinks
A sick child is likely to have a reduced appetite, but in the short term this in itself is no cause for concern. No special diet is necessary for most illnesses but, if you are worried that your child is not eating enough, you may be able to persuade him or her to eat a favorite meal (it does not matter if the meal is not particularly nourishing). If loss of appetite continues through a long illness, ask your physician for advice. In most cases, it is important that your child drink plenty of fluids, especially if he or she is feverish, has been vomiting or has diarrhea. Although water or plain, unsweetened fruit juices are preferable, offer whatever fluids your child seems to enjoy, including carbonated drinks.

Giving your child food and drink
Your child will probably not feel like eating, though you may successfully encourage him or her to eat a favorite food. Always make sure he or she drinks plenty of fluids.

Fresh air
The room your child is resting in should be a comfortable temperature, around 65°F (18°C), and have plenty of ventilation. Don't overheat the room, as this may increase any fever. If your child is well enough to play in the house, there is no reason why he or she should not be allowed to play outside, providing the weather is not too cold and he or she is not feverish. However, your child should not play near others if he or she has an infectious disease (opposite).

Infectious diseases
If your child has an infectious illness, there is a risk that it will be passed on to others. If your child is infectious, keep him or her, in the early stages, away from children and any adults who may be vulnerable to infection. In the case of German measles, keep your child away from public places and especially pregnant women, who are at risk of contracting the disease. The table on p.75 gives the infectious period of the common childhood infectious diseases. Your physician will advise you on any disease not covered there. If your child is lonely, you may want to invite children who have already had the disease to play at your house. The danger of their developing the disease again is remote.

When to call your physician
The charts further on in this book give advice on when to call your physician about particular symptoms. However, as a general rule, you should seek medical advice about your child's condition in the following cases:
- If you are unsure about the cause of the symptoms
- If home treatment fails to help or if the symptoms start to get worse
- If you are worried because your child is still an infant
- If your child refuses to drink or becomes excessively drowsy

Remember that diseases tend to develop more quickly in a child than in an adult, so a delay in seeking medical help that may seem acceptable for an adult may not be safe for a young child. It is better to call your physician than to risk serious complications.

Medicines
Medicines are usually prescribed for children in fruit-flavored liquid form to encourage the child to take the medicine without trouble. You can give a young baby accurately measured amounts of medicine in a calibrated "eye-dropper." For an older child, use a measuring spoon. If your child resists, try pouring the medicine down the back of the throat (the taste buds are at the front). Always consult your physician before giving aspirin to children or teenagers who have flu or chickenpox.

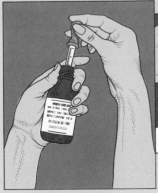
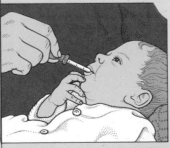
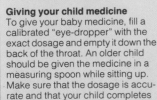

Giving your child medicine
To give your baby medicine, fill a calibrated "eye-dropper" with the exact dosage and empty it down the back of the throat. An older child should be given the medicine in a measuring spoon while sitting up. Make sure that the dosage is accurate and that your child completes the whole course.

Treating the most common symptoms and disorders at home
The following boxes give advice on treatment to combat childhood infection and when to consult your physician.
Feverish convulsions (babies), p.32
Feverish convulsions (children), p.54
Treating gastroenteritis in babies, p.41
Relieving your child's headache, p.61
Treating your child's cold, p.84
Treating your child's sore throat, p.85
What to do when your child vomits, p.93
Treating your child's gastroenteritis, p.99
How to relieve your child's toothache, p.90

Children in the hospital
Admission to the hospital – even for a short time – can be a traumatic experience for a young child. It may be the first time he or she has been away from home without you, and the surroundings are likely to be strange and frightening. The fact that your child also feels sick will obviously increase any distress. It is therefore extremely important for parents to spend as much time as possible at the hospital with their child. Most pediatric facilities allow unlimited visiting for parents and are often able to provide overnight accommodations for you as well. You will usually be able to participate in the day-to-day care (feeding, bathing) of your child. This will provide valuable reassurance for him or her and may help speed recovery. If your child needs to have an operation, it is a good idea for you to arrange to be present when he or she is put under the anesthetic and when he or she awakens afterward.

Preparing for a hospital stay
You can prepare your child for a planned stay in the hospital by talking about what is going to happen and by giving reassurance that he or she will then be returning home. Spending time with your child in the hospital, taking familiar toys to him or her and making sure that he or she has plenty of amusement will help your child during the stay.

Medication guide

If your child becomes ill, part of the treatment may include giving prescribed or over-the-counter drugs. Special care should be taken when giving drugs to babies and children because the liver, which processes chemicals from the bloodstream, is immature. Potentially dangerous levels of a drug may build up more quickly in a child than in an adult. It is vital that the precise dose for a child be given. Some drugs that can be used without risk by adults can be damaging to children (see *Poisoning,* p. 21). For these reasons it is important to use an accurate measure for liquid medicines (usually a calibrated spoon or dropper from the pharmacist) and give only the exact dose prescribed. Do not dilute medicines yourself or add them to your baby's bottle (see also *Medications*, below). Never give a child any drug that has been prescribed for an adult or for another child. If you are giving over-the-counter medicines, make sure that you read the instructions carefully. If you are in any doubt about their proper use, ask your physician or pharmacist for advice. Never give over-the-counter medicines for prolonged periods without seeking medical advice. And never use a drug to which your child has exhibited previous sensitivity such as nausea, vomiting, diarrhea, rash or swollen joints. Replace over-the-counter drugs after 1 year.

Prescribed drugs

When your physician prescribes a drug for your child, make sure that you ask the following:
- How much to give in each dose.
- How often a dose should be given.
- If it matters when you give the drug in relation to meals and whether you should wake your child at night for medication.
- If there are any side effects.
- If you should look out for any unusual or dangerous reactions to the drug.
- How soon you should expect to see an improvement in your child's condition.
- How long you should continue to give the drug before returning to your physician.

Drugs and breast-feeding

Many mothers worry that it may be harmful for them to take drugs while breast-feeding. Some drugs (for example, antibiotics, some tranquilizers, laxatives and thyroid hormone tablets) do pass from the bloodstream into breast milk, but their concentration in the milk is usually minimal. It is rare, however, for these drugs to necessitate stopping breast-feeding.

Medications

It will help you understand the treatment given to your child and the likely progress of his or her recovery if you have some background information on the drug your child is taking. The alphabetical Medication Guide includes a description of each major category of prescribed and over-the-counter drugs most frequently used to treat children. It outlines their major effects on the body and possible side effects.

ANALGESICS
Drugs that relieve pain. Some analgesics are also effective in reducing a raised temperature. An aspirin substitute in liquid form is the safest over-the-counter analgesic to use for painful and feverish symptoms in children. Aspirin, another analgesic often used by adults, is no longer considered entirely safe for children with certain viral infections because it may be linked with Reye's syndrome, a rare and dangerous condition affecting the brain and liver. For more severe pain – perhaps following an operation – a narcotic analgesic (e.g., codeine) may be prescribed. Analgesics may make a child sleepy and can cause transient constipation, nausea and dizziness.

ANTIANXIETY DRUGS
These drugs are rarely used to treat children. As an emergency treatment for convulsions, diazepam is used intravenously. The newer antianxiety drugs may occasionally be used to treat older children suffering from psychological stress. Side effects include drowsiness and confusion, and these drugs may be habit-forming.

ANTIASTHMATICS
Drugs that relax constricted air passages in the lungs. In children such narrowing usually occurs as a result of asthma or respiratory infections (bronchitis and bronchiolitis). There are two primary groups of drugs used to treat asthma. First are those that treat an acute attack (bronchodilators), including albuterol, terbutaline and the theophyllines. These may also be given routinely orally or by injection. Second are those that act to prevent an attack (cromolyn sodium). These are not effective in an acute attack. CORTICOSTEROIDS (see ANTI-INFLAMMATORIES) are reserved for asthma that is resistant to the above-mentioned drugs. Children over 3 can be taught to use inhalers very effectively. Side effects of the antiasthmatics include increased heart rate, tremor and irritability.

ANTIBIOTICS
Drugs that treat bacterial infections. Any one type of antibiotic is effective only against certain strains of bacteria, although some broad-spectrum antibiotics combat a wide range of bacterial infections. Sometimes a strain of bacteria becomes resistant to a particular antibiotic and an alternative is chosen on the basis of laboratory tests. No antibiotic is effective against viruses. The following are the antibiotics most commonly used to treat children: ampicillin, amoxicillin, erythromycin and penicillin. When antibiotics are prescribed, always ensure that the full course of treatment is completed. Stopping treatment too soon may lead to a relapse and may encourage the emergence of resistant bacteria. Antibiotics may cause side effects, and some children may be particularly sensitive to penicillin and similar antibiotics. Side effects may include rashes, nausea, vomiting, diarrhea and wheezing. Always consult your physician about any reaction to an antibiotic.

ANTICONVULSANTS
Drugs used to prevent and treat epileptic seizures. These usually are given at least twice a day. Careful calculation of the best dose for the individual child is necessary to minimize side effects. Regular blood tests are usually given to monitor drug concentrations in the blood. Usually the drug is given over a prolonged period until the child has gone 2 to 4 years without a seizure. The drugs most commonly used to treat children who have grand mal seizures are phenytoin, valproate sodium and carbamazepine. Their side effects may include drowsiness, gastrointestinal disturbances, rashes, an increase in body hair, overgrowth of the gums, enlargement of the lymph glands, blood abnormalities and liver damage. Phenobarbital is less often prescribed for children because it may cause behavior disturbances. Petit mal seizures (periods in which the child stares off into space and does not seem to hear or see) may be treated with valproate sodium or ethosuximide.

ANTIDEPRESSANTS
Drugs to counter depression. These may occasionally be prescribed for older children suffering from depression. In addition, some physicians may prescribe antidepressant drugs such as amitriptyline for bed-wetting in children over the age of 6 when other forms of treatment have failed. This use of antidepressants is controversial, however. Side effects may include behavioral disturbances and abnormal heart rate and rhythm.

ANTIFUNGALS
Drugs to treat fungal infections such as ringworm, athlete's foot, thrush and fungal diaper rash. They may be applied directly to the skin or administered orally over a prolonged period. The principal oral antifungal is griseofulvin. It, too, has several side effects including nausea, vomiting, diarrhea and/or headaches. Antifungals applied to the skin include clotrimazole and miconazole. Locally applied (topical) preparations may cause irritation.

ANTIHISTAMINES
Drugs to counteract allergic symptoms produced by the release of a substance called histamine in the body. Such symptoms may include runny nose and watering eyes (allergic rhinitis), itching and urticaria (hives). Antihistamines may be given orally or applied to skin rashes in the form of creams or sprays. Antihistamine drugs also act on the organs of balance in the middle ear and therefore are often used to prevent motion sickness. Their sedative effect may also be used to treat sleeplessness (on your physician's advice). They are also the most common routine medicine given as a medication before operations. They ensure that a child is in a relaxed, drowsy state prior to going to the operating room. The antihistamines most commonly given to children are trimeprazine tartate and promethazine hydrochloride. The main side effect is drowsiness, but some children may become unusually excited instead.

ANTI-INFLAMMATORIES
Drugs that reduce redness, heat, pain and swelling either as a result of infection or from noninfective inflammatory diseases such as certain rheumatic conditions. There are two main categories of anti-inflammatory drugs used

Home medical supplies

Safety note: Remember that it is important to keep all medicines safely out of the reach of children. A locked wall cabinet is usually the best place.

Home medicine cabinet

A family with children need not add many items to their usual stock of medicines. However, it is a good idea to keep the following basic medical supplies in the house at all times:

Aspirin substitute (for painful and feverish symptoms)
Antiseptic cream or spray (for minor wounds)
Calamine lotion (for inflamed or itchy skin)
Syrup of ipecac (to induce vomiting – for example, in cases of poisoning – see p. 21)
Rehydration treatments (for diarrhea)
Adhesive plasters of various shapes and sizes
Selection of bandages
Calibrated spoon or dropper
Clinical thermometer

Home first-aid kit

In cases of emergency, you are likely to need additional supplies. These should be stored in a well-sealed metal or plastic box that is clearly labeled and easy for you to open. It should be kept in a dry place, out of reach of children and should include:

1 Packet of sterile cotton
2 Sterile prepared bandages (2 large, 2 medium, 2 small)
3 Sterile gauze squares in several sizes
4 Sterile triangular bandages (2)
5 Gauze bandages (2) and at least 1 crepe bandage
6 Finger-size gauze with applicator
7 Waterproof plasters in assorted sizes
8 Surgical tape in wide and narrow widths
9 Rubbing alcohol
10 Small mirror

11 Tweezers
12 Scissors
13 Safety pins

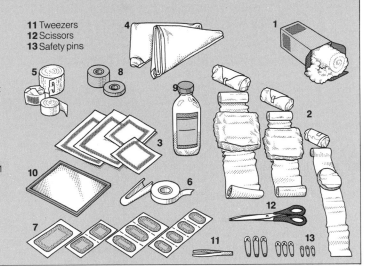

---

in the treatment of children: CORTI-COSTEROIDS and nonsteroidal anti-inflammatories. Commonly prescribed drugs of the latter type include aspirin (although this is now used with caution in the treatment of children – see ANALGESICS), ibuprofen and mefenamic acid. These drugs may cause transient constipation and often minor digestive disturbances.

ANTIVIRALS

Drugs that combat viral infections. Effective drug treatment is not yet available for the majority of viral infections such as colds and flu. However, severe cold sores caused by the herpes simplex virus can be treated by the application of idoxuridine ointment – also used to treat shingles – to the skin as soon as symptoms appear. Another antiviral drug, acyclovir, may be given orally or by injection or applied directly to the skin in the form of a cream to treat more severe types of herpes infection.

CORTICOSTEROIDS

A group of anti-inflammatory drugs (see ANTI-INFLAMMATORIES) that are chemically similar to certain naturally produced hormones from the adrenal glands that help the body respond to stress. They may be given orally, injected, applied to the skin as a cream or inhaled into the lungs. Corticosteroid inhalations such as beclomethasone may be prescribed when other ANTI-ASTHMATIC drugs have failed. There are few side effects to such treatment when used for limited periods of time. Corticosteroids such as hydrocortisone or prednisolone given orally or by injection are used for acute conditions (e.g., shock, severe allergic reactions or severe asthma). They are used in the long-term treatment of a wide variety of inflammatory conditions. They are not curative but do reduce inflammation,

which sometimes enables the body to repair itself. The conditions of children who are prescribed these drugs should be carefully monitored because of the side effects. These include fluid retention with excessive weight gain, a moon-shaped face, and growth retardation.

COUGH SUPPRESSANTS

Medicines that relieve coughing – usually as a result of a cold. There are many over-the-counter products, including lozenges and syrups, which contain soothing substances such as honey and glycerin to act on the surface of the throat, pleasant-tasting flavorings and minute doses of antiseptic chemicals. They may give temporary relief to a child's tickly throat and the taste may be comforting, but it is doubtful whether such products are any more effective than a home-made honey drink.

CYTOTOXICS

Drugs used to counter abnormal cells. They are used in the treatment of some types of cancer in children, notably leukemia. These powerful drugs are given under close specialist supervision. The most effective dosage is calculated, giving the minimum of side effects. Frequent blood tests are usually necessary. Cytotoxics may be given orally, by injection or by intravenous drip. Side effects include temporary hair loss, nausea, vomiting, diarrhea and a lowered resistance to infections.

DECONGESTANTS

Drugs that act on the mucous membranes lining the nose to reduce mucus production and so relieve a runny or a stuffed-up nose resulting from the common cold or an allergy. These drugs can be applied directly in the form of nose drops or spray or may be taken

orally. In children such drugs are usually recommended only for occasional use on your physician's advice – for example, when a stuffed-up nose prevents a young baby from sucking. If used excessively or for prolonged periods, nose drops may cause increased congestion.

HORMONES

Hormones may occasionally be given to children when a glandular disorder prevents insufficient quantities of that hormone from being produced by the body. The most common deficiencies are in the thyroid-stimulating hormone, the growth hormone and insulin (diabetes). If your child needs to take supplements of any of these hormones, regular blood tests are likely to be taken so that the dosage can be accurately controlled.

LAXATIVES

Substances that treat constipation by stimulating the action of the bowel muscles (softening the feces) or by increasing the volume of indigestible matter passing through the bowel. Laxatives should never be given to children except on the advice of your physician.

REHYDRATING TREATMENTS

These specially formulated powders and solutions contain glucose and essential mineral salts in measured quantities that, when added to boiled water, can be used to prevent and treat dehydration resulting from diarrhea or vomiting. These powders and solutions are useful for treating gastroenteritis in babies and children at home (see also p.41 and p.99). Similar solutions may be given intravenously in the hospital.

SKIN CREAMS

A wide variety of skin creams, ointments and lotions are available to treat

and/or prevent skin disorders (for example, to combat infection or relieve irritation). They usually consist of a base to which various active ingredients are added. Creams commonly used to treat children include the following: antiseptic creams, containing a drug such as cetrimide to prevent infection of minor wounds; soothing barrier creams such as zinc and cod liver oil to prevent and treat diaper rash; (ANTI-BIOTIC creams to treat skin infections such as impetigo; CORTICOSTEROID creams; ANTIFUNGAL creams; acne preparations (see p. 120); local anesthetic and antipruritic (itch relieving) creams containing calamine, ANTIHISTAMINES or a local anesthetic such as benzocaine. When selecting a cream to treat a child's skin condition, always ask your physician for advice.

SLEEPING DRUGS (HYPNOTICS)

Adult sleeping drugs are not used to treat sleeplessness in children. A young child who persistently wakes at night may be given ANTIHISTAMINES, which cause drowsiness. In rare cases an older child may be prescribed an ANTIANXIETY DRUG to promote sleep during a period of psychological distress.

VITAMINS

Vitamins are complex chemicals needed by the body in minute quantities. They are often prescribed routinely for babies and young children, especially if the children are breast-fed or premature, but are probably unnecessary for healthy children receiving an adequate diet (see *The components of a healthy diet*, p.97). Small doses of vitamin supplements are harmless, but exceeding the recommended daily dose may be dangerous.

Essential first aid

Children are naturally adventurous, often careless, and prone to accidental injuries of all kinds. Luckily, most injuries are minor and easily treated, but every parent should be prepared for the possibility of a serious accident that may require lifesaving first aid. On the following pages and on charts elsewhere in this book, you will find instructions on major lifesaving techniques. Familiarize yourself with these so that, if necessary, you will be able to act quickly and effectively. Consult the first-aid index to find instructions on a particular technique. For life-threatening emergencies, go first to the *Emergency action checklist,* below.

Seeking emergency help

Usually, the quickest way to obtain medical treatment is for you to take your child by car to the emergency room of your local hospital. DO NOT attempt to take the child yourself in either of the following circumstances:

- If your child has a suspected back injury and/or any other injury (for example, broken bones) that makes moving the child inadvisable without a stretcher.
- If you are alone, and your child needs supervision because he or she is very distressed or unconscious.

In such cases, or if you have no means of transportation, call for an ambulance at once. In any event, remaining as calm as possible is best for the child.

Emergency action checklist

If your child suffers any type of serious accident, carry out emergency first aid in the order listed below before seeking help. If possible, send someone else for help while you carry out first aid.

1 Check breathing. If this has stopped, carry out mouth-to-mouth resuscitation (right).
2 Attempt to control any severe bleeding (opposite).
3 If the child is unconscious, place him or her in the recovery position (p.20).
4 Treat any severe burns (p.20).
5 Watch for signs of shock (p.20) and carry out treatment if necessary.

Index of first~aid techniques

Mouth-to-mouth resuscitation

A child may stop breathing after falling into water, being knocked unconscious by an electric shock, or taking poisonous medicines. In such circumstances, or if you find your child unconscious and apparently not breathing, your first priority is to restart breathing by mouth-to-mouth resuscitation. Do this before summoning medical help and before dealing with any other injury. The only exception to this rule is when the cause of the trouble is choking. In this case you should try to remove the obstruction as described under Choking (opposite).

Resuscitating an older child

1 Lay the child face upward. Support the back of the neck and tip the head well back. Clear his or her mouth with your finger to remove any blockage from the windpipe.

2 Pinch the child's nose shut, take a deep breath and seal your mouth around his or her mouth. Blow strongly into the lungs four times.

3 Continue to give a breath every 5 seconds. After each breath remove your mouth. Listen for air leaving the lungs and watch for the chest to fall. Continue until medical help arrives or until the child is able to breathe on his or her own.

Resuscitating babies and young children

1 Lay the baby on his or her back and clear the mouth as in step 1 above.

2 Tilt the baby's head back slightly, take a deep breath and seal your mouth over the baby's mouth and nose. Blow gently into the baby's lungs.

3 Remove your mouth and watch for the baby's chest to fall as air leaves the lungs. Repeat a breath every 2 to 3 seconds until medical help arrives or the baby starts to breathe on his or her own.

Drowning

In a drowning accident, first check breathing. Do this as soon as you reach the child, whether or not you are still in the water. If the child is not breathing, start mouth-to-mouth resuscitation at once. Do not wait to get the child out of the water or concern yourself with removing water from the lungs. Once you have managed to restore breathing and are out of the water, place the child in the recovery position (see p.20) and keep him or her warmly covered with blankets or clothes. Seek medical help.

Bleeding

Bleeding, whether from a small cut or a serious wound, is usually distressing for a child and should be dealt with promptly and calmly. Minor cuts and scrapes should be treated as described below. **Treat bleeding as severe in the following cases:**

■ If blood spurts forcefully from the wound.
■ If bleeding continues for more than 5 minutes.

Minor cuts and scrapes

Bleeding from a minor cut or scrape normally stops spontaneously after a few minutes. Pressing a clean pad over the wound for a few minutes helps to stop bleeding. When the bleeding has stopped, clean around the cut with clean gauze or cotton, and hydrogen peroxide or soap and water. You can hold gaping edges closed using strips of surgical tape, but any cut more than about ½ in. (1 cm) long may need to be stitched to help healing. Consult your physician or go to your local hospital emergency room for professional help if the wound might need stitching, if it is very dirty, or if a tetanus shot is needed. A tetanus booster shot is necessary if the cut occurred outdoors or if the wound is dirty, and your child's last tetanus shot was given more than five years ago.

Severe bleeding

Your main objective is to reduce blood flow so as to encourage the clotting of blood in the wound, sealing the damaged blood vessels. This can be done by applying pressure to the wound itself, as described below. As a general rule you should try to keep the injured part raised above the level of the heart. Do not try to clean a serious wound with water or antiseptic. As soon as you have carried out first aid, seek emergency medical help.

How to stop severe bleeding

1 Lay the injured child down and raise the injured part.

2 Remove any easily accessible foreign objects such as pieces of glass from the wound, but do not probe for anything that is deeply embedded.

3 Press hard on the wound with a cloth pad, holding any gaping edges together. If there is anything still embedded in the wound, avoid exerting direct pressure on it.

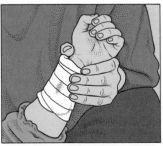

4 Maintain pressure on the wound by binding the pad firmly over the wound using a bandage or strips of material. Do not wrap the wound so tightly that you cut off blood flow to the extremity.

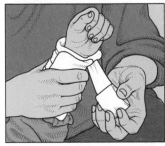

5 If the pad becomes soaked with blood, do not remove it. Instead, apply more padding over the wound and hold this in place firmly with another bandage.

Nosebleeds

Nosebleeds are common in childhood and may be brought on by a minor injury to the nose.

If your child has a nosebleed, sit him or her down, leaning slightly forward. Make sure that he or she breathes through the mouth and firmly pinch both nostrils closed for 10 minutes. Continue the pinch pressure for the entire 10 minutes.

Seek medical help if this technique does not stop the nosebleed and bleeding continues for longer than 20 minutes, or if you suspect that the nose may be broken (for example, if bleeding followed a severe blow to the nose). If you think the nose may be broken, apply ice. Emergency medical attention should be sought if bleeding from the nose follows a blow to another part of the head; this may indicate a fractured skull.

Choking

If your child chokes on a piece of food or any other object – for example, an accidentally swallowed small toy – and is unable to cough it up, you should take action to remove the blockage without delay. The technique you use depends on the size of the child. Following successful removal of the blockage, you should always seek medical advice promptly.

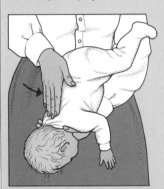

Babies (under 1 year)
Lay the baby face down on your forearm, supporting the baby's chest, with the head lower than the body. Give several firm, but not forceful, blows with the heel of your hand between the shoulder blades.

Small children (1 to 9 years)
Sit down and place the child face down across your lap. Give several sharp blows with the heel of your hand between the shoulder blades. Be careful not to use excessive force. If the blockage is not dislodged, repeat.

Older children (over 9 years)

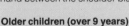

1 Hold the child up from behind in a standing position, pressing one fist with one thumb upward against the waist. Hold your other hand over the fist and thrust hard in and up under the rib cage. If this does not clear the blockage, repeat 3 more times.

2 If breathing does not restart following removal of the blockage, carry out mouth-to-mouth resuscitation (opposite).

The recovery position

The recovery position is a safe position for an unconscious child. It allows him or her to breathe freely and prevents choking and inhalation of vomit. The arrangement of the limbs supports the body in a stable and comfortable position. Place the child in this position after you have ensured that he or she is breathing normally and have dealt with any obvious injury. Then keep the child still and warm. DO NOT use the recovery position if the child has fallen or collided with another object, since there may be a neck or back injury.

The position
Place the child on his or her stomach, with one leg drawn up at a right angle. The head should be turned to one side with the chin jutting forward. The arms should be raised above the head.

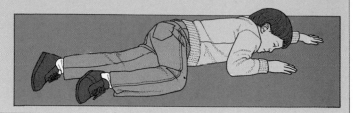

Burns

Burns may be caused by dry heat (fire), moist heat (steam or hot liquids), electricity, or corrosive chemicals. For treatment of electric shock, see below right.

All burns should be treated first by removing their cause — for example, putting out flames, or by washing off corrosive chemicals. The affected area should then be cooled as rapidly as possible by immersing the area in cold water or by holding it beneath a running, cold water tap. DO NOT apply any type of ointment or cream to the burn or burst any blisters that may form.

Following first aid, seek emergency medical help if the burn affects an extensive area, if the skin is broken, severely blistered, or charred, or if your child is in severe pain. Even small burns on the face or hands require special treatment. Always seek medical advice about burns.

Dealing with burns

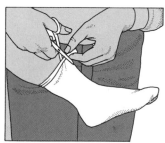

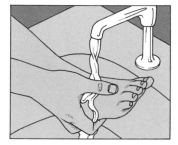

1 Remove clothing that has been soaked in hot fat, boiling water, or chemical agents from the burned area unless it is firmly stuck to the skin. Dry, burned clothing should be left.

2 Immerse the burn in cold, preferably running water for at least 10 minutes. If the area affected is large, cover it with a clean towel or sheet soaked in cold water.

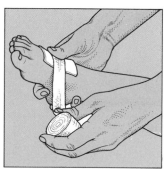

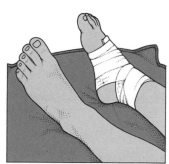

3 When you have cooled the burn, cover it with a clean, dry gauze or cloth dressing. Do not use cotton balls or other fluffy materials. If you are taking your child to the hospital, do not cover the burn; any dressing will have to be removed, possibly causing your child further pain.

4 Keep a burned limb raised and, if your child is conscious, give sips of cold water while waiting for medical help to arrive.

Shock

Shock is a life-threatening condition that may be caused by severe injuries, a large loss of blood, burns, or overwhelming infection. Its main feature is a dramatic drop in blood pressure. Suspect that your child is in shock if he or she becomes pale and sweaty, and possibly drowsy or confused following such an injury. Seek medical help at once.

Treating shock
If your child seems to be in shock, lay him or her down on his or her back with legs raised. Loosen any tight clothing and cover the child to keep him or her warm. Offer plenty of reassurance.

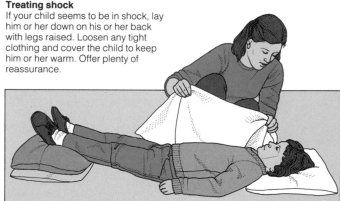

Electric shock

A severe electric shock is likely to knock a child unconscious and may stop breathing. There may also be deep burns at the point where the current entered the body and possibly internal damage as well. Always seek medical advice after an electric shock even if your child seems to have suffered only minor burns.

What to do
First, switch off the current or break the contact between the child and the appliance. Do not try to pull the child away or you may receive a shock yourself. Instead, use an object such as a wooden broom handle to push away the source of the current. Check your child's breathing. If this has stopped, start mouth-to-mouth resuscitation (see p.18) at once. You may need to continue with this for up to half an hour. Once your child is breathing, place him or her in the recovery position (above), treat any burns (above left) and summon medical help.

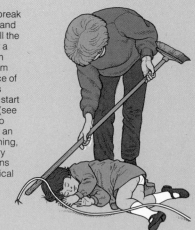

Unconsciousness

Loss of consciousness may result from a simple fainting spell or a more serious problem requiring urgent medical attention. For *First aid for fainting,* see p.58. When loss of consciousness is accompanied by uncontrolled movements, suspect a seizure (see *Seizures,* p.59).

In any child who has lost consciousness, check breathing first. If breathing has stopped, roll the child carefully onto his or her back and carry out mouth-to-mouth resuscitation immediately (see p.18).

If unconsciousness followed a fall or collision, avoid moving the child further in case of a neck or back injury.

If no collision or fall preceded unconsciousness, place the child in the recovery position (opposite), loosen any tight clothing and keep the child warm, making sure there is plenty of ventilation.

While waiting for medical help, do not give anything to eat or drink and do not leave the child alone.

Bites and stings

The bites and stings of most animals and insects are minor and, although they may cause local pain and irritation, are no threat to your child's general health. If you are traveling with your child, make sure you know how to identify animals and insects that may have poisonous bites or stings and seek advice about antidotes and treatments. Occasionally, a child may develop a severe allergic reaction to an apparently minor bite or sting. This requires emergency treatment (see *Anaphylactic shock,* below).

Animal bites: If your child is bitten by an animal such as a dog, cat or horse, seek medical help, since most bite wounds are likely to become infected if not quickly treated. Your child may need to have a tetanus injection, stitches or rabies injections.

Insect bites and stings: Bites and stings from most common insects – for example, gnats and mosquitoes – cause local itching, redness and swelling. Calamine lotion may relieve discomfort. If your child is stung by a bee or hornet, first try to remove the sting from the wound by gently scraping it out with a fingernail or knife blade. Do not try to remove the sting with tweezers, as you may squeeze more venom into the wound. Watch for signs of allergic reaction, which may include redness around the sting that spreads to a large area and swells; hives; difficulty breathing; and anaphylactic shock (below).

Snake bites: If your child receives a snake bite, wash around the wound, give the child aspirin or an aspirin substitute to relieve any pain and encourage the child to rest. Seek medical advice promptly.

Anaphylactic shock

In rare cases a child may become hypersensitive to a particular type of bite or sting – usually after having been bitten previously. If the child is bitten or stung again he or she develops a severe allergic reaction known as anaphylactic shock. Symptoms may include difficult breathing as a result of narrowing of the air passages and/or any of the signs of shock (opposite). If your child shows such symptoms after receiving a bite or sting, treat as for shock and seek emergency medical help.

Poisoning

Accidental poisoning is one of the most common reasons for a child to need emergency treatment, especially among children under 5. For households with young children, it is therefore imperative to post the telephone number of the local poison control center. Poisoning may be caused by swallowing alcohol, medicines, household cleaning fluids or chemicals, or poisonous plants or berries. In some cases a child will admit to having taken something poisonous, but you may also suspect that your child has swallowed poison if he or she suddenly and inexplicably starts to vomit, becomes drowsy or confused, loses consciousness or starts to breathe abnormally. If you think that your child may have taken any type of poison, even if he or she seems well at the moment, seek expert advice at once. Telephone your physician, your local hospital emergency room or poison control center. You should try to give the following information:

- What has been swallowed.
- How much has been swallowed. In the case of medicines, try to find out how many tablets were taken.
- When it was swallowed.
- If you take your child to the hospital or to your physician, take with you any containers that you think may be involved.

If you are unable to obtain expert advice and cannot easily get to a hospital, follow the advice given below.

Chemical poisons
(including household cleaning fluids, paraffin, gasoline, polishes and paint)

1 If your child is conscious, you may give a glass of milk to drink at once.

2 DO NOT try to induce vomiting, but if your child vomits spontaneously, hold him or her face down over your lap to prevent inhalation of chemicals in the vomit.

3 If your child loses consciousness, place him or her in the recovery position (opposite). If breathing stops, carry out mouth-to-mouth resuscitation (p.18).

4 Seek medical help as soon as possible.

Medicines, alcohol, poisonous plants and berries

1 If your child is conscious, you may try to induce vomiting (see below).

2 If your child is unconscious, do not give anything by mouth. Lay the child down in the recovery position (opposite) and if breathing stops carry out mouth-to-mouth resuscitation (p.18).

3 Seek medical help as soon as possible.

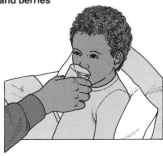

How to induce vomiting
Never try to induce vomiting in a child who is unconscious or who has swallowed chemical products such as cleaning fluids, paraffin or gasoline (see above). In other cases, give 3 teaspoonfuls (15 ml) of syrup of ipecac followed by 2 glasses of water or other liquid. If this does not lead to vomiting within 20 minutes, repeat the dose *once only.* When your child vomits, keep his or her face down with head lowered to prevent choking or inhalation of vomit.

How to use the charts

The 53 diagnostic charts in this book have been compiled to help you find probable reasons for your child's symptoms. Each chart shows in detail a single symptom – for instance, vomiting, headache or a rash – and explores the possible causes of the symptom by means of a logically organized sequence of questions, each answerable by a simple YES or NO. Your responses will lead you toward a clearly worded end point, which suggests what may be wrong and offers advice on whether your child's disorder requires professional attention. To see how the charts work, examine the accompanying sample chart and study the explanatory notes. In particular, make sure you understand the exact meanings of the systematized action codes that indicate the relative urgency of the need to consult a physician (see *What the instructions mean,* opposite).

Note that every chart is numbered and bears a label defining or describing the key symptom. An introductory paragraph provides further description and explanation of the purpose of the chart. Read this paragraph carefully to make sure you have chosen the most appropriate pathway toward an analysis of your child's problem; then proceed as indicated in the chart itself. Always begin with the first question and follow through to the end point that fits your child's special situation. In many cases, extensive boxed information accompanying the chart will enhance your understanding of specific diagnoses as well as likely treatment for underlying disorders. Always read through such information texts (except, of course, in emergencies, when swift action is essential). It is important to consult the *correct* chart at the *correct* time. For instructions on how to choose the precise chart you need, turn to p.18.

Chart group
The charts are divided into sections according to the age of your child. Before using a chart, make sure you have chosen one from the right age group.

Chart number
Each chart has a number so that it can be easily found and cross-referenced. Occasionally, you will be advised to turn to a more appropriate chart.

Go to chart

Chart title

Chart title
A short, descriptive term for the symptom heads each chart.

Definition
Each symptom is defined in simple, nontechnical terms and an indication of when a symptom is severe enough to cause concern is given.

The questions
These are structured so that you follow either a YES or a NO pathway from each question. Follow the series of questions, answering as appropriate in your case. In almost all cases you will then arrive at a possible reason for your symptoms.

The diagnosis
Each series of questions usually leads to a possible diagnosis and the treatment you are likely to need. The diagnoses take various forms according to the potential seriousness of a complaint. For example, it takes the form of a warning in cases where you may need urgent medical attention (see *What the instructions mean,* opposite). You are usually referred to other sections of the book for further information.

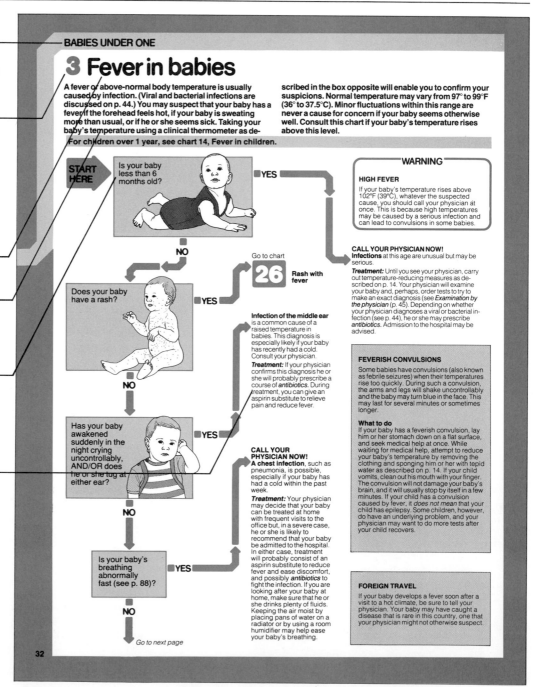

BABIES UNDER ONE

3 Fever in babies

A fever or above-normal body temperature is usually caused by infection. (Viral and bacterial infections are discussed on p. 44.) You may suspect that your baby has a fever if the forehead feels hot, if your baby is sweating more than usual, or if he or she seems sick. Taking your baby's temperature using a clinical thermometer as described in the box opposite will enable you to confirm your suspicions. Normal temperature may vary from 97° to 99°F (36° to 37.5°C). Minor fluctuations within this range are never a cause for concern if your baby seems otherwise well. Consult this chart if your baby's temperature rises above this level.

For children over 1 year, see chart 14, Fever in children.

START HERE → Is your baby less than 6 months old? **YES** →

NO ↓

Does your baby have a rash? **YES** → Go to chart **26** Rash with fever

NO ↓

Has your baby awakened suddenly in the night crying uncontrollably, AND/OR does he or she tug at either ear? **YES** →

NO ↓

Is your baby's breathing abnormally fast (see p. 88)? **YES** →

NO ↓

Go to next page

WARNING

HIGH FEVER
If your baby's temperature rises above 102°F (39°C), whatever the suspected cause, you should call your physician at once. This is because high temperatures may be caused by a serious infection and can lead to convulsions in some babies.

CALL YOUR PHYSICIAN NOW!
Infections at this age are unusual but may be serious.

Treatment: Until you see your physician, carry out temperature-reducing measures as described on p. 14. Your physician will examine your baby and, perhaps, order tests to try to make an exact diagnosis (see *Examination by the physician* (p. 45). Depending on whether your physician diagnoses a viral or bacterial infection (see p. 44), he or she may prescribe *antibiotics.* Admission to the hospital may be advised.

Infection of the middle ear is a common cause of a raised temperature in babies. This diagnosis is especially likely if your baby has recently had a cold. Consult your physician.
Treatment: If your physician confirms this diagnosis he or she will probably prescribe a course of *antibiotics.* During treatment, you can give an aspirin substitute to relieve pain and reduce fever.

CALL YOUR PHYSICIAN NOW!
A chest infection, such as pneumonia, is possible, especially if your baby has had a cold within the past week.
Treatment: Your physician may decide that your baby can be treated at home with frequent visits to the office but, in a severe case, he or she is likely to recommend that your baby be admitted to the hospital. In either case, treatment will probably consist of an aspirin substitute to reduce fever and ease discomfort, and possibly *antibiotics* to fight the infection. If you are looking after your baby at home, make sure that he or she drinks plenty of fluids. Keeping the air moist by placing pans of water on a radiator or by using a room humidifier may help ease your baby's breathing.

FEVERISH CONVULSIONS

Some babies have convulsions (also known as febrile seizures) when their temperatures rise too quickly. During such a convulsion, the arms and legs will shake uncontrollably and the baby may turn blue in the face. This may last for several minutes or sometimes longer.

What to do
If your baby has a feverish convulsion, lay him or her stomach down on a flat surface, and seek medical help at once. While waiting for medical help, attempt to reduce your baby's temperature by removing the clothing and sponging him or her with tepid water as described on p. 14. If your child vomits, clean out his mouth with your finger. The convulsion will not damage your baby's brain, and it will usually stop by itself in a few minutes. If your child has a convulsion caused by fever, it *does not mean* that your child has epilepsy. Some children, however, do have an underlying problem, and your physician may want to do more tests after your child recovers.

FOREIGN TRAVEL

If your baby develops a fever soon after a visit to a hot climate, be sure to tell your physician. Your baby may have caught a disease that is rare in this country, one that your physician might not otherwise suspect.

> **WARNING:** Though self-treatment is recommended for many minor disorders, remember that the charts provide only *likely* diagnoses. If you have any doubt about the diagnosis or treatment of any symptom, *always consult your physician.*

What the instructions mean

EMERGENCY
GET MEDICAL HELP NOW!

The condition may threaten life or lead to permanent disability if not given immediate medical attention. Get medical help by the fastest means possible, usually by calling an ambulance. In some cases it may be better to call your physician or take the patient to the hospital yourself.

CALL YOUR PHYSICIAN NOW!
There is a possibility of a serious condition that may warrant immediate treatment and perhaps hospital admission. Seek medical advice immediately – day or night – usually by telephoning your physician, who will then decide on further action. If you are unable to make contact with your physician within an hour or so, emergency action (left) may be justified.

CONSULT YOUR PHYSICIAN WITHOUT DELAY!
The condition is serious and needs urgent medical assessment, but a few hours' delay in seeking treatment is unlikely to be damaging. Seek your physician's advice within 24 hours. This will usually mean telephoning for an appointment the same day.

Consult your physician.
A condition for which medical treatment is advisable, but for which reasonable delay is unlikely to lead to problems. Seek medical advice as soon as practical.

Discuss with your physician.
The condition is nonurgent and specific treatment is unlikely. However, your physician's advice may be helpful. Seek medical advice as soon as practical.

Boxed information
On most charts there are boxes containing important additional information to expand on either a diagnosis or a form of treatment. See the information and self-help boxes below.

> ### WARNING
> Symptoms that indicate an immediate danger to life are highlighted in these boxes. Where appropriate, steps that can be taken while waiting for medical help to arrive are explained.

> **FIRST AID**
> Wherever first-aid measures are applicable, a cross-reference to the *Essential first-aid* section is provided.

INFORMATION
These boxes expand on the possible diagnoses and likely forms of treatment for specific symptoms. For example, several of them contain an explanation of a particular medical procedure. Where applicable, self-help treatment is included.

SELF-HELP
Where self-help measures may be effective in dealing with a symptom, advice is given on ways in which you may alleviate the problem.

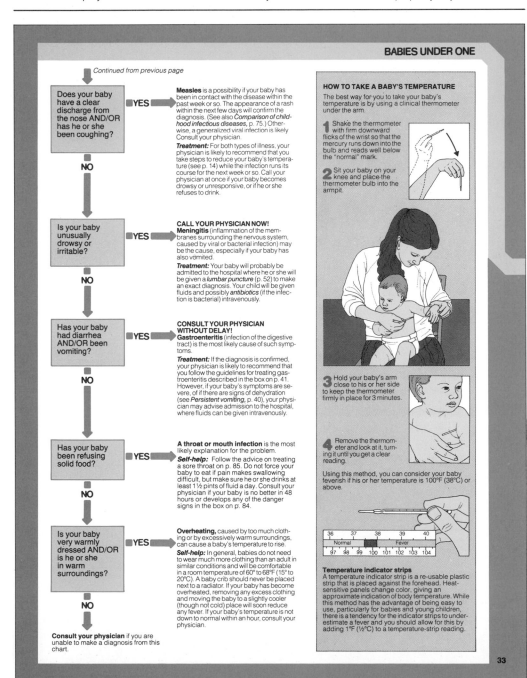

BABIES UNDER ONE

Continued from previous page

Does your baby have a clear discharge from the nose AND/OR has he or she been coughing? — **YES**

Measles is a possibility if your baby has been in contact with the disease within the past week or so. The appearance of a rash within the next few days will confirm the diagnosis. (See also *Comparison of childhood infectious diseases*, p. 75.) Otherwise, a generalized viral infection is likely Consult your physician.
Treatment: For both types of illness, your physician is likely to recommend that you take steps to reduce your baby's temperature (see p. 14) while the infection runs its course for the next week or so. Call your physician at once if your baby becomes drowsy or unresponsive, or if he or she refuses to drink.

NO

Is your baby unusually drowsy or irritable? — **YES**

CALL YOUR PHYSICIAN NOW!
Meningitis (inflammation of the membranes surrounding the nervous system, caused by viral or bacterial infection) may be the cause, especially if your baby has also vomited.
Treatment: Your baby will probably be admitted to the hospital where he or she will be given a *lumbar puncture* (p. 52) to make an exact diagnosis. Your child will be given fluids and possibly *antibiotics* (if the infection is bacterial) intravenously.

NO

Has your baby had diarrhea AND/OR been vomiting? — **YES**

CONSULT YOUR PHYSICIAN WITHOUT DELAY!
Gastroenteritis (infection of the digestive tract) is the most likely cause of such symptoms.
Treatment: If the diagnosis is confirmed, your physician is likely to recommend that you follow the guidelines for treating gastroenteritis described in the box on p. 41. However, if your baby's symptoms are severe, or if there are signs of dehydration (see *Persistent vomiting*, p. 40), your physician may advise admission to the hospital, where fluids can be given intravenously.

NO

Has your baby been refusing solid food? — **YES**

A throat or mouth infection is the most likely explanation for the problem.
Self-help: Follow the advice on treating a sore throat on p. 85. Do not force your baby to eat if pain makes swallowing difficult, but make sure he or she drinks at least 1½ pints of fluid a day. Consult your physician if your baby is no better in 48 hours or develops any of the danger signs in the box on p. 84.

NO

Is your baby very warmly dressed AND/OR is he or she in warm surroundings? — **YES**

Overheating, caused by too much clothing or by excessively warm surroundings, can cause a baby's temperature to rise.
Self-help: In general, babies do not need to wear much more clothing than an adult in similar conditions and will be comfortable in a room temperature of 60° to 68°F (15° to 20°C). A baby crib should never be placed next to a radiator. If your baby has become overheated, removing any excess clothing and moving the baby to a slightly cooler (though not cold) place will soon reduce any fever. If your baby's temperature is not down to normal within an hour, consult your physician.

NO

Consult your physician if you are unable to make a diagnosis from this chart.

HOW TO TAKE A BABY'S TEMPERATURE
The best way for you to take your baby's temperature is by using a clinical thermometer under the arm.

1 Shake the thermometer with firm downward flicks of the wrist so that the mercury runs down into the bulb and reads well below the "normal" mark.

2 Sit your baby on your knee and place the thermometer bulb into the armpit.

3 Hold your baby's arm close to his or her side to keep the thermometer firmly in place for 3 minutes.

4 Remove the thermometer and look at it, turning it until you get a clear reading.

Using this method, you can consider your baby feverish if his or her temperature is 100°F (38°C) or above.

Temperature indicator strips
A temperature indicator strip is a re-usable plastic strip that is placed against the forehead. Heat-sensitive panels change color, giving an approximate indication of body temperature. While this method has the advantage of being easy to use, particularly for babies and young children, there is a tendency for the indicator strips to underestimate a fever and you should allow for this by adding 1°F (½°C) to a temperature-strip reading.

33

How to find the correct chart

There are three ways to find the appropriate diagnostic chart for your child's symptom. You can use the *Pain-site map*, the *System-by-system chartfinder* or the *Chart index*, depending on the nature of the symptom and where it is located. Whatever method you choose to find the correct chart, you will be given the title of the appropriate chart and its number.

1 Pain-site map

If your child is in pain, the quickest way to find the correct chart is by reference to the pain-site map (below).

2 System-by-system chartfinder

If you know the body system affected but are unsure how to define your child's symptom, consult the system-by-system chartfinder (opposite).

3 Chart index

When you have no difficulty naming your child's symptom, consult the chart index (p. 20). If your child is suffering from more than one symptom at the same time, concentrate on the symptom that causes your child the most distress.

1 Pain-site map

Consult this section to find the correct diagnostic chart for your child's symptom if he or she is suffering from pain in any part of the body. The illustrations below indicate possible areas of pain and are keyed in to the titles and numbers of the charts that deal with pain in that part of the body.

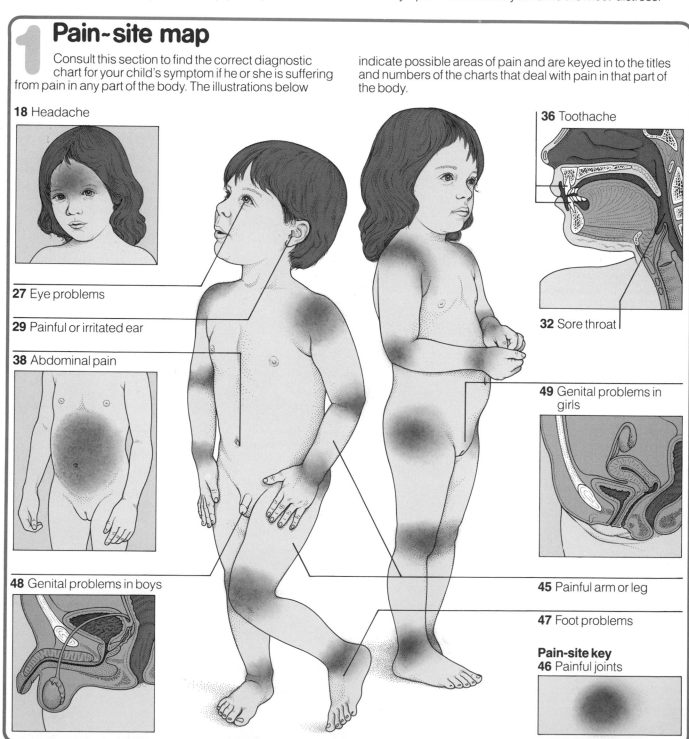

18 Headache

27 Eye problems

29 Painful or irritated ear

38 Abdominal pain

48 Genital problems in boys

36 Toothache

32 Sore throat

49 Genital problems in girls

45 Painful arm or leg

47 Foot problems

Pain-site key
46 Painful joints

24

2 System-by-system chartfinder

Consult this section if you know what part of the body or which body system your child's symptom originates in. A list of the charts that deal with each of the main body systems is given under each main heading. Select the chart that most closely seems to fit your child's symptom.

General symptoms

Babies under one
1 Slow weight gain
2 Waking at night
3 Fever in babies
5 Excessive crying
6 Feeding problems

Children of all ages
9 Feeling sick
10 Slow growth
11 Excessive weight gain
12 Sleeping problems
13 Drowsiness
14 Fever in children
15 Swollen glands

Adolescents
50 Delayed puberty
53 Adolescent weight problems

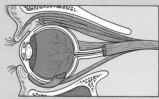

Eye and sight symptoms

27 Eye problems
28 Disturbed or impaired vision

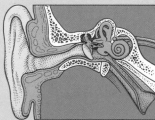

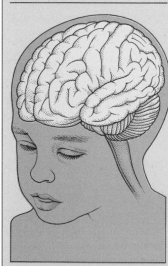

Head, brain and psychological symptoms

Children of all ages
13 Drowsiness
17 Fainting, dizzy spells and seizures
18 Headache
19 Clumsiness
20 Confusion
21 Speech difficulties
22 Behavior problems
23 School difficulties

Adolescents
51 Adolescent behavior problems
53 Adolescent weight problems

Ear and hearing symptoms

29 Painful or irritated ear
30 Deafness

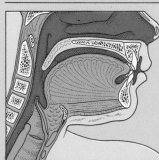

Mouth, tongue and throat symptoms

32 Sore throat
36 Toothache

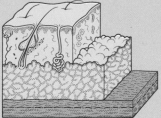

Skin, hair and nail symptoms

Babies under one
4 Skin problems in babies

Children of all ages
16 Itching
25 Spots and rashes
26 Rash with fever

Adolescents
52 Adolescent skin problems

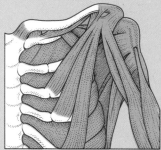

Muscle, bone and joint symptoms

45 Painful arm or leg
46 Painful joints
47 Foot problems

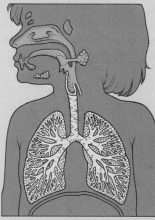

Respiratory symptoms

31 Runny or stuffed-up nose
32 Sore throat
33 Coughing
34 Fast breathing
35 Noisy breathing

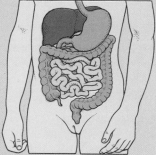

Abdominal and digestive symptoms

Babies under one
7 Vomiting in babies
8 Diarrhea in babies

Children of all ages
37 Vomiting in children
38 Abdominal pain
39 Loss of appetite
40 Diarrhea in children
41 Constipation
42 Abnormal-looking bowel movements

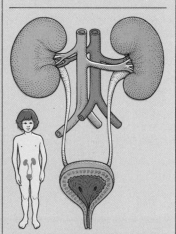

Urinary symptoms

43 Urinary problems
44 Toilet-training problems

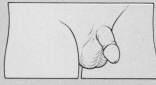

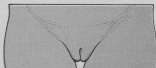

Genital symptoms

48 Genital problems in boys
49 Genital problems in girls

3 Chart index

Consult this index if you think that you know the correct name for your symptom. The chart titles and their numbers are listed alphabetically together with possible alternative names for symptoms (for example, *Raised temperature* for *Fever* or *Swellings* for *Swollen glands*). In this section you will also find the titles of information boxes dealing with symptoms that do not have a separate diagnostic chart.

A

Abdominal pain **38**
Abnormal-looking bowel movements **42**
Abnormal-looking urine **43**
Acne **52**
Adolescent behavior problems **51**
Adolescent skin problems **52**
Adolescent weight problems **53**
Aggressiveness **22**
Anorexia nervosa **53**
Appetite, loss of **39, 53**
Arm, painful **45**

B

Balance, loss of **17**
Behavior problems, children **22, 23**; adolescents **51**
Blackheads **52**
Blood in the bowel movements **42**
Boils **25**
Bowel movements, abnormal-looking **42**
Breathing, fast **34**; noisy **35**
Bulimia **53**

C

Clumsiness **19**
Confusion **20**
Constipation **41**
Convulsions **17**
Coughing **33**
Crying, excessive **5**

D

Deafness **30**
Delayed puberty **50**
Destructiveness **22**
Diarrhea, babies **8**; children **40**
Disobedience **22**
Disturbed vision **28**
Dizzy spells **17**
Drooping eyelid **27**
Drowsiness **13**

E

Ear, painful or irritated **29**
Excessive crying **5**
Excessive weight gain, children **11**; adolescents **53**
Eye problems **27, 28**

F

Fainting **17**
Fast breathing **34**
Feeding problems **6**
Feeling sick **9**
Fever, babies **3**; children **14**
Fever, rash with **26**
Feverish seizures, babies **3**; children **14, 17**
Foot problems **47**

G

Gas, babies **5**; children **38**
Genital problems, boys **48**; girls **49**
Glands, swollen **15**
Growth, slow **10**

H

Hair problems **24**
Headache **18**
Hearing difficulties **30**
High temperature, babies **3**; children **14**

I

Impaired vision **28**
Irritated ear **29**
Itching **16**

J

Joints, painful **46**

L

Late-rising in the morning **13**
Loss of appetite **39**
Loss of consciousness **17**
Leg, painful **45**
Lumps **15**

N

Nail problems **24**
Nose, runny or stuffed-up **31**
Noisy breathing **35**

O

Overweight, children **11**; adolescent **53**

P

Painful arm **45**
Painful ear **29**
Painful joints **46**
Painful leg **45**
Puberty, delayed **50**

R

Raised temperature, babies **3**; children **14**
Rashes **25, 26**
Rash with fever **26**
Regurgitation **7**
Run down, feeling **9, 13**
Runny nose **31**

S

Scalp problems **24**
School difficulties **23**
Seizures **17**
Sickness, babies **7**; children **37**
Sight, disturbed or impaired **28**
Skin problems, babies **4**; adolescents **52**

L

Sleeping problems, babies **2**; children **12**
Slow growth **10**
Slow weight gain, babies **1**; adolescents **53**
Sore throat **32**
Speech difficulties **21**
Spots **25**
Squint **27, 28**
Stomachache **38**
Stuffed-up nose **31**
Swellings **15**
Swollen glands **15**

T

Temperature, high, babies **3**; children **14**
Throat, sore **32**
Tiredness **13**
Toilet-training problems **44**
Toothache **36**

U

Urinary problems **43, 44**

V

Violence **22**
Vision, disturbed or impaired **28**
Vomiting, babies **7**; children **37**

W

Waking at night, babies **2**; children **12**
Warts **25**
Weight gain, excessive, children **11**; adolescents **53**
Weight loss, babies **1**; adolescents **53**
Weight gain, slow **1**
Withdrawal **22**

1 Babies under one

1 Slow weight gain

It is important to keep a regular check on your baby's weight gain because failure to put on weight can be a sign of problems. Your baby is likely to be weighed whenever you visit your pediatrician, where any problems are likely to be noticed and dealt with. It is also a good idea for you to keep your own chart of your baby's progress so you can reassure yourself that your baby is developing normally. Using the growth charts below, compare your baby's weight gain and increase in head circumference as

measured by your pediatrician with the average for babies of similar birth weight. Do not worry if your baby's progress does not exactly follow the curve shown; there can be many normal variations to this pattern (see Growth patterns in infancy, below). Only if you can find no normal explanation for your baby's failure to gain weight at the expected rate should you consult the diagnostic pathways on the facing page. Use the growth charts on pp. 122-123 to record your baby's length and weight.

For children over 1 year, see chart 10, Slow growth

GROWTH PATTERNS IN INFANCY

The growth charts on pp. 122-123 allow you to record your baby's growth and to compare his or her progress with the standard weight gain for small, average and large babies. Most babies follow these standard curves, but there are many possible variations, most of which are quite normal. The charts on this page show some common examples of how

your baby's growth may differ from the usual pattern. Remember that length, weight and head circumference are interrelated. When your pediatrician assesses the size of your baby, he or she is looking at the relationship among them. Above all, don't worry if your child appears to be growing slowly; consult your pediatrician.

Short mother and tall father
A short mother is likely to have a smaller-than-average baby. But, if the father is tall and the baby is ultimately going to take after him, the baby's growth chart is likely to show a rapid increase in both weight and head circumference in the first few months of life.

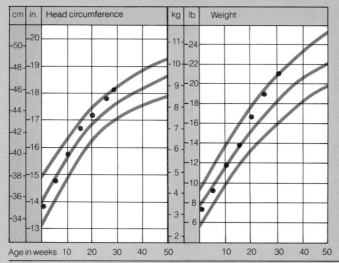

Age in weeks 10 20 30 40 50   10 20 30 40 50

Tall mother and short father
A tall mother is likely to have a larger-than-average baby. However, if the father is short and the baby is going to take after him, the baby is likely to gain weight and increase his or her head circumference at a slower rate than normal for the first few months.

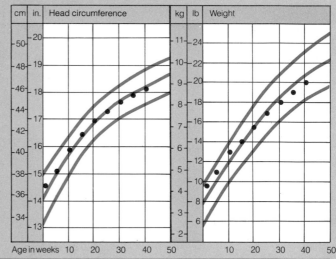

Age in weeks 10 20 30 40 50   10 20 30 40 50

Gaining too little weight
This chart shows a baby who is gaining too little weight. The head is growing normally for an average-sized baby, but the weight gain curve is flattening out and approaching that for a small baby. In this case you should consult the diagnostic chart opposite.

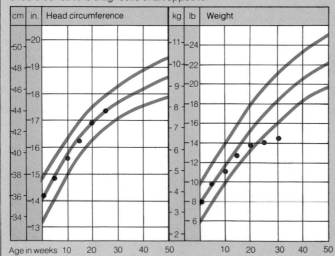

Age in weeks 10 20 30 40 50   10 20 30 40 50

Gaining too much weight
This chart shows a baby who was of average weight at birth, but whose weight has consistently risen at a faster rate than his or her head circumference, so that the weight curve now relates to that of a larger-than-average baby (see chart 11, *Excessive weight gain*).

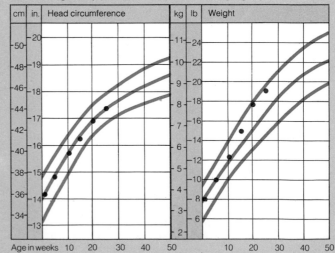

Age in weeks 10 20 30 40 50   10 20 30 40 50

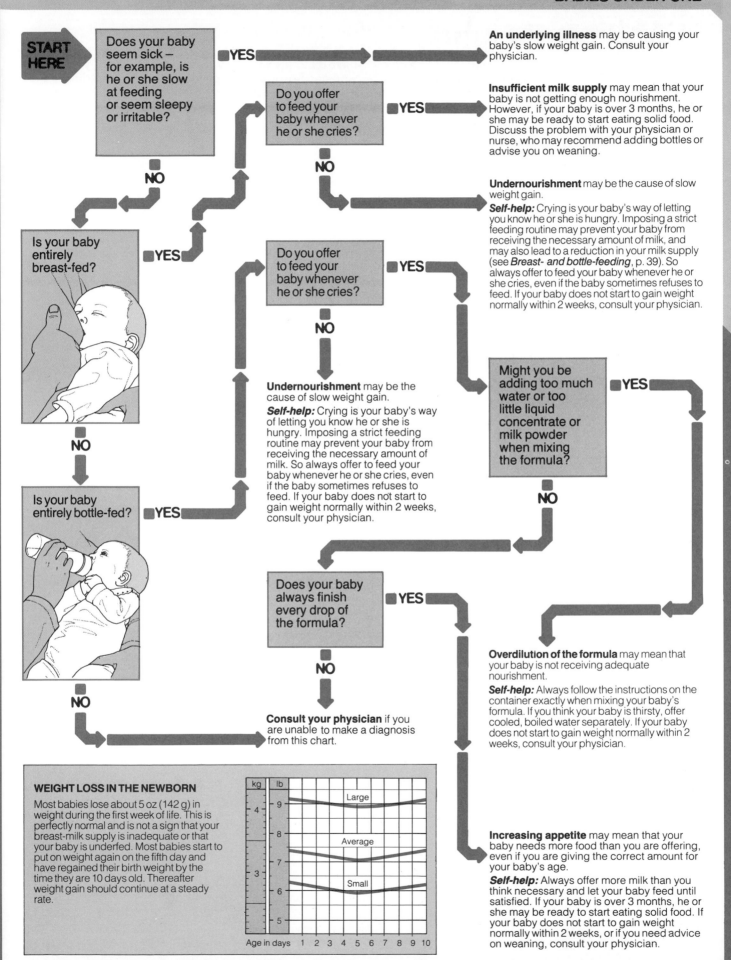

START HERE → Does your baby seem sick — for example, is he or she slow at feeding or seem sleepy or irritable?

YES → **An underlying illness** may be causing your baby's slow weight gain. Consult your physician.

NO → Is your baby entirely breast-fed?

Do you offer to feed your baby whenever he or she cries?

YES → **Insufficient milk supply** may mean that your baby is not getting enough nourishment. However, if your baby is over 3 months, he or she may be ready to start eating solid food. Discuss the problem with your physician or nurse, who may recommend adding bottles or advise you on weaning.

NO → **Undernourishment** may be the cause of slow weight gain.

Self-help: Crying is your baby's way of letting you know he or she is hungry. Imposing a strict feeding routine may prevent your baby from receiving the necessary amount of milk, and may also lead to a reduction in your milk supply (see *Breast- and bottle-feeding*, p. 39). So always offer to feed your baby whenever he or she cries, even if the baby sometimes refuses to feed. If your baby does not start to gain weight normally within 2 weeks, consult your physician.

YES → Do you offer to feed your baby whenever he or she cries?

YES (from breast-fed NO path)

NO → **Undernourishment** may be the cause of slow weight gain.

Self-help: Crying is your baby's way of letting you know he or she is hungry. Imposing a strict feeding routine may prevent your baby from receiving the necessary amount of milk. So always offer to feed your baby whenever he or she cries, even if the baby sometimes refuses to feed. If your baby does not start to gain weight normally within 2 weeks, consult your physician.

NO → Is your baby entirely bottle-fed?

YES →

Might you be adding too much water or too little liquid concentrate or milk powder when mixing the formula?

YES →

NO →

Does your baby always finish every drop of the formula?

YES →

NO → **Consult your physician** if you are unable to make a diagnosis from this chart.

Overdilution of the formula may mean that your baby is not receiving adequate nourishment.

Self-help: Always follow the instructions on the container exactly when mixing your baby's formula. If you think your baby is thirsty, offer cooled, boiled water separately. If your baby does not start to gain weight normally within 2 weeks, consult your physician.

Increasing appetite may mean that your baby needs more food than you are offering, even if you are giving the correct amount for your baby's age.

Self-help: Always offer more milk than you think necessary and let your baby feed until satisfied. If your baby is over 3 months, he or she may be ready to start eating solid food. If your baby does not start to gain weight normally within 2 weeks, or if you need advice on weaning, consult your physician.

WEIGHT LOSS IN THE NEWBORN

Most babies lose about 5 oz (142 g) in weight during the first week of life. This is perfectly normal and is not a sign that your breast-milk supply is inadequate or that your baby is underfed. Most babies start to put on weight again on the fifth day and have regained their birth weight by the time they are 10 days old. Thereafter weight gain should continue at a steady rate.

Large

Average

Small

Age in days 1 2 3 4 5 6 7 8 9 10

2 Waking at night

Most babies wake at regular intervals through the day and night for feedings during the first few months. Consult this chart only if you think your baby is waking more frequently than is normal for his or her age, if you have difficulty settling your baby at night or if your baby who has previously slept well starts to wake during the night. Diaper rash can sometimes cause a baby to wake at night; see p.135.

For children over 1 year, see chart 12, Sleeping problems

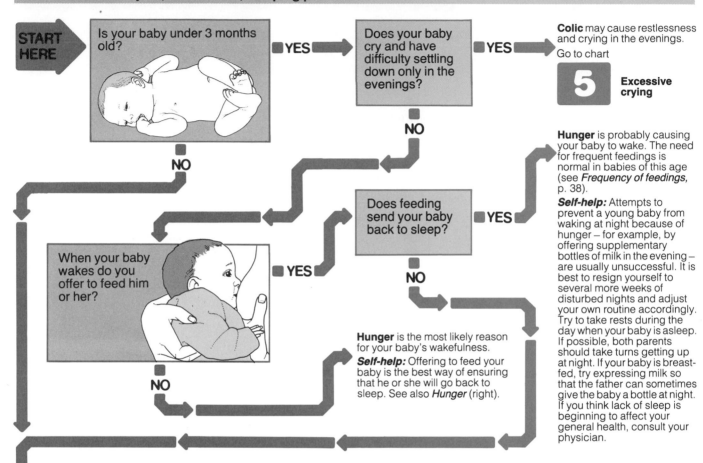

START HERE

Is your baby under 3 months old?

YES ▶ Does your baby cry and have difficulty settling down only in the evenings?

YES ▶ **Colic** may cause restlessness and crying in the evenings.

Go to chart

5 **Excessive crying**

NO

When your baby wakes do you offer to feed him or her?

YES Does feeding send your baby back to sleep?

NO (below "evenings?" box)

YES **Hunger** is probably causing your baby to wake. The need for frequent feedings is normal in babies of this age (see *Frequency of feedings*, p. 38).

Self-help: Attempts to prevent a young baby from waking at night because of hunger – for example, by offering supplementary bottles of milk in the evening – are usually unsuccessful. It is best to resign yourself to several more weeks of disturbed nights and adjust your own routine accordingly. Try to take rests during the day when your baby is asleep. If possible, both parents should take turns getting up at night. If your baby is breast-fed, try expressing milk so that the father can sometimes give the baby a bottle at night. If you think lack of sleep is beginning to affect your general health, consult your physician.

NO

Hunger is the most likely reason for your baby's wakefulness.
Self-help: Offering to feed your baby is the best way of ensuring that he or she will go back to sleep. See also *Hunger* (right).

HELPING YOUR BABY SLEEP

Young babies (under 4 months)
In the first few months of life a baby will sleep when fed and comfortable; the most you can do to help your baby sleep is to ensure that these basic needs of food, warmth and comfort are provided. Concentrate on adjusting your own routine so that you sleep when your baby does to prevent yourself from becoming overtired by disturbed nights. The following suggestions may help you to cope more easily:

- Try to take rests during the day when your baby is asleep.
- Take turns with your partner getting up at night when your baby cries.
- If your baby is breast-fed, express some milk so that your partner can sometimes give the baby a bottle at night.
- Move your baby into a separate room as soon as you feel ready, preferably before the age of 6 months.

Older babies (4 to 12 months)
Most babies who are past the stage of needing frequent night feedings benefit from a regular bedtime routine. A baby who has learned to go to bed without fuss during the first year is less likely to have problems later on. In general, it is best to be firm and predictable, but this should

not prevent you from making the bedtime ritual affectionate and fun. Your baby needs to be reassured that going to bed is not a form of punishment. Some suggestions for increasing the chances of problem-free bedtimes are listed below:

- Always carry out the preparations for bed in the same order – for example, supper, bath, quiet playtime, a breast- or bottle-feeding, and then into the crib for the night.
- Avoid too much excitement in the hour or so before bed.
- Make your baby's room as inviting as possible with plenty to look at on the walls and favorite toys in the crib.
- Provide a night-light if your baby seems to be frightened of the dark.
- Do not be too ready to go to your baby if he or she whimpers in the night. He or she may simply be making noises while asleep, and going into the room may wake your baby unnecessarily.
- If your baby cries in the night, do whatever is necessary to settle him or her (giving a drink or changing a diaper) as quickly and quietly as possible. Do not let your baby persuade you to play, otherwise he or she may learn that waking at night can be fun.

Help your baby not to feel lonely or bored in the crib by providing plenty of interesting things to look at.

Go to next page

Continued from previous page

Has your baby previously slept well at night?

YES →

Does your baby seem sick in any way – for example, is his or her temperature 100°F (38°C) or above?

YES →

A physical illness can easily disrupt a baby's sleep. Depending on your baby's additional symptoms, go to the appropriate chart elsewhere in this book.

↓ **NO** (from previously slept well)

↓ **NO** (from seem sick)

When your baby woke, was he or she crying and difficult to console?

YES →

↓ **NO**

Does your baby sleep in the same room as you?

YES →

Sharing the same room can result in unnecessarily disturbed nights for you and your baby. This may be because you make sounds that disturb your baby or – and this is more likely – the closeness of your baby may make you overaware of his or her movements during sleep. This may cause you to think that your baby is waking when he or she is only whimpering in his or her sleep. Many babies are restless sleepers and, if left alone (unless actually crying), will continue to sleep.

Self-help: If possible, move your baby into his or her own room. You are less likely to be disturbed by anything less than a true cry.

Earache, possibly as a result of an infection of the middle ear, is a common cause of waking at night and distress in a baby who has previously slept well.

Go to chart

29 **Painful or irritated ear**

↓ **NO**

Is the room where your baby sleeps cold AND do you usually find your baby's covers have been kicked off during the night?

YES →

Cold may be waking your baby.
Self-help: A baby who moves a great deal while asleep and kicks off the bedclothes can be kept warm at night by a sleeping sack or a warm sleeper suit.

↓ **NO**

Has there been any domestic crisis or possible cause for anxiety in recent weeks – for example, a move to a new house or a recent absence of the mother or father?

YES →

Anxiety is a possible cause for disrupted sleep even in a young baby. Even comparatively small changes in domestic routine can upset some babies.
Self-help: It may take several days to reassure your baby that there is no cause for anxiety. During this time try to ensure that there are no further changes of routine. When your baby wakes at night, offer a drink and a hug, but make sure that he or she understands that he or she will be put back in the crib. Otherwise, there is a danger that your baby will get into the habit of waking and expecting to play. See also *Helping your baby sleep* (opposite).

↓ **NO**

The need for the comfort and reassurance of your presence is the most common explanation for waking at night when a baby is past the stage of needing night feedings.
Self-help: From an early age, make every effort to stick to a set routine for putting your baby to bed. Your baby should be taught to understand that you will not allow him or her to get up again until morning. If your baby wakes at night, offer a drink but try to avoid picking him or her up. Do not stay with your baby any longer than is necessary to reassure him or her of your presence and to reassure yourself that all is well. If your baby cries when you leave the room, resist going back in. Crying for a few minutes will do your baby no harm and he or she will soon go back to sleep.

SLEEPING PATTERNS

No two babies have the same sleeping pattern or the same sleep requirements, so do not make the mistake of thinking that your baby is abnormal if he or she sleeps less than a friend's baby of the same age. The typical sleeping patterns described here are given simply as examples, and your own baby's routine will almost certainly be different. However, the gradual transition from spending most of the day and night asleep to spending nearly the whole day awake and nearly the whole night asleep is likely to apply to most babies.

Newborn
A newborn baby spends most of the time asleep, waking for feedings about every 3 hours. After the first few months, most babies will sleep longer at night, perhaps only waking once. Wakeful periods in the day will probably become more prolonged.

6 months
By the time a baby is 6 months old, he or she is likely to sleep most of the night, but may wake briefly for a feeding in the early hours of the morning. He or she will be awake for most of the day, but will probably need a nap in the morning and in the afternoon.

1 year
A 1-year-old baby usually sleeps throughout the night without waking (between 10 and 12 hours on average). At this age, a baby will probably need only one major nap during the day.

☐ Awake
▨ Asleep

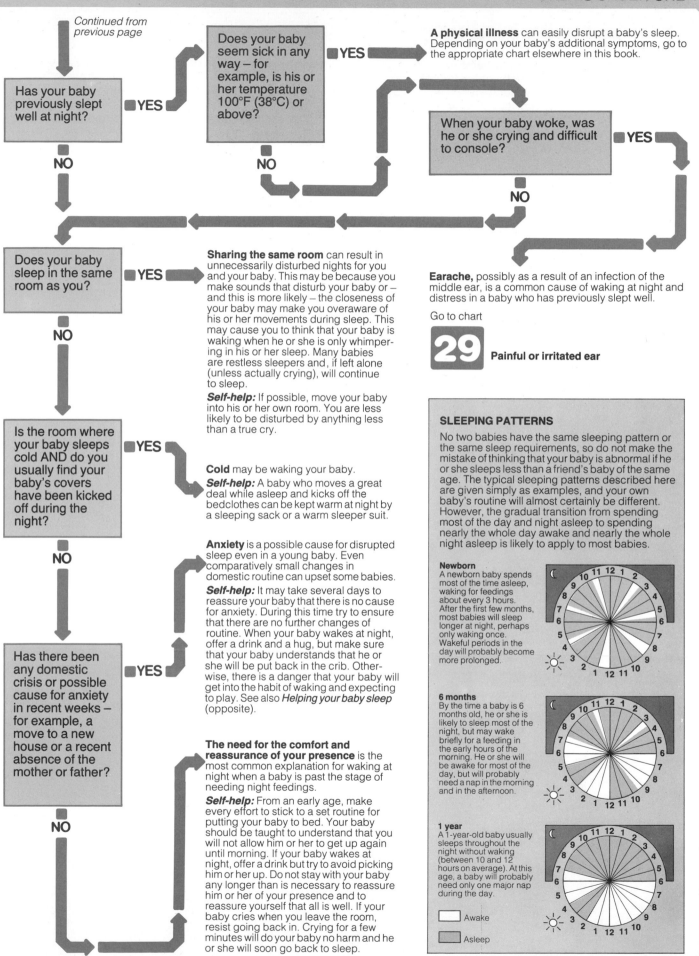

3 Fever in babies

A fever or above-normal body temperature is usually caused by infection. (Viral and bacterial infections are discussed on p. 44.) You may suspect that your baby has a fever if the forehead feels hot, if your baby is sweating more than usual, or if he or she seems sick. Taking your baby's temperature using a clinical thermometer as de-

scribed in the box opposite will enable you to confirm your suspicions. Normal temperature may vary from 97° to 99°F (36° to 37.5°C). Minor fluctuations within this range are never a cause for concern if your baby seems otherwise well. Consult this chart if your baby's temperature rises above this level.

For children over 1 year, see chart 14, Fever in children

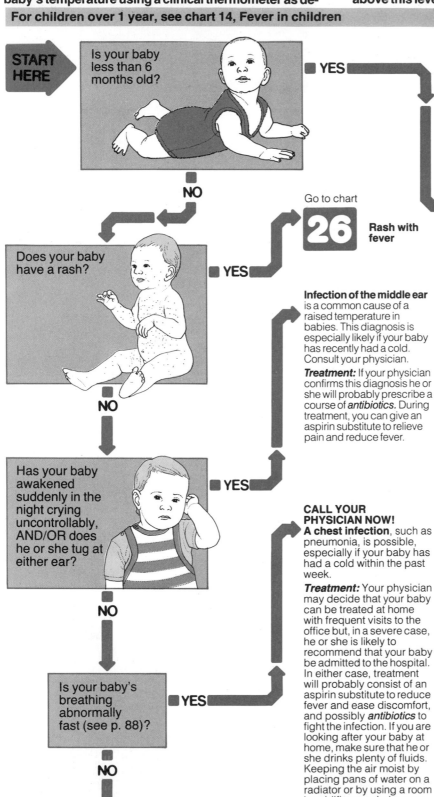

START HERE

Is your baby less than 6 months old?

YES

NO

Does your baby have a rash?

YES → Go to chart **26** **Rash with fever**

NO

Has your baby awakened suddenly in the night crying uncontrollably, AND/OR does he or she tug at either ear?

YES

NO

Is your baby's breathing abnormally fast (see p. 88)?

YES

NO

Go to next page

Infection of the middle ear is a common cause of a raised temperature in babies. This diagnosis is especially likely if your baby has recently had a cold. Consult your physician.

Treatment: If your physician confirms this diagnosis he or she will probably prescribe a course of *antibiotics*. During treatment, you can give an aspirin substitute to relieve pain and reduce fever.

CALL YOUR PHYSICIAN NOW!
A chest infection, such as pneumonia, is possible, especially if your baby has had a cold within the past week.

Treatment: Your physician may decide that your baby can be treated at home with frequent visits to the office but, in a severe case, he or she is likely to recommend that your baby be admitted to the hospital. In either case, treatment will probably consist of an aspirin substitute to reduce fever and ease discomfort, and possibly *antibiotics* to fight the infection. If you are looking after your baby at home, make sure that he or she drinks plenty of fluids. Keeping the air moist by placing pans of water on a radiator or by using a room humidifier may help ease your baby's breathing.

WARNING

HIGH FEVER

If your baby's temperature rises above 102°F (39°C), whatever the suspected cause, you should call your physician at once. This is because high temperatures may be caused by a serious infection and can lead to convulsions in some babies.

CALL YOUR PHYSICIAN NOW!
Infections at this age are unusual but may be serious.

Treatment: Until you see your physician, carry out temperature-reducing measures as described on p. 14. Your physician will examine your baby and, perhaps, order tests to try to make an exact diagnosis (see *Examination by the physician* (p. 45). Depending on whether your physician diagnoses a viral or bacterial infection (see p. 44), he or she may prescribe *antibiotics.* Admission to the hospital may be advised.

FEVERISH CONVULSIONS

Some babies have convulsions (also known as febrile seizures) when their temperatures rise too quickly. During such a convulsion, the arms and legs will shake uncontrollably and the baby may turn blue in the face. This may last for several minutes or sometimes longer.

What to do

If your baby has a feverish convulsion, lay him or her stomach down on a flat surface, and seek medical help at once. While waiting for medical help, attempt to reduce your baby's temperature by removing the clothing and sponging him or her with tepid water as described on p. 14. If your child vomits, clean out his mouth with your finger. The convulsion will not damage your baby's brain, and it will usually stop by itself in a few minutes. If your child has a convulsion caused by fever, it *does not mean* that your child has epilepsy. Some children, however, do have an underlying problem, and your physician may want to do more tests after your child recovers.

FOREIGN TRAVEL

If your baby develops a fever soon after a visit to a hot climate, be sure to tell your physician. Your baby may have caught a disease that is rare in this country, one that your physician might not otherwise suspect.

Continued from previous page

Does your baby have a clear discharge from the nose AND/OR has he or she been coughing? ▶ **YES**

Measles is a possibility if your baby has been in contact with the disease within the past week or so. The appearance of a rash within the next few days will confirm the diagnosis. (See also *Comparison of childhood infectious diseases,* p. 75.) Otherwise, a generalized viral infection is likely. Consult your physician.

Treatment: For both types of illness, your physician is likely to recommend that you take steps to reduce your baby's temperature (see p. 14) while the infection runs its course for the next week or so. Call your physician at once if your baby becomes drowsy or unresponsive, or if he or she refuses to drink.

NO

Is your baby unusually drowsy or irritable? ▶ **YES**

CALL YOUR PHYSICIAN NOW!
Meningitis (inflammation of the membranes surrounding the nervous system, caused by viral or bacterial infection) may be the cause, especially if your baby has also vomited.

Treatment: Your baby will probably be admitted to the hospital where he or she will be given a *lumbar puncture* (p. 52) to make an exact diagnosis. Your child will be given fluids and possibly *antibiotics* (if the infection is bacterial) intravenously.

NO

Has your baby had diarrhea AND/OR been vomiting? ▶ **YES**

CONSULT YOUR PHYSICIAN WITHOUT DELAY!
Gastroenteritis (infection of the digestive tract) is the most likely cause of such symptoms.

Treatment: If the diagnosis is confirmed, your physician is likely to recommend that you follow the guidelines for treating gastroenteritis described in the box on p. 41. However, if your baby's symptoms are severe, of if there are signs of dehydration (see *Persistent vomiting,* p. 40), your physician may advise admission to the hospital, where fluids can be given intravenously.

NO

Has your baby been refusing solid food? ▶ **YES**

A throat or mouth infection is the most likely explanation for the problem.

Self-help: Follow the advice on treating a sore throat on p. 85. Do not force your baby to eat if pain makes swallowing difficult, but make sure he or she drinks at least 1½ pints of fluid a day. Consult your physician if your baby is no better in 48 hours or develops any of the danger signs in the box on p. 84.

NO

Is your baby very warmly dressed AND/OR is he or she in warm surroundings? ▶ **YES**

Overheating, caused by too much clothing or by excessively warm surroundings, can cause a baby's temperature to rise.

Self-help: In general, babies do not need to wear much more clothing than an adult in similar conditions and will be comfortable in a room temperature of 60° to 68°F (15° to 20°C). A baby crib should never be placed next to a radiator. If your baby has become overheated, removing any excess clothing and moving the baby to a slightly cooler (though not cold) place will soon reduce any fever. If your baby's temperature is not down to normal within an hour, consult your physician.

NO

Consult your physician if you are unable to make a diagnosis from this chart.

HOW TO TAKE A BABY'S TEMPERATURE
The best way for you to take your baby's temperature is by using a clinical thermometer under the arm.

1 Shake the thermometer with firm downward flicks of the wrist so that the mercury runs down into the bulb and reads well below the "normal" mark.

2 Sit your baby on your knee and place the thermometer bulb into the armpit.

3 Hold your baby's arm close to his or her side to keep the thermometer firmly in place for 3 minutes.

4 Remove the thermometer and look at it, turning it until you get a clear reading.

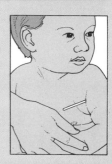

Using this method, you can consider your baby feverish if his or her temperature is 100°F (38°C) or above.

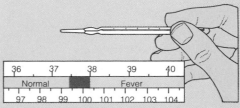

36	37	38	39	40
Normal			Fever	
97 98	99 100	101 102	103	104

Temperature indicator strips
A temperature indicator strip is a re-usable plastic strip that is placed against the forehead. Heat-sensitive panels change color, giving an approximate indication of body temperature. While this method has the advantage of being easy to use, particularly for babies and young children, there is a tendency for the indicator strips to underestimate a fever and you should allow for this by adding 1°F (½°C) to a temperature-strip reading.

4 Skin problems in babies

The skin of newborn babies is sensitive and can easily become inflamed as a result of minor irritations such as prolonged contact with urine or stools, overheating or rubbing against rough fabrics. Such rashes are usually no cause for concern, although you should deal with the cause. Rashes and other skin abnormalities that occur for no apparent reason, or that persist, should always be brought to your physician's attention. Medical advice should be sought promptly if your baby has a rash and seems sick.

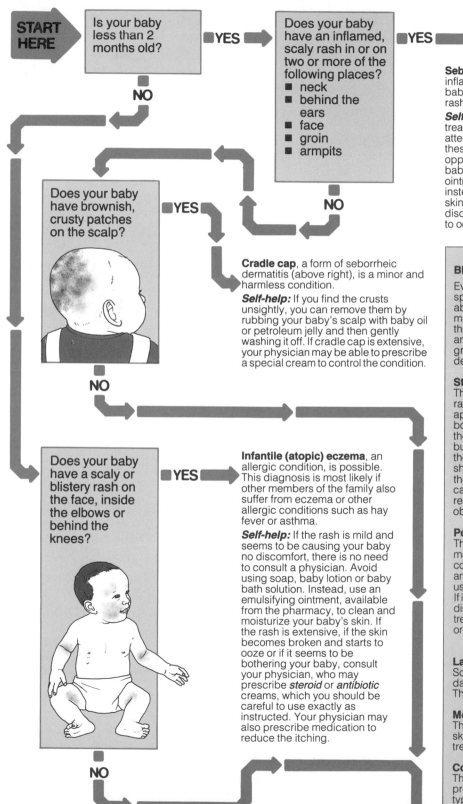

START HERE

Is your baby less than 2 months old?

YES → **Does your baby have an inflamed, scaly rash in or on two or more of the following places?**
- neck
- behind the ears
- face
- groin
- armpits

YES →

Seborrheic dermatitis is a possible cause of skin inflammation in these areas. It is more likely if your baby has been suffering from an extensive diaper rash and/or cradle cap (below left).

Self-help: In mild cases of this condition, no special treatment is needed other than paying special attention to washing and drying the folds of skin in these areas (see *Caring for your baby's skin*, opposite). You should, however, avoid using soap, baby lotion or baby bath solution. An emulsifying ointment, available from the pharmacy, can be used instead for cleansing and moisturizing your baby's skin. If the rash is extensive or seems to be causing discomfort, or if the skin becomes broken and starts to ooze, consult your physician.

NO

Does your baby have brownish, crusty patches on the scalp?

YES →

Cradle cap, a form of seborrheic dermatitis (above right), is a minor and harmless condition.

Self-help: If you find the crusts unsightly, you can remove them by rubbing your baby's scalp with baby oil or petroleum jelly and then gently washing it off. If cradle cap is extensive, your physician may be able to prescribe a special cream to control the condition.

NO

NO

Does your baby have a scaly or blistery rash on the face, inside the elbows or behind the knees?

YES →

Infantile (atopic) eczema, an allergic condition, is possible. This diagnosis is most likely if other members of the family also suffer from eczema or other allergic conditions such as hay fever or asthma.

Self-help: If the rash is mild and seems to be causing your baby no discomfort, there is no need to consult a physician. Avoid using soap, baby lotion or baby bath solution. Instead, use an emulsifying ointment, available from the pharmacy, to clean and moisturize your baby's skin. If the rash is extensive, if the skin becomes broken and starts to ooze or if it seems to be bothering your baby, consult your physician, who may prescribe *steroid* or *antibiotic* creams, which you should be careful to use exactly as instructed. Your physician may also prescribe medication to reduce the itching.

NO

Go to next page

BIRTHMARKS

Every baby has a few moles and pigmented spots. Some babies are born with large areas of abnormally colored skin. The sight of such marks on a new baby can be alarming, but these marks usually become less prominent and may disappear completely as the child grows older. The main types of birthmarks are described here.

Strawberry hemangioma
This is a bright red, usually raised, mark that can appear anywhere on the body. It may grow during the first few months of life, but, in the second half of the first year starts to shrink. The mark continues to shrink until about the age of 7 years, when, in 80 percent of the cases, it disappears completely. Treatment to remove the hemangioma is necessary only if it obscures vision.

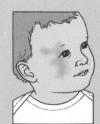

Port-wine stain
This is purplish-red skin that may be slightly raised. It commonly affects the face and limbs. This birthmark usually remains unchanged. If it is disfiguring it can be disguised with make-up or treated by plastic surgery or lasers.

Large pigmented spots
Some babies are born with flat patches of darkened skin known as café-au-lait spots. They can be disguised with cosmetics.

Mongolian blue spots
These are bruise-like marks that appear in dark-skinned races. These marks disappear without treatment before the second birthday.

Congenital brown nevus
This is similar to the ordinary brown mole but is present at birth. If you notice changes in this type of mole, consult your physician.

Continued from previous page

Does your baby have an area of inflamed skin or spots confined to or spreading from the diaper area?

YES →

Is the rash mainly around the anus?

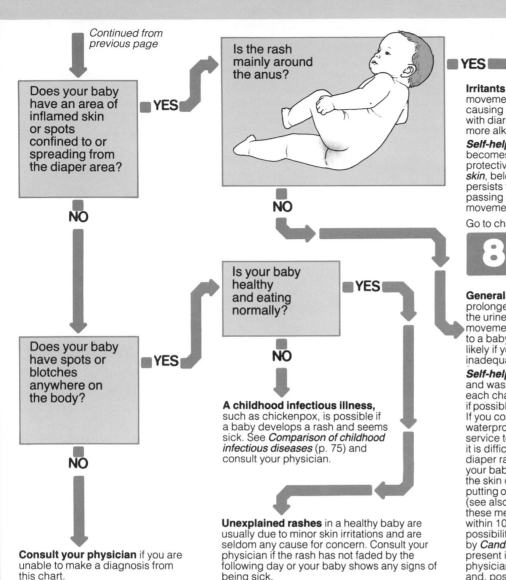

YES →

Irritants that occur naturally in your baby's bowel movements may inflame the skin around the anus, causing diaper rash. This is most likely to occur with diarrhea, which makes the bowel movements more alkaline.

Self-help: Change the diaper as soon as it becomes soiled. Wash your baby well and apply a protective cream (see also *Caring for your baby's skin*, below). Consult your physician if diaper rash persists for more than 10 days. If your baby is passing unusually watery or frequent bowel movements, he or she may have an infection.

Go to chart

8 Diarrhea in babies

NO ↓

Generalized diaper rash is usually due to prolonged contact with wet diapers. Substances in the urine react with chemicals in the bowel movements to produce ammonia, which is irritating to a baby's skin. This type of diaper rash is most likely if you use cloth diapers that have been inadequately sterilized.

Self-help: Change your baby's diapers frequently and wash the diaper area thoroughly between each change. It is best to use disposable diapers, if possible, because these are certain to be sterile. If you continue to use cloth diapers, try not to put waterproof pants on your baby. Hiring a diaper service to clean the diapers may be helpful, since it is difficult to get rid of the ammonia that causes diaper rash by simple home laundering. Leave off your baby's diapers as often as possible to help the skin dry out and promote healing. Before putting on a clean diaper, apply a protective cream (see also *Caring for your baby's skin*, below). If these measures fail to clear up the diaper rash within 10 days, or if it starts to get worse, there is a possibility that the skin may have become infected by *Candida* (or thrush), a fungus that is often present in the bowel. In this case, consult your physician, who may prescribe a special cream and, possibly, medication to treat the infection.

NO ↓

Does your baby have spots or blotches anywhere on the body?

YES →

Is your baby healthy and eating normally?

YES →

NO ↓

A childhood infectious illness, such as chickenpox, is possible if a baby develops a rash and seems sick. See *Comparison of childhood infectious diseases* (p. 75) and consult your physician.

NO ↓

Consult your physician if you are unable to make a diagnosis from this chart.

Unexplained rashes in a healthy baby are usually due to minor skin irritations and seldom any cause for concern. Consult your physician if the rash has not faded by the following day or your baby shows any signs of being sick.

CARING FOR YOUR BABY'S SKIN

A baby's skin is delicate and needs protection from severe cold or heat and strong sunlight (or it may become inflamed, dry and sore). Regular, careful washing is necessary to prevent skin infections and diaper rash.

Washing and bathing

A baby's skin should always be kept clean. Usually the best way to ensure this is to give your baby a daily bath. However, providing that you wash the diaper area thoroughly at each diaper change (see *Diapers*, right) and wipe away any excess spills elsewhere on your baby, less frequent bathing is adequate. When you bathe your baby, remember the following points:

■ Make sure that the water is not too hot (check it using your elbow).
■ Always hold your baby securely in the bath and, even when he or she can sit up unaided, never leave your baby in the bath unattended.
■ Use a mild, unscented soap or baby bath solution. If your baby has dry skin, infantile eczema or seborrheic dermatitis, use emulsifying ointment and wash it away with plain water.
■ When your baby's hair starts to grow thickly, wash it once a week with a mild shampoo.
■ Dry your baby, using his or her own towel, making sure all moisture is removed from the skin folds.
■ If you use talcum powder, apply it sparingly.

Hold your baby securely in the bath.

Diapers

Cloth diapers need careful washing and sterilizing and should be used with a "one-way" diaper liner to keep moisture away from the skin. Disposables are more convenient and are always sterile, but may hold less moisture than cloth diapers. Whichever you choose, change them regularly to prevent diaper rash.

Diaper changing

When you change your baby's diaper, wipe away all traces of urine and bowel movements with a clean washcloth and water or alcohol-free baby wipes. If your baby's skin is dry, baby oil or cream will help. Before putting on a clean diaper, apply petroleum jelly liberally to the area around the genitals and anus.

If possible, try to set aside some time at least once a day for your baby to be without diapers. Exposure to air helps the skin dry out thoroughly and helps prevent diaper rash. If your baby has a sore bottom, try leaving the diapers off for long periods and let your baby lie in a warm room on a towel or diaper. This assists healing, as will the use of a diaper rash ointment contining zinc oxide. If your baby develops a fever or the rash persists, consult your physician.

Use a clean washcloth moistened with water or baby lotion to clean your baby's bottom.

5 Excessive crying

Crying is a young baby's only means of communicating physical discomfort or emotional distress. All babies cry sometimes when they are hungry, wet, upset or in pain, and some babies often seem to cry for no obvious reason. Crying does not necessarily indicate a serious problem. Most parents learn to recognize the most common causes of their baby's crying. Consult this chart if your baby regularly cries more often than you think is normal, or if your baby suddenly starts to cry in an unusual way or for no apparent reason.

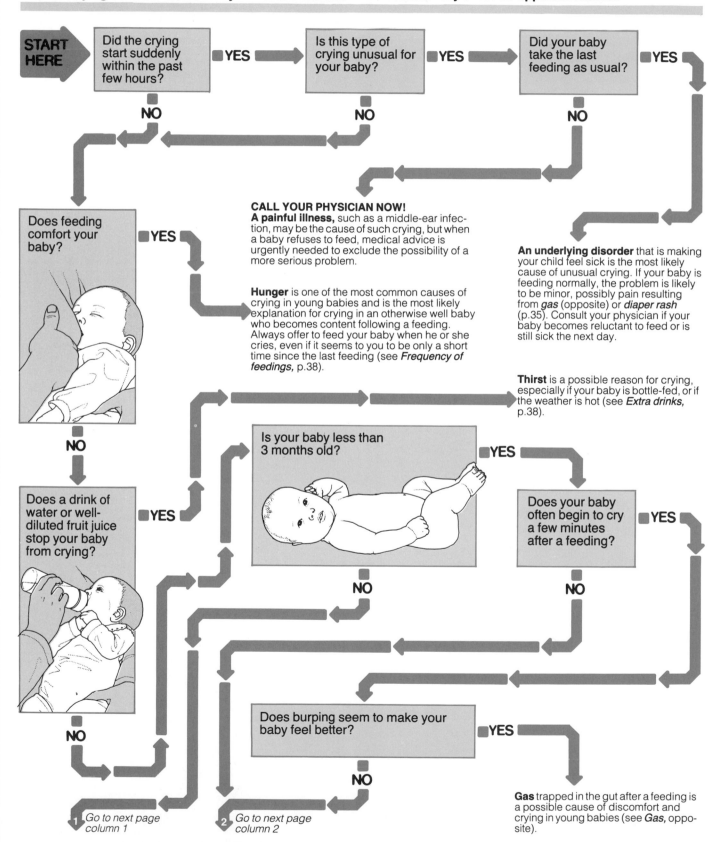

START HERE

Did the crying start suddenly within the past few hours? **YES**

Is this type of crying unusual for your baby? **YES**

Did your baby take the last feeding as usual? **YES**

NO

NO

NO

Does feeding comfort your baby? **YES**

CALL YOUR PHYSICIAN NOW!
A painful illness, such as a middle-ear infection, may be the cause of such crying, but when a baby refuses to feed, medical advice is urgently needed to exclude the possibility of a more serious problem.

Hunger is one of the most common causes of crying in young babies and is the most likely explanation for crying in an otherwise well baby who becomes content following a feeding. Always offer to feed your baby when he or she cries, even if it seems to you to be only a short time since the last feeding (see *Frequency of feedings,* p.38).

An underlying disorder that is making your child feel sick is the most likely cause of unusual crying. If your baby is feeding normally, the problem is likely to be minor, possibly pain resulting from *gas* (opposite) or *diaper rash* (p.35). Consult your physician if your baby becomes reluctant to feed or is still sick the next day.

Thirst is a possible reason for crying, especially if your baby is bottle-fed, or if the weather is hot (see *Extra drinks,* p.38).

NO

Does a drink of water or well-diluted fruit juice stop your baby from crying? **YES**

Is your baby less than 3 months old? **YES**

Does your baby often begin to cry a few minutes after a feeding? **YES**

NO

NO

Does burping seem to make your baby feel better? **YES**

NO

NO

Go to next page column 1

Go to next page column 2

Gas trapped in the gut after a feeding is a possible cause of discomfort and crying in young babies (see *Gas,* opposite).

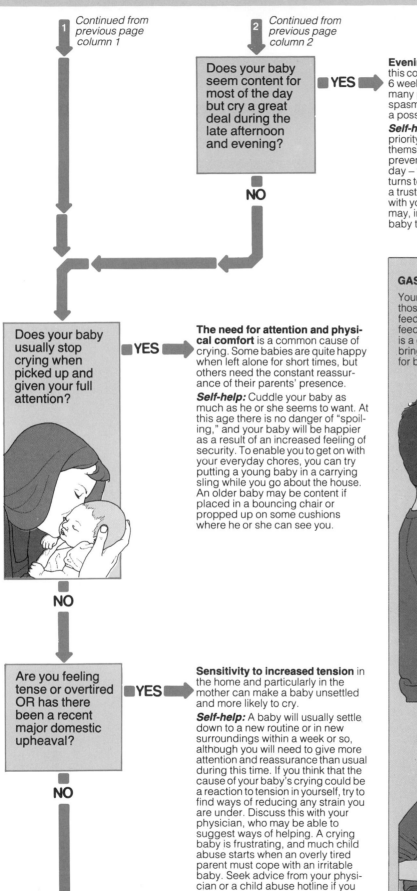

1 Continued from previous page column 1

2 Continued from previous page column 2

Does your baby seem content for most of the day but cry a great deal during the late afternoon and evening?

YES →

Evening (or 3-month) colic is the term often used to describe this common type of crying. It usually starts when a baby is about 6 weeks old and ceases after the age of 3 months. There are many possible explanations for this problem, including painful spasm of the intestines, tiredness and tension in the mother and a possible reduction in her milk supply at this time of day.

Self-help: There is no effective cure for evening colic. The main priority for parents is to find a way of minimizing the strain on themselves from a constantly crying baby. Try to find ways of preventing yourself from becoming too tired at the end of the day – for example, by taking an afternoon rest. Parents can take turns to give each other an evening off or you can sometimes ask a trusted babysitter to look after the baby. Discuss the problem with your physician, who may advise you on how to cope and may, in extreme cases, prescribe a medicine that helps your baby to settle down.

NO

Does your baby usually stop crying when picked up and given your full attention?

YES →

The need for attention and physical comfort is a common cause of crying. Some babies are quite happy when left alone for short times, but others need the constant reassurance of their parents' presence.

Self-help: Cuddle your baby as much as he or she seems to want. At this age there is no danger of "spoiling," and your baby will be happier as a result of an increased feeling of security. To enable you to get on with your everyday chores, you can try putting a young baby in a carrying sling while you go about the house. An older baby may be content if placed in a bouncing chair or propped up on some cushions where he or she can see you.

NO

Are you feeling tense or overtired OR has there been a recent major domestic upheaval?

YES →

Sensitivity to increased tension in the home and particularly in the mother can make a baby unsettled and more likely to cry.

Self-help: A baby will usually settle down to a new routine or in new surroundings within a week or so, although you will need to give more attention and reassurance than usual during this time. If you think that the cause of your baby's crying could be a reaction to tension in yourself, try to find ways of reducing any strain you are under. Discuss this with your physician, who may be able to suggest ways of helping. A crying baby is frustrating, and much child abuse starts when an overly tired parent must cope with an irritable baby. Seek advice from your physician or a child abuse hotline if you think you could lose your temper and become abusive.

NO

Consult your physician if you are unable to make a diagnosis from this chart.

GAS

Young babies often swallow air during feedings, especially those eager feeders who gulp greedily at the start of every feeding. Excess gas in the gut causes regurgitation of feedings and may be linked to discomfort and crying, so it is a good idea to spend a little time helping your baby to bring up gas after each feeding. Some of the best positions for burping are shown below.

Positions for burping
When feeding your baby, make sure that he or she is supported in a semi-upright position (above). After feeding, help your baby to bring up gas by holding him or her against your shoulder (left), over your knee (below left) or on your lap (below).

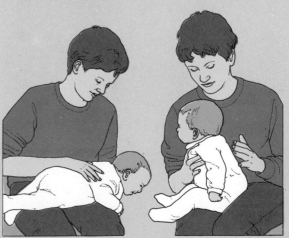

6 Feeding problems

Feeding problems are a common source of irritability and crying in young babies and of concern to their parents. Such problems may include a reluctance to feed, constant hungry crying, and swallowing too much air, leading to regurgitation. There may also be special problems for mothers who are breast-feeding. The diagnostic chart and the boxes on these pages deal with most of the common problems that may arise.

For children over one, see chart 39, Loss of appetite

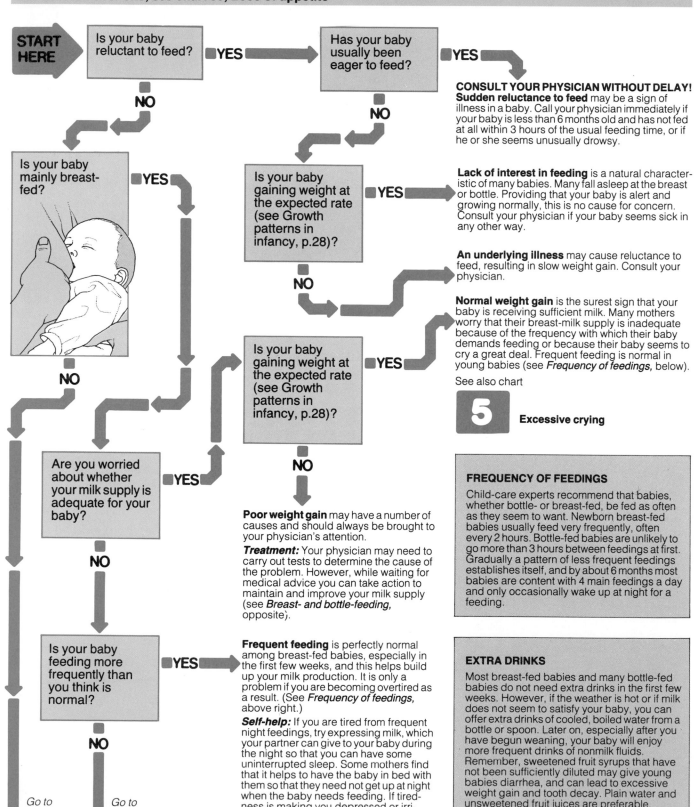

START HERE

Is your baby reluctant to feed? — YES → **Has your baby usually been eager to feed?** — YES →

CONSULT YOUR PHYSICIAN WITHOUT DELAY!
Sudden reluctance to feed may be a sign of illness in a baby. Call your physician immediately if your baby is less than 6 months old and has not fed at all within 3 hours of the usual feeding time, or if he or she seems unusually drowsy.

Is your baby reluctant to feed? — NO ↓

Has your baby usually been eager to feed? — NO ↓

Is your baby mainly breast-fed? — YES ↓

Is your baby gaining weight at the expected rate (see Growth patterns in infancy, p.28)? — YES →

Lack of interest in feeding is a natural characteristic of many babies. Many fall asleep at the breast or bottle. Providing that your baby is alert and growing normally, this is no cause for concern. Consult your physician if your baby seems sick in any other way.

Is your baby gaining weight at the expected rate (see Growth patterns in infancy, p.28)? — NO ↓

An underlying illness may cause reluctance to feed, resulting in slow weight gain. Consult your physician.

Is your baby mainly breast-fed? — NO ↓

Is your baby gaining weight at the expected rate (see Growth patterns in infancy, p.28)? — YES →

Normal weight gain is the surest sign that your baby is receiving sufficient milk. Many mothers worry that their breast-milk supply is inadequate because of the frequency with which their baby demands feeding or because their baby seems to cry a great deal. Frequent feeding is normal in young babies (see *Frequency of feedings*, below).

See also chart

5 **Excessive crying**

Are you worried about whether your milk supply is adequate for your baby? — YES ↑

Is your baby gaining weight at the expected rate (see Growth patterns in infancy, p.28)? — NO ↓

Poor weight gain may have a number of causes and should always be brought to your physician's attention.
Treatment: Your physician may need to carry out tests to determine the cause of the problem. However, while waiting for medical advice you can take action to maintain and improve your milk supply (see *Breast- and bottle-feeding*, opposite).

Are you worried about whether your milk supply is adequate for your baby? — NO ↓

Is your baby feeding more frequently than you think is normal? — YES →

Frequent feeding is perfectly normal among breast-fed babies, especially in the first few weeks, and this helps build up your milk production. It is only a problem if you are becoming overtired as a result. (See *Frequency of feedings*, above right.)
Self-help: If you are tired from frequent night feedings, try expressing milk, which your partner can give to your baby during the night so that you can have some uninterrupted sleep. Some mothers find that it helps to have the baby in bed with them so that they need not get up at night when the baby needs feeding. If tiredness is making you depressed or irritable, consult your physician.

Is your baby feeding more frequently than you think is normal? — NO ↓

1 Go to next page column 1

2 Go to next page column 2

FREQUENCY OF FEEDINGS

Child-care experts recommend that babies, whether bottle- or breast-fed, be fed as often as they seem to want. Newborn breast-fed babies usually feed very frequently, often every 2 hours. Bottle-fed babies are unlikely to go more than 3 hours between feedings at first. Gradually a pattern of less frequent feedings establishes itself, and by about 6 months most babies are content with 4 main feedings a day and only occasionally wake up at night for a feeding.

EXTRA DRINKS

Most breast-fed babies and many bottle-fed babies do not need extra drinks in the first few weeks. However, if the weather is hot or if milk does not seem to satisfy your baby, you can offer extra drinks of cooled, boiled water from a bottle or spoon. Later on, especially after you have begun weaning, your baby will enjoy more frequent drinks of nonmilk fluids. Remember, sweetened fruit syrups that have not been sufficiently diluted may give young babies diarrhea, and can lead to excessive weight gain and tooth decay. Plain water and unsweetened fruit juices are preferable.

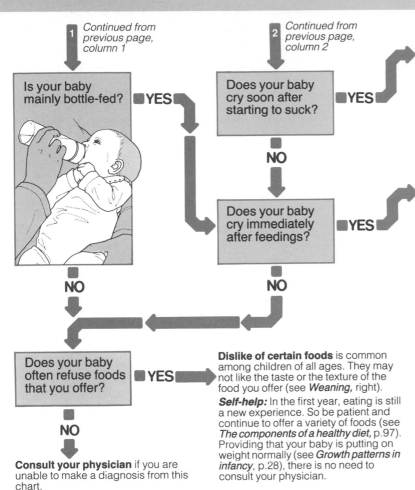

1 Continued from previous page, column 1

Is your baby mainly bottle-fed? ■ YES

2 Continued from previous page, column 2

Does your baby cry soon after starting to suck? ■ YES

NO

Does your baby cry immediately after feedings? ■ YES

Delayed "let-down" reflex is often the cause of such crying. This means that milk is not immediately released from the glands in the breast when your baby starts to suck. Alternatively, the milk may be let down too forcefully and your baby is choked by it.

Self-help: If you think that the problem is delayed let-down, the best cure is to relax. Make sure you are comfortable and undistracted. If necessary, go into a room away from the rest of the family and take the telephone off the hook. If your let-down reflex is too strong for your baby, try expressing a little milk before starting to feed.

Gas or thirst are possible explanations for this

Go to chart

5 Excessive crying

NO

NO

Does your baby often refuse foods that you offer? ■ YES

Dislike of certain foods is common among children of all ages. They may not like the taste or the texture of the food you offer (see *Weaning,* right).

Self-help: In the first year, eating is still a new experience. So be patient and continue to offer a variety of foods (see *The components of a healthy diet,* p.97). Providing that your baby is putting on weight normally (see *Growth patterns in infancy,* p.28), there is no need to consult your physician.

NO

Consult your physician if you are unable to make a diagnosis from this chart.

WEANING

The age at which you start to introduce your baby to solid foods is largely a matter of a baby's individual development and routine. Here are some broad guidelines:

■ Do not give nonmilk foods before 3 months.
■ Start by giving about one teaspoonful of ground rice cereal, or fruit or vegetable puree, once a day.
■ Never add salt or sugar to your baby's food.
■ Make sure early foods are smooth and not too thick.
■ Gradually give a wider variety of tastes and textures. At around 6 months you can introduce foods like pieces of toast or peeled raw fruit and vegetables.
■ Do not give cow's milk before 6 months.
■ As soon as your baby shows an interest, allow him or her to hold the spoon.
■ Remember gradually to reduce your baby's milk intake as more solid food is given.

See also *The components of a healthy diet,* p.97.

BREAST- and BOTTLE-FEEDING

Breast-feeding
All physicians agree that, when possible, breast-feeding is the best way to feed a baby. Breast milk contains all the nutrients a baby needs in the ideal proportions and in the most easily digested form. In addition, a baby who is breast-fed receives antibodies in the milk that protect against infection.

There are very few women who cannot or should not breast-feed their babies if they want to. Most early difficulties can be overcome with patience and determination. Some common breast-feeding problems are discussed below.

Sore nipples
Most new mothers experience some soreness in the first few days of breast-feeding. This normally gets better without special treatment, but here are some suggestions for minimizing discomfort:

■ Ensure that your baby is latching on properly (see right).
■ Prevent your breasts from becoming overfull (see right).
■ Keep your nipples as dry as possible between feedings.
■ If necessary, apply a bland, lanolin-based cream.

Consult your physician if the skin around the nipple becomes cracked or if pain continues throughout the feeding.

Maintaining your milk supply
Most mothers produce exactly the right amount of milk to meet their baby's needs. The following measures will ensure that your milk supply remains plentiful:

■ Eat a nourishing diet (you may need 800 calories a day more than usual).
■ Do not allow yourself to become overtired.
■ Offer your baby a feeding whenever either of you feels the need.
■ If you are temporarily unable to nurse, express milk at normal feeding times so that you can resume normal feeding later.
■ Unless there is a special reason, avoid giving your baby supplementary bottles of formula; these will satisfy your baby's hunger but prevent your breasts from receiving the stimulation they need to produce more milk.

Latching on
When you put your baby to the breast, make sure that he or she takes the whole of the nipple and areola (colored area) into the mouth (far left); otherwise, your nipples may become sore. If your breasts are overfull, latching on may be difficult (left) and you should follow the advice below.

Engorged breasts
This is a common problem during the first few weeks of breast-feeding that can be uncomfortable for you and frustrating for your baby because it makes latching on difficult. Some suggestions:

■ Encourage your baby to feed frequently.
■ If latching on has become difficult for your baby, express a little milk from the nipple before each feeding.
■ If your breasts are very full and your baby is not ready to feed, express some milk.

Consult your physician if your breasts become generally painful and/or red.

Bottle-feeding
For mothers who are unable or unwilling to breast feed, modern formulas provide a satisfactory alternative.

Making up the formula
If it is concentrated, formula should always be made up exactly according to the manufacturer's instructions. Ask your physician if you can use water straight from the tap or if you should boil and cool it first.

Washing feeding equipment
Bottle-fed babies are more susceptible to gastroenteritis than breast-fed babies because germs grow very easily in inadequately washed and rinsed bottles and utensils. Make sure you wash and rinse all your baby's feeding equipment thoroughly.

7 Vomiting in babies

Vomiting is the forceful throwing up of the contents of the stomach as a result of sudden contraction of the muscles around the stomach. Almost any minor upset can cause a baby to regurgitate, but persistent vomiting can be a sign of serious disease and needs prompt medical attention.

For children over 1 year, consult chart 37, Vomiting in children

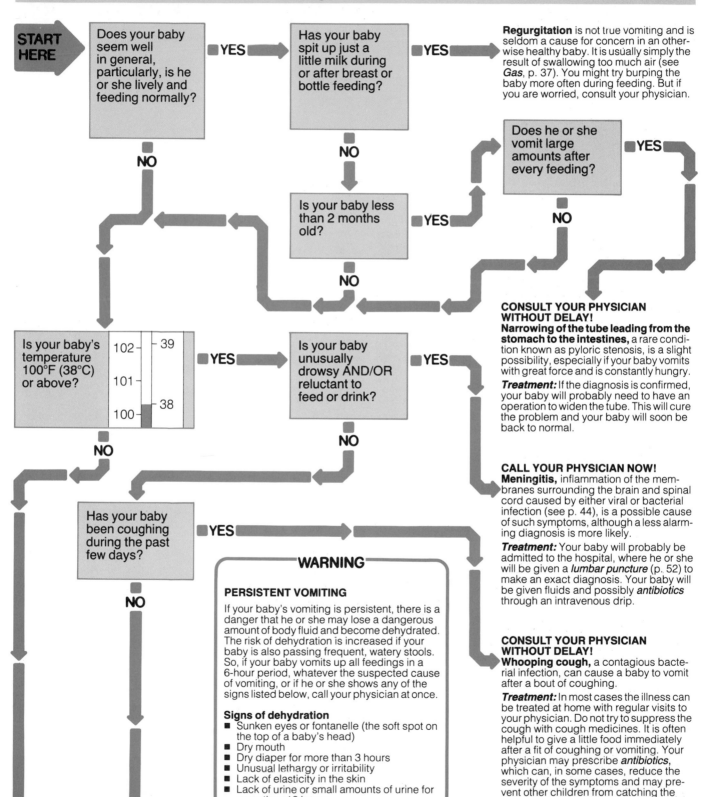

START HERE

Does your baby seem well in general, particularly, is he or she lively and feeding normally? — **YES** →

Has your baby spit up just a little milk during or after breast or bottle feeding? — **YES** →

Regurgitation is not true vomiting and is seldom a cause for concern in an otherwise healthy baby. It is usually simply the result of swallowing too much air (see *Gas*, p. 37). You might try burping the baby more often during feeding. But if you are worried, consult your physician.

NO (from first box) ↓

NO (from second box) ↓

Does he or she vomit large amounts after every feeding? — **YES** →

Is your baby less than 2 months old? — **YES** →

NO (from "Does he or she vomit large amounts")

NO (from "Is your baby less than 2 months old?")

CONSULT YOUR PHYSICIAN WITHOUT DELAY!
Narrowing of the tube leading from the stomach to the intestines, a rare condition known as pyloric stenosis, is a slight possibility, especially if your baby vomits with great force and is constantly hungry.

Treatment: If the diagnosis is confirmed, your baby will probably need to have an operation to widen the tube. This will cure the problem and your baby will soon be back to normal.

Is your baby's temperature 100°F (38°C) or above?

102 / 39
101
100 / 38

— **YES** →

Is your baby unusually drowsy AND/OR reluctant to feed or drink? — **YES** →

NO (from temperature box) ↓

NO (from "Is your baby unusually drowsy") ↓

CALL YOUR PHYSICIAN NOW!
Meningitis, inflammation of the membranes surrounding the brain and spinal cord caused by either viral or bacterial infection (see p. 44), is a possible cause of such symptoms, although a less alarming diagnosis is more likely.

Treatment: Your baby will probably be admitted to the hospital, where he or she will be given a *lumbar puncture* (p. 52) to make an exact diagnosis. Your baby will be given fluids and possibly *antibiotics* through an intravenous drip.

Has your baby been coughing during the past few days? — **YES** →

NO ↓

WARNING

PERSISTENT VOMITING
If your baby's vomiting is persistent, there is a danger that he or she may lose a dangerous amount of body fluid and become dehydrated. The risk of dehydration is increased if your baby is also passing frequent, watery stools. So, if your baby vomits up all feedings in a 6-hour period, whatever the suspected cause of vomiting, or if he or she shows any of the signs listed below, call your physician at once.

Signs of dehydration
- Sunken eyes or fontanelle (the soft spot on the top of a baby's head)
- Dry mouth
- Dry diaper for more than 3 hours
- Unusual lethargy or irritability
- Lack of elasticity in the skin
- Lack of urine or small amounts of urine for more than 12 hours

Call your physician now!

CONSULT YOUR PHYSICIAN WITHOUT DELAY!
Whooping cough, a contagious bacterial infection, can cause a baby to vomit after a bout of coughing.

Treatment: In most cases the illness can be treated at home with regular visits to your physician. Do not try to suppress the cough with cough medicines. It is often helpful to give a little food immediately after a fit of coughing or vomiting. Your physician may prescribe *antibiotics*, which can, in some cases, reduce the severity of the symptoms and may prevent other children from catching the disease. Call your physician at once if your baby has any difficulty breathing or turns bluish during a bout of coughing.

1 Go to next page column 1

2 Go to next page column 2

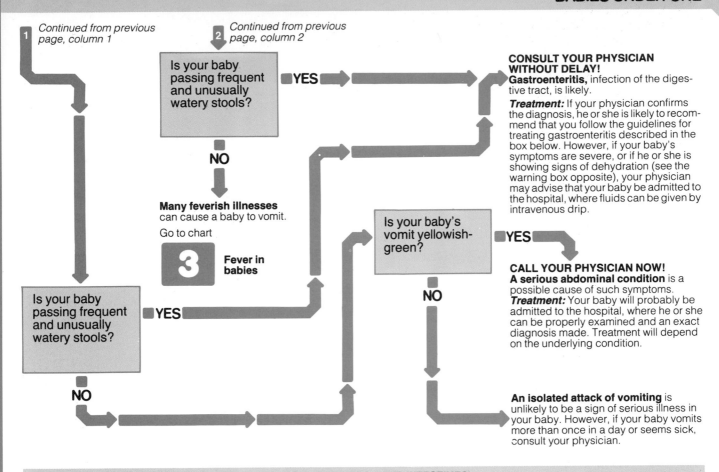

1 *Continued from previous page, column 1*

2 *Continued from previous page, column 2*

Is your baby passing frequent and unusually watery stools?

→ **YES** → **CONSULT YOUR PHYSICIAN WITHOUT DELAY!**
Gastroenteritis, infection of the digestive tract, is likely.

Treatment: If your physician confirms the diagnosis, he or she is likely to recommend that you follow the guidelines for treating gastroenteritis described in the box below. However, if your baby's symptoms are severe, or if he or she is showing signs of dehydration (see the warning box opposite), your physician may advise that your baby be admitted to the hospital, where fluids can be given by intravenous drip.

NO ↓

Many feverish illnesses can cause a baby to vomit.

Go to chart

3 **Fever in babies**

Is your baby passing frequent and unusually watery stools?

→ **YES**

NO ↓

Is your baby's vomit yellowish-green?

→ **YES** → **CALL YOUR PHYSICIAN NOW!**
A serious abdominal condition is a possible cause of such symptoms.
Treatment: Your baby will probably be admitted to the hospital, where he or she can be properly examined and an exact diagnosis made. Treatment will depend on the underlying condition.

NO ↓

An isolated attack of vomiting is unlikely to be a sign of serious illness in your baby. However, if your baby vomits more than once in a day or seems sick, consult your physician.

TREATING GASTROENTERITIS (INFLAMMATION OF THE STOMACH AND INTESTINES)

If your physician decides that your baby can be safely treated at home, he or she will probably recommend that you stop all milk and solids for at least 24 hours and gradually reintroduce a normal diet over the following days. Example schemes are described here. Instead of milk and other drinks you may be advised to give your baby a glucose solution.

Making up a glucose solution
You can make up your own glucose solution by using 5 tablespoons of sugar to 1 quart of boiled water. Do not use for more than 24 hours without consulting your physician. Alternatively, you can use packets of glucose and mineral powder or ready-to-use mixtures of salt and sugar, available without a prescription at your pharmacy. A homemade mixture can be made by adding 3 tablespoons of sugar and ½ teaspoon of salt to 1 quart of water.

Baby's weight	Daily fluid intake
(pounds)	(ounces)
8 and under	16
9	18
10	20
11	22
12	24
13	26
14	28
15	30
16 – 17	33
18	36
19	38
20	40
21	42
22 and over	44

Calculating your baby's fluid needs
Babies with gastroenteritis need to receive a carefully regulated amount of fluid each day to prevent dehydration. To calculate an adequate amount for your baby, find his or her weight in the left-hand column of the table (below left) and then look across to the right-hand column to find an appropriate volume of fluid. No baby, regardless of weight, should receive less than ½ quart (16 oz) or more than 1½ quarts (48 oz).

Breast-fed babies
If your breast-fed baby has gastroenteritis, do not breast feed for the first 24 hours of the illness, but give the recommended amount of glucose solution. On each successive day reduce the amount of glucose solution you offer at each feeding by one fifth of the total recommended, and put your baby to the breast afterward. During the days of treatment you can relieve the discomfort of overfull breasts by expressing the excess breast milk.

Weaned babies
If your baby is already weaned, give no milk or dairy products for 5 days, but give the recommended amount of glucose solution for his or her weight. (Apple juice, jello or bouillon could also be given.) Give no solids on Day 1, but you can gradually introduce increased amounts of strained fruit or vegetables from Day 2 until Day 6, when you can resume your normal feeding routine. If your child's condition continues to improve in 24 to 28 hours, bananas, apple sauce and/or saltine crackers can be given, if introduced into the diet slowly.

Treatment scheme
While your baby is sick you must ensure that he or she drinks the correct amount of fluid for his or her weight each day (see **Calculating your baby's fluid needs**, above). While your baby is vomiting you will need to give fluids at frequent intervals (about every hour).

Bottle-fed babies

Day 1
Give no milk. Instead, give the glucose solution at regular intervals.

Day 2
Give your baby a mixture of 1 part made-up milk formula to 4 parts glucose solution at each feeding.

Day 3
Give a mixture of 2 parts milk formula to 3 parts glucose solution at each feeding.

Day 4
Give a mixture of 3 parts milk formula to 2 parts glucose solution at each feeding.

Day 5
Give a mixture of 4 parts milk formula to 1 part glucose solution at each feeding.

Day 6
Return to normal feeding.

Note: If at any time your baby's symptoms recur, go back to Day 1 and call your physician.

8 Diarrhea in babies

Diarrhea is the more frequent passage of runny, watery bowel movements than is usual for your baby. Remember, it is quite normal for a fully breast-fed baby to pass very soft bowel movements. However, if your baby has diarrhea, whatever the suspected cause, it is important to prevent dehydration (see below).

For children over 1 year, see chart 40, Diarrhea in children

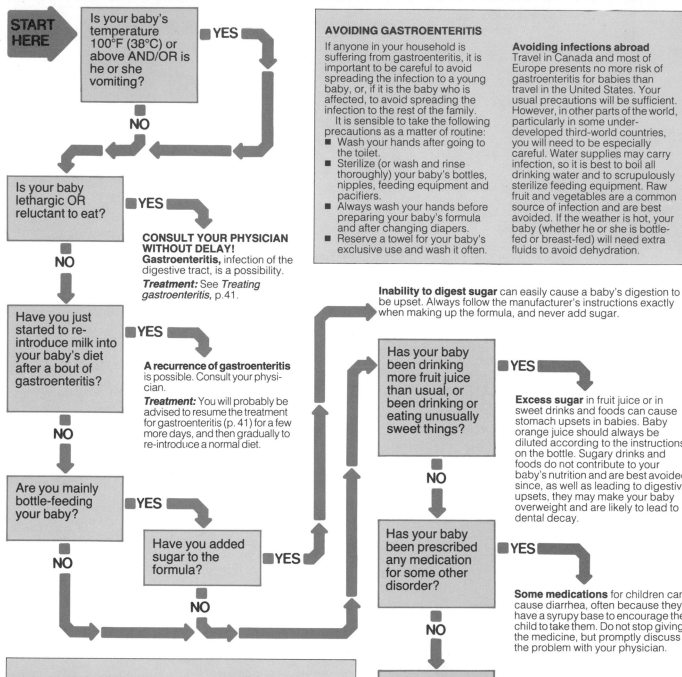

START HERE

Is your baby's temperature 100°F (38°C) or above AND/OR is he or she vomiting?

YES

NO

Is your baby lethargic OR reluctant to eat?

YES

NO

CONSULT YOUR PHYSICIAN WITHOUT DELAY!
Gastroenteritis, infection of the digestive tract, is a possibility.
Treatment: See *Treating gastroenteritis,* p.41.

Have you just started to re-introduce milk into your baby's diet after a bout of gastroenteritis?

YES

NO

A recurrence of gastroenteritis is possible. Consult your physician.
Treatment: You will probably be advised to resume the treatment for gastroenteritis (p. 41) for a few more days, and then gradually to re-introduce a normal diet.

Are you mainly bottle-feeding your baby?

YES

NO

Have you added sugar to the formula?

YES

NO

AVOIDING GASTROENTERITIS

If anyone in your household is suffering from gastroenteritis, it is important to be careful to avoid spreading the infection to a young baby, or, if it is the baby who is affected, to avoid spreading the infection to the rest of the family.
It is sensible to take the following precautions as a matter of routine:
■ Wash your hands after going to the toilet.
■ Sterilize (or wash and rinse thoroughly) your baby's bottles, nipples, feeding equipment and pacifiers.
■ Always wash your hands before preparing your baby's formula and after changing diapers.
■ Reserve a towel for your baby's exclusive use and wash it often.

Avoiding infections abroad
Travel in Canada and most of Europe presents no more risk of gastroenteritis for babies than travel in the United States. Your usual precautions will be sufficient. However, in other parts of the world, particularly in some under-developed third-world countries, you will need to be especially careful. Water supplies may carry infection, so it is best to boil all drinking water and to scrupulously sterilize feeding equipment. Raw fruit and vegetables are a common source of infection and are best avoided. If the weather is hot, your baby (whether he or she is bottle-fed or breast-fed) will need extra fluids to avoid dehydration.

Inability to digest sugar can easily cause a baby's digestion to be upset. Always follow the manufacturer's instructions exactly when making up the formula, and never add sugar.

Has your baby been drinking more fruit juice than usual, or been drinking or eating unusually sweet things?

YES

NO

Excess sugar in fruit juice or in sweet drinks and foods can cause stomach upsets in babies. Baby orange juice should always be diluted according to the instructions on the bottle. Sugary drinks and foods do not contribute to your baby's nutrition and are best avoided since, as well as leading to digestive upsets, they may make your baby overweight and are likely to lead to dental decay.

Has your baby been prescribed any medication for some other disorder?

YES

NO

Some medications for children can cause diarrhea, often because they have a syrupy base to encourage the child to take them. Do not stop giving the medicine, but promptly discuss the problem with your physician.

Have you just started your baby on solids?

YES

NO

Unfamiliar foods may cause digestive upsets in babies. This is no cause for concern if it happens only occasionally and your baby's bowel movements quickly return to normal. But if the problem persists, or seems to happen only when a particular type of food is eaten, consult your physician.

Consult your physician if you are unable to make a diagnosis from this chart.

PREVENTING DEHYDRATION

If your baby has persistent diarrhea, especially if it is accompanied by vomiting, there is a danger of dehydration (loss of body fluids). So it is important to give your baby plenty of extra fluids, even if he or she does not take in any food or milk (see *Treating gastroenteritis,* p.41).
Even if you think your baby is taking in adequate amounts of fluid, you should be on the lookout for signs of dehydration (see *Persistent vomiting,* p.40).

Signs of dehydration
■ Sunken eyes or fontanelle (the soft spot on the top of a baby's head)
■ Dry mouth
■ Dry diaper for more than 3 hours
■ Unusual lethargy or irritability
■ Lack of elasticity in the skin

2 Children of all ages

9 Feeling sick

A child may sometimes complain of feeling sick without giving you a clear idea of what exactly is the matter. Or you may suspect that your child is sick if he or she seems less lively or more irritable than usual. If this happens, you may be able to find a possible explanation for the problem by looking for specific signs of illness as described in this chart. If your child is under 2 years old, see the box below.

For unusual drowsiness, see chart 13, Drowsiness

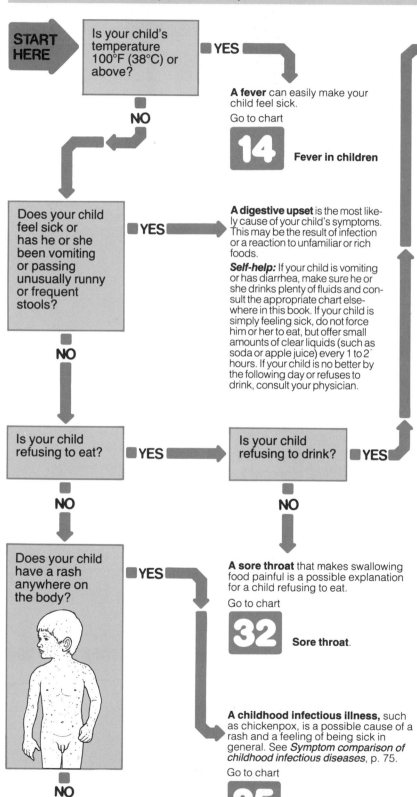

START HERE

Is your child's temperature 100°F (38°C) or above?

YES → A **fever** can easily make your child feel sick.

Go to chart

14 Fever in children

NO

Does your child feel sick or has he or she been vomiting or passing unusually runny or frequent stools?

YES → A **digestive upset** is the most likely cause of your child's symptoms. This may be the result of infection or a reaction to unfamiliar or rich foods.

Self-help: If your child is vomiting or has diarrhea, make sure he or she drinks plenty of fluids and consult the appropriate chart elsewhere in this book. If your child is simply feeling sick, do not force him or her to eat, but offer small amounts of clear liquids (such as soda or apple juice) every 1 to 2 hours. If your child is no better by the following day or refuses to drink, consult your physician.

NO

Is your child refusing to eat? **YES** → **Is your child refusing to drink?** **YES** →

NO **NO**

Does your child have a rash anywhere on the body? **YES** → A **sore throat** that makes swallowing food painful is a possible explanation for a child refusing to eat.

Go to chart

32 Sore throat.

A **childhood infectious illness,** such as chickenpox, is a possible cause of a rash and a feeling of being sick in general. See *Symptom comparison of childhood infectious diseases,* p. 75.

Go to chart

25 Spots and rashes.

NO

Go to next page

CALL YOUR PHYSICIAN NOW!
Refusal to eat or drink, when combined with other signs of illness such as listlessness or irritability, is a serious symptom requiring urgent medical attention.

CHILDREN UNDER TWO

It is usually easy for you to tell when your baby or young child is sick: he or she may seem irritable, or may cry continuously and the sound of the cry may be quite different from the healthy yell you are used to. However, since a baby cannot describe his or her feelings to you, it is often quite difficult to find the cause of the problem. In addition, illnesses in young children tend to develop much faster than in older children and adults. It is therefore usually best to seek your physician's advice if your baby or toddler seems sick in general for no obvious reason. You should call your physician as a matter of urgency if your baby has any of the following symptoms:

- abnormal drowsiness or unresponsiveness
- temperature over 102°F (39°C)
- repeated vomiting
- diarrhea for more than 24 hours
- abnormally rapid breathing (see p. 88)
- noisy breathing
- refusal to drink
- red or purple rash
- has not urinated in 12 hours

VIRAL AND BACTERIAL INFECTIONS

Childhood infections may be caused by two different types of microbe – bacteria or viruses. These microbes and the illnesses they cause differ from each other in several important ways.

Bacteria
Bacteria multiply in body fluids, they are large enough to be seen under a microscope and are destroyed by *antibiotics*. A child can be infected by the same bacteria many times.

Viruses
Viruses are much smaller than bacteria and multiply inside body cells. They cannot be seen under a microscope and are unaffected by standard antibiotics. A single attack by a particular virus usually gives lifelong immunity; this is why children normally have mumps or chickenpox only once. Unfortunately, dozens of different viruses can cause coughs, sore throats and runny noses, and every child has to suffer repeated attacks until he or she has developed immunity to the most common ones.

Treatment
A physician examining a sick child has to decide whether the cause is likely to be a viral or bacterial infection. Often the two are difficult to distinguish. In most cases, he or she will make a diagnosis based on the history and physical examination. Sometimes laboratory tests may be helpful. If a virus is thought to be responsible, treatment is aimed at relieving symptoms, such as pain and fever. If there is bacterial infection, your physician may prescribe antibiotics.

Continued from previous page

Has your child been in contact with an infectious illness within the past 3 weeks?

YES → **Childhood infectious illnesses** often start by making the child feel sick in general. The appearance of a specific symptom, such as a rash, within a few days should make diagnosis easier. (See *Symptom comparison of childhood infectious diseases*, p. 75.) Consult your physician if your child is no better in 24 hours or develops further symptoms.

NO ↓

Does your child complain of stomachache or does he or she cry and draw his or her legs up toward the stomach?

YES → **Abdominal pain** may occur in a child for a variety of reasons.

Go to chart

38 **Abdominal pain**

NO ↓

Can you think of any reason why your child may wish to stay at home (if he or she goes to school) or why he or she may want extra attention from you?

YES → **School difficulties or insecurity at home** can often make a child feel physically sick.
Self-help: If this is the first time that this has happened, keep your child at home for a day and try to discover what the underlying problem is and, if possible, reassure your child. If your child still feels sick the following day, call your physician. If your child regularly refuses to go to school, you may need special help.

Go to chart

23 **School difficulties**.

NO ↓

Consult your physician if you are unable to make a diagnosis from this chart and your child is no better in 24 hours.

EXAMINATION BY THE PHYSICIAN

The examination that your physician performs on your sick child follows a methodical routine of assessment. The physician decides whether the child looks sick—in particular whether he or she is lively or apathetic.

Your physician then checks the pulse and breathing rates and examines the different body systems in turn.

Lymph glands
The physician feels along the jaw (left) and in the armpits and groin for signs of swelling that may suggest infection.

Throat and mouth
The inside of the mouth and throat is examined for inflammation and spots using a wooden spatula and small flashlight (right).

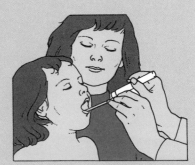

Heart and lungs
The health of heart and lungs are assessed by listening to the child's chest and back through a stethoscope (below).

Ears
Ear examination is described on p. 81.

Abdomen
The abdomen is gently pressed (palpated) to check for swelling of any of the internal organs (e.g., liver or spleen) (below).

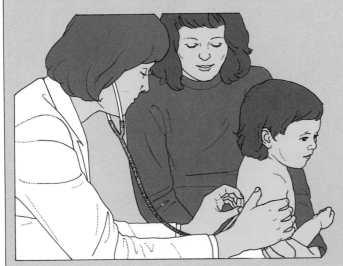

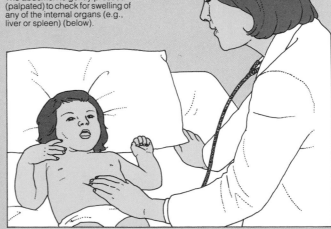

10 Slow growth

Many parents worry that their child is too short or too thin. Some children are naturally smaller than average as a result of heredity or other factors. However, serious growth disorders affecting general health are rare. The best way for you to avoid unnecessary anxiety is to keep a regular record of your child's height and weight so that you will know that your child is growing in proportion as well as at a normal rate (see the growth charts on pp. 124-125). Consult the diagnostic chart below only if your child's weight is increasing at a much slower rate than you would expect from his or her height, or if your child fails to grow in height as much as expected.

For children under 1 year, see chart 1, Slow weight gain

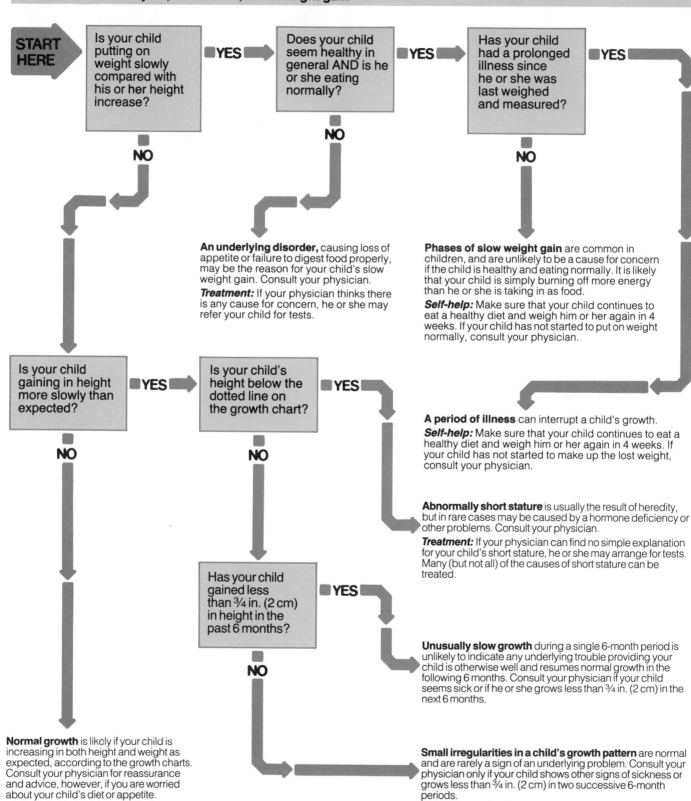

START HERE

Is your child putting on weight slowly compared with his or her height increase?

YES → **Does your child seem healthy in general AND is he or she eating normally?**

YES → **Has your child had a prolonged illness since he or she was last weighed and measured?**

YES →

NO ↓ (from first box)

NO ↓ (from second box)

An underlying disorder, causing loss of appetite or failure to digest food properly, may be the reason for your child's slow weight gain. Consult your physician.
Treatment: If your physician thinks there is any cause for concern, he or she may refer your child for tests.

NO ↓ (from third box)

Phases of slow weight gain are common in children, and are unlikely to be a cause for concern if the child is healthy and eating normally. It is likely that your child is simply burning off more energy than he or she is taking in as food.
Self-help: Make sure that your child continues to eat a healthy diet and weigh him or her again in 4 weeks. If your child has not started to put on weight normally, consult your physician.

Is your child gaining in height more slowly than expected?

YES → **Is your child's height below the dotted line on the growth chart?**

YES →

A period of illness can interrupt a child's growth.
Self-help: Make sure that your child continues to eat a healthy diet and weigh him or her again in 4 weeks. If your child has not started to make up the lost weight, consult your physician.

NO ↓ (from "Is your child gaining in height")

NO ↓ (from "Is your child's height below")

Abnormally short stature is usually the result of heredity, but in rare cases may be caused by a hormone deficiency or other problems. Consult your physician.
Treatment: If your physician can find no simple explanation for your child's short stature, he or she may arrange for tests. Many (but not all) of the causes of short stature can be treated.

Has your child gained less than ¾ in. (2 cm) in height in the past 6 months?

YES →

Unusually slow growth during a single 6-month period is unlikely to indicate any underlying trouble providing your child is otherwise well and resumes normal growth in the following 6 months. Consult your physician if your child seems sick or if he or she grows less than ¾ in. (2 cm) in the next 6 months.

NO ↓ (from "Has your child gained less")

Normal growth is likely if your child is increasing in both height and weight as expected, according to the growth charts. Consult your physician for reassurance and advice, however, if you are worried about your child's diet or appetite.

Small irregularities in a child's growth pattern are normal and are rarely a sign of an underlying problem. Consult your physician only if your child shows other signs of sickness or grows less than ¾ in. (2 cm) in two successive 6-month periods.

GROWTH PATTERNS IN CHILDHOOD

The growth charts on pp. 124-125 enable you to record your child's height and weight at regular intervals and to compare his or her progress with the standard growth rates for large, average and small children.

Usually, a child's growth will remain close to a standard curve for both height and weight throughout childhood. However, sometimes growth patterns can vary, as shown by the charts below.

Naturally slim

Some children are naturally slim. This is unlikely to be a cause for concern in a healthy child if both height and weight increase at a constant rate, and providing that the child's weight is only a little less than expected. The chart shown is that of a normal child who has always been light for his or her own height.

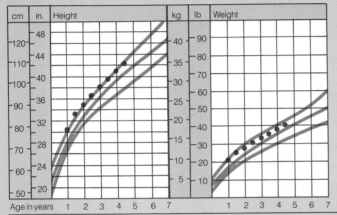

Losing excess weight

An overweight child may at first appear to be gaining insufficient weight as he or she slims down. The chart shows a child whose height is average, but whose weight was above average at 2 years. Over the next 2 years he or she gained little weight so that, by the age of 4, the child's weight was normal for his or her height.

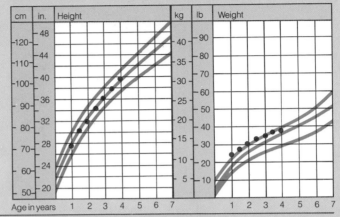

Too light

This chart shows a tall child whose weight is increasing much slower than normal, although he or she is growing in height as expected. If your child's weight is increasing at less than the normal rate, you should consult your physician.

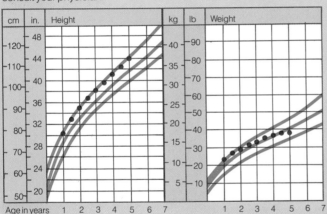

Too small

This chart shows both weight and height increasing at a much slower rate than is normal, even for a small child. If your child's growth chart looks like this, you should seek medical advice.

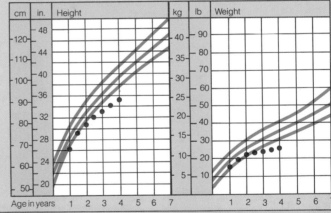

Overweight

The chart of a child who is overweight shows a normal rate of height increase – in this example the child is just below average height – but the weight increase curve is similar to that of a much taller child. If your child's growth chart looks like this, consult diagnostic chart 11, *Excessive weight gain.*

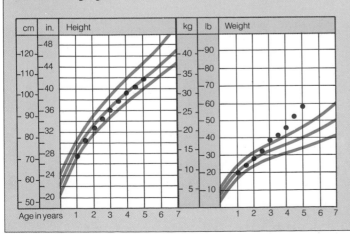

Late puberty

A child approaching puberty who is a late developer may appear to be growing more slowly than normal at an age when many of his or her contemporaries have reached a period of rapid growth. This is, however, no cause for concern; the child will usually make up for the delay later, as shown in this example. See also diagnostic chart 50, *Delayed puberty.*

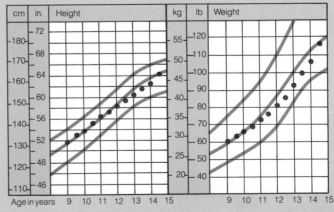

11 Excessive weight gain

Growing appreciation of the dangers of obesity in adults has led to an increasing awareness that the problem often starts in childhood, when eating habits are established. In addition, being overweight carries particular health risks for a child and may contribute to emotional and social problems as he or she gets older. It is therefore most important for parents to be alert to the possibility of excessive weight gain in their child. The appearance of a young baby is not always a reliable sign of obesity, as babies and toddlers are naturally chubby. The best way of ensuring that you quickly notice any weight problem in your child (whatever his or her age) is to keep a regular record of your child's growth (see the growth charts on pp. 122-125). If your child's weight-gain curve is rising more steeply than the curve for height, your child is probably becoming fat. Consult this diagnostic chart to find out what may be the reason.

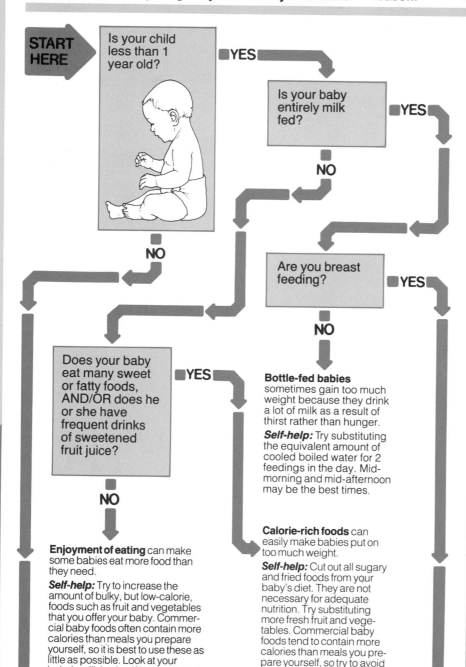

START HERE

Is your child less than 1 year old?

YES → **Is your baby entirely milk fed?**

YES →

NO ↓

NO ↓

Are you breast feeding?

YES →

NO ↓

Does your baby eat many sweet or fatty foods, AND/OR does he or she have frequent drinks of sweetened fruit juice?

YES →

NO ↓

Enjoyment of eating can make some babies eat more food than they need.

Self-help: Try to increase the amount of bulky, but low-calorie, foods such as fruit and vegetables that you offer your baby. Commercial baby foods often contain more calories than meals you prepare yourself, so it is best to use these as little as possible. Look at your baby's milk intake. If he or she is still drinking more than about 1 pint a day, try substituting plain cooled boiled water or well-diluted, fresh fruit juice sometimes. See also *The components of a healthy diet,* p. 97.

Bottle-fed babies sometimes gain too much weight because they drink a lot of milk as a result of thirst rather than hunger.

Self-help: Try substituting the equivalent amount of cooled boiled water for 2 feedings in the day. Mid-morning and mid-afternoon may be the best times.

Calorie-rich foods can easily make babies put on too much weight.

Self-help: Cut out all sugary and fried foods from your baby's diet. They are not necessary for adequate nutrition. Try substituting more fresh fruit and vegetables. Commercial baby foods tend to contain more calories than meals you prepare yourself, so try to avoid these. If your baby drinks large quantities of sweetened drinks, offer plain water or well-diluted unsweetened fruit juice instead. See also *The components of a healthy diet,* p. 97.

CAUSES OF EXCESSIVE WEIGHT GAIN

The vast majority of children who become overweight do so because they regularly eat more food than they burn up to produce energy. The excess calories are then deposited under the skin as fat. Normally, children will adjust their intake of food according to their energy needs. However, the body's natural appetite-regulating mechanism can be upset by a number of factors.

Family overeating
The most common cause of obesity in children is habitual overeating in the family, so that the child loses touch with the body's real needs. The family may eat too many of the wrong foods (mainly sugar and fat) or may simply eat too much. So, if your child is overweight, look at yourself and the rest of the family; the chances are that you are all fatter than you should be. In this case, the best way to help your child to slim down will be for the whole family to adopt healthier eating habits.

Enforced eating
A child who is brought up to finish everything on the plate, regardless of appetite, may also become overweight, because he or she will become used to eating more than necessary to please his or her parents.

Eating for comfort
Less commonly, a child may turn to eating in reaction to stress and anxiety. In this situation, food is used for comfort rather than to satisfy hunger, and over time the child may get into the habit of eating too much.

Medical causes
Medical problems that cause obesity are extremely rare and should be considered only if your child shows other signs of ill health or if genuine attempts at dieting fail.

Three golden rules for preventing your child from becoming overweight
- Make sure that the whole family is eating a healthy diet (see *The components of a healthy diet,* p. 97).
- Always be guided by your child's appetite and never force him or her to eat. He or she will not starve.
- Try to avoid giving or withholding food as a form of reward or punishment. This may give food emotional significance for your child, which can lead to eating problems in the future.

Breast-fed babies often gain weight quickly between 2 and 4 months. This is perfectly normal and no special action is necessary.

Go to next page

Continued from previous page

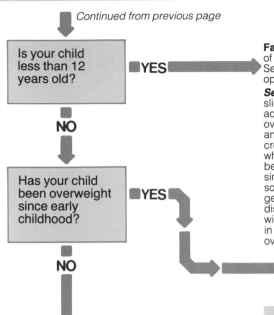

Is your child less than 12 years old? ▪YES▪ → **Family overeating** is almost always the cause of excessive weight gain in this age group. See *Causes of excessive weight gain*, opposite.

Self-help: Suggestions for helping your child slim down are given below. Do not try to achieve a rapid weight loss or you will become overanxious about your child's eating habits and may transmit your anxiety to your child, creating additional problems. At this age, when children have plenty of growing to do before they reach adult size, concentrate simply on preventing additional weight gain, so that your child "stretches out" as he or she gets taller. If your child is severely overweight, discuss the problem with your physician, who will help you with diet advice, and may put you in contact with a self-help support group for overweight children.

NO

Has your child been overweight since early childhood? ▪YES▪

NO

Unhealthy eating habits established in early childhood are likely to persist into adolescence and adulthood unless action is taken.

Self-help: Your child probably realizes that he or she has a weight problem. Plenty of moral support from you is necessary to make any diet successful. This includes the cooperation of the whole family in eating sensibly. It is difficult for a child to lose weight if either parent is overeating. Look at the diet suggestions below and discuss the best methods of losing weight with your child. Your child's cooperation is essential; if you try to enforce a diet, he or she may only start to eat secretly. Crash dieting can be harmful physically and emotionally. Gradual weight loss is far more effective.

Sudden weight gain as a child approaches adolescence is common, particularly in girls. Slight weight gain may be the result of hormonal changes, but excessive weight gain is more likely to be the result of overeating, possibly as a result of emotional insecurity.

Self-help: If your child is only slightly overweight, no special action is necessary other than paying a little extra attention to providing a healthy diet. If your child has put on a lot of weight, try to find out why he or she is overeating. Does your child have any reason to feel insecure? Are there any problems in the family or at school? Tackling the underlying cause of any unhappiness as well as adopting a sensible reducing diet (see *How to help your child lose weight*, right) will help your child feel more self-confident.

THE DANGERS OF OBESITY IN CHILDHOOD

Dangers to health
The principal danger to physical health of obesity in childhood is that children who become fat are more likely to remain so and become fat adults, who in turn are at greater-than-average risk from disorders of the heart and circulation, and other problems. There are also risks to the health of the child. Some physicians believe that overweight children suffer from more chest infections than those who are slimmer. Tooth decay is more common in overweight children, who tend to eat more sugary foods than other children. A child who is overweight is likely to be less physically active than a slimmer child, making it more difficult to burn off the excess fat or to become physically fit in other ways.

Social and psychological risks
An important risk for obese children is that of social isolation. Fat children are often the butt of other children's cruel ribbing, leading to much unhappiness. And, as these children approach adolescence, they will feel more self-conscious and less secure than other children at a time when self-confidence may be low in any case, and the need for social acceptance is at its greatest.

HOW TO HELP YOUR CHILD LOSE WEIGHT

Diet
The principal adjustment to your child's diet should be to cut out all foods that contain calories but few nutrients. Foods in this category include cakes, cookies, white bread and sweetened drinks. At mealtimes substitute fresh fruit for dessert, and encourage your child to drink plain water or unsweetened fruit juice instead of cola or pop. In many cases this change of diet alone is enough to help a child lose weight.

You should also look at the way you cook and serve food. Butter, margarine, oil and lard are all high in calories. So cut down on the amount of fat you use in cooking; grill rather than fry, bake rather than roast. Do not coat vegetables in butter, and avoid heavy gravies and sauces. Spread butter and margarine very thinly on bread.

Replace the foods you have cut down on with plenty of fruit and vegetables. These will help satisfy hunger and supply vitamins without making your child fat.

The importance of exercise
The more physically active a child is, the easier it is to burn up excess fat.

Persuade your young child to walk rather than ride in a carriage or stroller, and encourage outdoor games that involve running or bicycling. An older child may need to be persuaded to take part in sports. Less competitive activities such as swimming, dancing and cycling may be more suitable for an overweight child.

Your support
For children to lose weight successfully, they must never be made to feel different or excluded. Adopt the diet suggestions for the whole family – it will do none of you any harm. Make exercise an enjoyable part of the family routine. Above all, never make your child feel that the diet is a form of punishment. Assure your child of your love no matter what, and you are far more likely to succeed.

You should be careful not to insist that your child be thin, especially if a girl. This may contribute to excessive dieting when she becomes a teenager. It is important that you are not extremely overweight – but this should not lead to the attitude that it is good to be underweight.

All the family can enjoy a healthy diet that helps your child to lose weight.

12 Sleeping problems

Most children over 1 year old will sleep through the night without interruption. The amount of sleep a child needs each night varies from about 9 to 12 hours according to age and individual requirements. Lack of sleep does not affect appetite, growth or development. However, refusal to go to bed at what you consider to be a reasonable time, and/or waking in the middle of the night, can be disruptive and sometimes distressing for the whole family. A number of factors may be responsible for such sleeping problems, including physical illness, emotional upset, nightmares and failure to establish a regular bedtime routine.

For children under 1 year, see chart 2, Waking at night

START HERE

Has your child been waking during the night?

→ YES → **Are there any signs of physical illness, such as earache (uncontrollable crying), fever or runny nose?** → YES →

Most illnesses will disrupt a child's sleep. Consult the appropriate diagnostic chart elsewhere in this book.

NO (from waking question)

NO (from physical illness question)

Is there any cause for your child to be anxious – for example, a domestic crisis, absence of a parent or starting at a new school? → YES →

Anxiety can easily disrupt a child's sleep, even if he or she seems untroubled during the day.

Self-help: Once the cause for worry has been removed or the child has become used to the new situation, he or she should begin to sleep well again. Meanwhile, offer your child plenty of reassurance during the day and quietly comfort your child back to sleep again when he or she wakes at night. If there is difficulty in removing the cause of anxiety or if your child remains disturbed for longer than you think normal, consult your physician.

Too much sleep during the day may mean that your child is not tired enough to sleep properly at night. Some children, especially after the age of 2, need very little sleep in the day.

Self-help: Try cutting down your child's daytime naps and increase the amount of physical activity during the day. This should make your child more tired and therefore more ready to sleep at night.

NO

Does your child seem frightened on waking? → YES →

Nightmares may be disturbing your child's sleep. Bad dreams can start at quite an early age. They may be triggered by a number of different factors, including stress or anxiety from the daytime

Self-help: If your child is frightened by a nightmare, make sure you awaken your child fully so that it becomes clear that the dream was not real. Let your child talk about the dream if he or she wants to and offer plenty of reassurance before tucking him or her in for the night again.

NO

Waking during the night to pass urine more than once or twice may be a sign of an underlying disorder – for example, a urinary tract infection.

Go to chart

43 **Urinary problems**

Does your child wake several times a night to pass urine? → YES →

Does your child sleep more than an hour or so during the day? → YES →

NO

NO

Go to next page

NIGHT-TIME WANDERING

Many children climb out of their cribs or beds at night. If you do not want this to become a habit that is hard to break, it is best to deal with it quickly and firmly. If your child is still in a crib, you may be able to lower the base to make climbing out more difficult. If this is not possible, you may not be able to prevent your child from getting up, but you should put him or her back to bed firmly and without hesitation each time it happens.

Sleepwalking
Walking while asleep is an uncommon usually harmless problem that mainly affects older children. It is not known why children do this, but it may be connected with anxiety. If you find your child sleepwalking, gently guide him or her back to bed. It is not necessary to wake your child unless you think he or she is having a nightmare as well.

Continued from previous page

> **Does your child usually cry as soon as you leave the room at night?**

YES ▸

NO ▸

Waking at night without obvious cause is usually the result of an irregular sleeping pattern. Your child may be in the habit of expecting attention from you during the night.

Self-help: To re-establish a regular sleeping rhythm, you will need to stick firmly to a plan such as the one described in the box on *Preventing and overcoming sleeping problems*, below. Your child will probably take up to 2 weeks to adjust to the new routine.

Fear of being left alone and a continuing need for the reassurance of your presence will often make a child reluctant to go to sleep at night.

Self-help: You will need to accustom your child gradually to the idea of going to sleep on his or her own each night. Try the suggestions for *Preventing and overcoming sleeping problems*, below. If you think your child may be frightened of the dark, leave a night-light on.

PREVENTING AND OVERCOMING SLEEPING PROBLEMS

Most children need to have a predictable bedtime ritual to help them settle down for the night. The suggestions made for establishing such a routine for babies under 1 year (see *Helping your baby to sleep*, p. 30) also apply, on the whole, to older children. However, even if there is an established bedtime routine, many young children develop sleeping problems. A child may start to refuse to go to bed, or may regularly wake at night. This may be triggered by an upset to the routine, such as a holiday away from home or a stay at the hospital, but often may have no

apparent cause. If your child has developed some bad sleeping habits, you will need to take steps to re-establish a more convenient pattern.

Refusal to go to sleep
If your child refuses to go to sleep and cries when put to bed for the night after the usual bedtime ritual, you can try one of the two "withdrawal" approaches that follow. Whichever method you choose, you will need to ensure total consistency from both parents; any exception to the rule will undermine the progress you have already made. Both

methods are likely to involve prolonged periods of crying.

Sudden withdrawal
Once you have settled your child in the crib or bed, say goodnight and leave the room, and do not return when your child starts to cry. The first night your child may take an hour or more to go to sleep, but each successive night the period of crying should get shorter until, after a week or so, he or she should go to bed without a fuss. Your child will come to no harm from the crying, but many parents find this method too much of an ordeal.

Gradual withdrawal
Having put your child to bed, say goodnight, tell your child you will return in 10 minutes, and leave the room. In 10 minutes, return for a few moments to reassure your child that you are still there, say goodnight again, tell him or her that you will return in 20 minutes, and then leave. Repeat this, reducing the amount of time you spend in the room, until your child falls asleep. This may take several hours the first night but, if you persevere, the time should get shorter until after a week or two there is no further trouble.

Waking during the night
If your child has gotten into the habit of waking during the night, you can try a program of conditioning similar to the one described for refusal to go to sleep. If your child only whimpers in the night, do not go into the room at once; wait a few moments, he or she may still be half-asleep and will drift off again, if undisturbed. If your child is truly crying, you will need to go into the room to check that there is nothing wrong – for example, an earache or a nightmare. Once you are satisfied that all is well, give a drink of water if it is wanted, tuck your child in again, and say goodnight. Then leave the room as quickly and quietly as possible. After this you can either allow your child to cry himself or herself to sleep or return every 10 to 20 minutes or so as described under *gradual withdrawal*, above.

How your physician can help
If these suggestions do not work for your child, or if you are worn out by many sleepless nights, consult your physician. An older child who has difficulty falling asleep and wakes up early may be depressed. Never give your child sleeping drugs prescribed for an adult. These can be extremely dangerous for children.

Your child's bedroom
It is important to make your child's room as pleasant and as welcoming as possible, so that he or she is always happy to be left there at night (right).

Bedtime ritual
Most young children respond to a predictable bedtime ritual, such as a bath, always followed by a story, before turning the lights out (below).

Comforting objects
Many children become attached to a particular toy or to another comforting item, such as a blanket. Hugging this object will often encourage sleep (below right).

13 Drowsiness

Drowsiness (or excessive sleepiness) may be a child's natural response to lack of sleep or an unusually late night. In addition, a child who is sick – for example, with flu – is likely to sleep more than usual. Consult this chart if your child suddenly becomes unusually sleepy or unresponsive, or if he or she is difficult to arouse from sleep and you can find no obvious explanation. This is a serious symptom that should never be ignored.

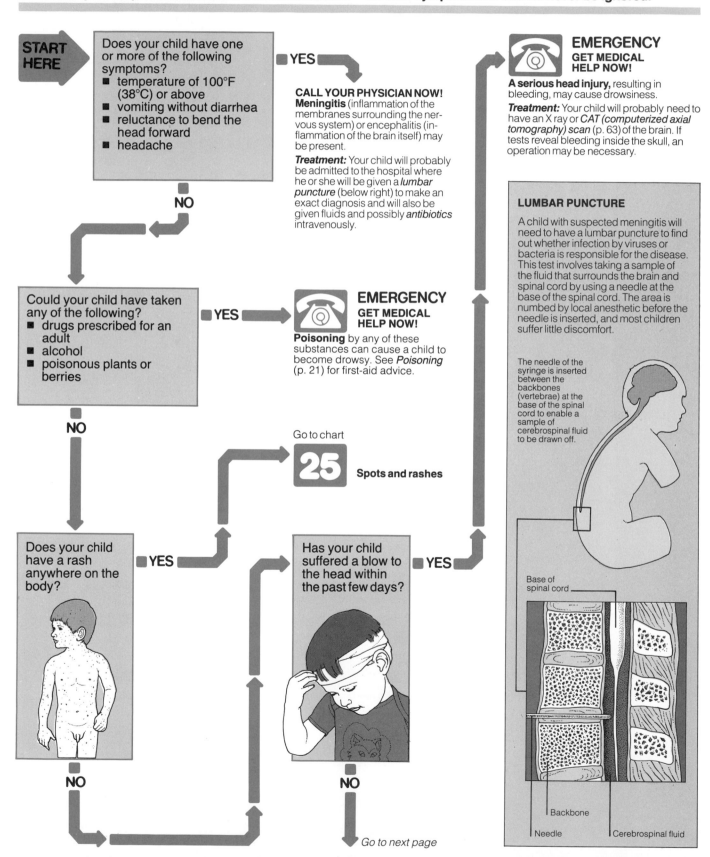

START HERE

Does your child have one or more of the following symptoms?
- temperature of 100°F (38°C) or above
- vomiting without diarrhea
- reluctance to bend the head forward
- headache

YES

CALL YOUR PHYSICIAN NOW!
Meningitis (inflammation of the membranes surrounding the nervous system) or encephalitis (inflammation of the brain itself) may be present.
Treatment: Your child will probably be admitted to the hospital where he or she will be given a *lumbar puncture* (below right) to make an exact diagnosis and will also be given fluids and possibly *antibiotics* intravenously.

NO

Could your child have taken any of the following?
- drugs prescribed for an adult
- alcohol
- poisonous plants or berries

YES

EMERGENCY
GET MEDICAL HELP NOW!
Poisoning by any of these substances can cause a child to become drowsy. See *Poisoning* (p. 21) for first-aid advice.

NO

Go to chart

25 **Spots and rashes**

Does your child have a rash anywhere on the body?

YES

Has your child suffered a blow to the head within the past few days?

YES

NO

NO

Go to next page

EMERGENCY
GET MEDICAL HELP NOW!
A serious head injury, resulting in bleeding, may cause drowsiness.
Treatment: Your child will probably need to have an X ray or CAT (*computerized axial tomography*) *scan* (p. 63) of the brain. If tests reveal bleeding inside the skull, an operation may be necessary.

LUMBAR PUNCTURE

A child with suspected meningitis will need to have a lumbar puncture to find out whether infection by viruses or bacteria is responsible for the disease. This test involves taking a sample of the fluid that surrounds the brain and spinal cord by using a needle at the base of the spinal cord. The area is numbed by local anesthetic before the needle is inserted, and most children suffer little discomfort.

The needle of the syringe is inserted between the backbones (vertebrae) at the base of the spinal cord to enable a sample of cerebrospinal fluid to be drawn off.

Base of spinal cord

Backbone

Needle   Cerebrospinal fluid

Continued from previous page

Does your child have diarrhea? — ■ **YES** →

CALL YOUR PHYSICIAN NOW!
Dehydration as a result of persistent diarrhea is possible, especially if your child has been vomiting as well. This may originally have been caused by an infection of the digestive tract (gastroenteritis). (See chart 40, *Diarrhea in children.)*

Treatment: If your physician confirms the diagnosis of dehydration, your child will be admitted to the hospital, where fluids can be given intravenously.

CALL YOUR PHYSICIAN NOW!
Too much sugar in the blood as a result of diabetes can cause drowsiness. Diabetes occurs when the body fails to make sufficient quantities of the hormone insulin, which helps convert sugar into energy.

Treatment: If your physician suspects this possibility, he or she will arrange for your child to be admitted to the hospital at once where tests will confirm the diagnosis. Your child will be given insulin injections and also fluids to reduce the level of sugar in the blood. If your child has diabetes, he or she will probably need injections of insulin for life.

↓ **NO**

Has your child been unusually thirsty lately? — ■ **YES** → **Has your child been passing large amounts of urine?** — ■ **YES** →

↓ **NO** ↓ **NO**

DROWSINESS AND DRUG AND ALCOHOL ABUSE IN OLDER CHILDREN

Parents of children over about 10 years of age should bear in mind the possibility of abuse of drugs (perhaps tranquilizers or marijuana), solvents (including glue and dry-cleaning fluids) or alcohol if the child has episodes of unusual sleepiness or lethargy over a period of days or weeks. Additional signs may include loss of appetite, red eyes, headaches or a falling off in school performance. There are, of course, a number of less worrisome explanations for such symptoms, such as a minor infection or temporary anxiety or depression. Whichever problem you suspect, your child's symptoms should be brought to your physician's attention.

See also *Smoking and drug abuse,* p. 118.

Has your child lost weight AND/OR been unusually tired during the past few weeks? — ■ **YES** →

Certain drugs, such as antihistamines given for allergic disorders, may cause mild drowsiness. Discuss the problem with your physician. If, however, your child becomes very drowsy and unresponsive, you should call your physician at once.

↓ **NO**

Is your child taking any medications prescribed by your physician? — ■ **YES** →

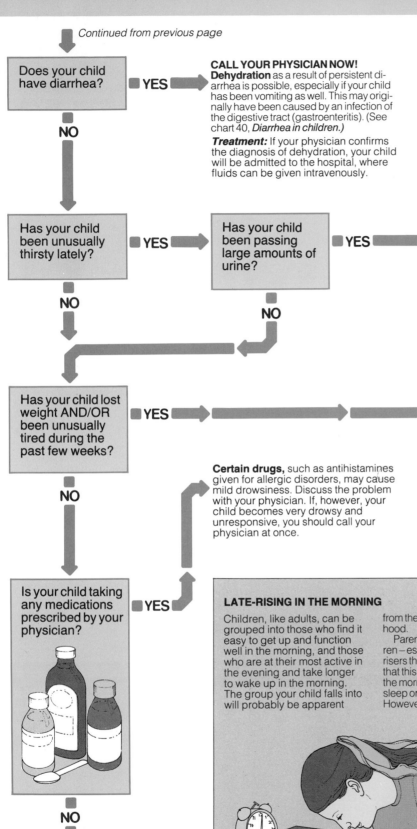

LATE-RISING IN THE MORNING

Children, like adults, can be grouped into those who find it easy to get up and function well in the morning, and those who are at their most active in the evening and take longer to wake up in the morning. The group your child falls into will probably be apparent from the early years of childhood.

Parents of late-waking children – especially if they are early risers themselves – often worry that this reluctance to get up in the morning is a sign of lack of sleep or of a physical disorder. However, there is rarely any cause for concern if an otherwise healthy child who is alert and energetic for most of the rest of the day takes an hour or so to become fully awake in the morning. Enforcing an early bedtime when a child feels full of energy is unlikely to help the problem and may lead to unnecessary conflict.

When to consult your physician
While there is no cause for concern if a child is regularly sluggish in the mornings only, you should consult your physician in the following cases:
- If your child starts to become drowsy at other times of the day.
- If a normally early-waking child is unusually drowsy in the morning for no obvious reason.

Call your physician at once if you cannot rouse your child from sleep in the morning.

↓ **NO**

Consult your physician without further delay if you are unable to make a diagnosis from this chart.

14 Fever in children

A fever (above-normal body temperature) is usually caused by infection either by viruses or bacteria (p. 44). However, a child may also become feverish if allowed to become overheated – for example, as a result of playing too long in hot sunshine. A raised temperature will make a child's forehead feel hot and will cause increased sweating and a sick feeling. If you suspect that your child has a fever, take his or her temperature (see opposite). Consult this chart if the temperature reading is 100°F (38°C) or above.

For children under 1 year, see chart 3, Fever in babies

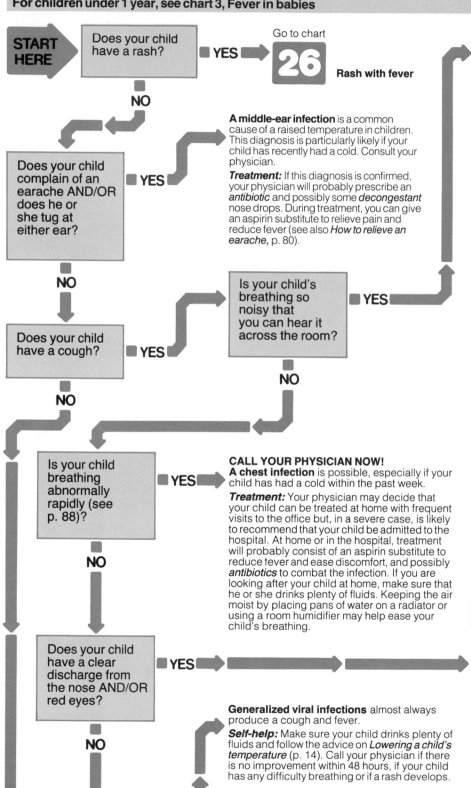

START HERE

Does your child have a rash? — YES → Go to chart **26** Rash with fever

NO

Does your child complain of an earache AND/OR does he or she tug at either ear? — YES →

A middle-ear infection is a common cause of a raised temperature in children. This diagnosis is particularly likely if your child has recently had a cold. Consult your physician.

Treatment: If this diagnosis is confirmed, your physician will probably prescribe an *antibiotic* and possibly some *decongestant* nose drops. During treatment, you can give an aspirin substitute to relieve pain and reduce fever (see also *How to relieve an earache*, p. 80).

NO

Does your child have a cough? — YES →

Is your child's breathing so noisy that you can hear it across the room? — YES →

NO

NO

Is your child breathing abnormally rapidly (see p. 88)? — YES →

CALL YOUR PHYSICIAN NOW!
A chest infection is possible, especially if your child has had a cold within the past week.

Treatment: Your physician may decide that your child can be treated at home with frequent visits to the office but, in a severe case, is likely to recommend that your child be admitted to the hospital. At home or in the hospital, treatment will probably consist of an aspirin substitute to reduce fever and ease discomfort, and possibly *antibiotics* to combat the infection. If you are looking after your child at home, make sure that he or she drinks plenty of fluids. Keeping the air moist by placing pans of water on a radiator or using a room humidifier may help ease your child's breathing.

NO

Does your child have a clear discharge from the nose AND/OR red eyes? — YES →

NO

Generalized viral infections almost always produce a cough and fever.

Self-help: Make sure your child drinks plenty of fluids and follow the advice on *Lowering a child's temperature* (p. 14). Call your physician if there is no improvement within 48 hours, if your child has any difficulty breathing or if a rash develops.

Go to next page

EMERGENCY
GET MEDICAL HELP NOW!

Narrowing of the air passages caused by inflammation of the tissues resulting from infection is a possibility.

Treatment: While waiting for medical help, you may be able to ease your child's breathing by moistening the air with steam. Taking your child into a bathroom where you have turned on the hot water tap or shower to make steam is often effective. Your child will probably need to be admitted to the hospital, where oxygen and intravenous fluids will be given. Your child may also be given *antibiotics*.

FEVERISH CONVULSIONS

Young children (under 5) sometimes have convulsions when their temperatures rise too quickly. During such a convulsion, a child's arms and legs will shake uncontrollably and he or she may turn blue in the face. This may last for several minutes or sometimes longer.

What to do
Lay the child flat on his or her stomach with the head turned to the side. If there is vomiting, clean out the mouth with your finger. The convulsion will not damage your child's brain and it will stop by itself in a few minutes. If your child has a convulsion caused by fever, it *does not mean* that your child has epilepsy. Some children, however, do have an underlying problem. Your physician may want to do more tests after your child recovers.

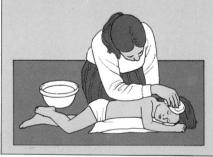

Measles often starts with a cough, fever, runny nose and/or inflamed eyes. The appearance of a red rash a few days later makes this diagnosis more likely, especially if your child has not been vaccinated against the disease (see *Comparison of childhood infectious diseases*, p. 75). Consult your physician.

Treatment: There is no specific treatment for measles. You will probably just be advised to keep your child's temperature down (see *Lowering a child's temperature*, p. 14). There is no need to darken your child's room as was once believed. Call your physician at once if your child develops an earache, has any difficulty breathing or becomes drowsy and difficult to wake. Full recovery normally takes about 10 days.

Continued from previous page

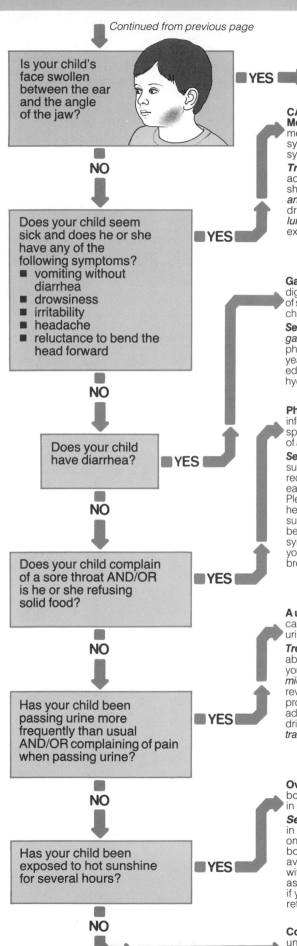

Is your child's face swollen between the ear and the angle of the jaw?

YES →

NO ↓

Does your child seem sick and does he or she have any of the following symptoms?
- vomiting without diarrhea
- drowsiness
- irritability
- headache
- reluctance to bend the head forward

YES →

NO ↓

Does your child have diarrhea?

YES →

NO ↓

Does your child complain of a sore throat AND/OR is he or she refusing solid food?

YES →

NO ↓

Has your child been passing urine more frequently than usual AND/OR complaining of pain when passing urine?

YES →

NO ↓

Has your child been exposed to hot sunshine for several hours?

YES →

NO ↓

Mumps, a viral infection that mainly affects the salivary glands, is a possibility, especially if your child has been in contact with the disease within the past 3 weeks. (See *Comparison of childhood infectious diseases*, p. 75.) Consult your physician.
Treatment: Your physician will probably advise you to keep your child at home and give him or her an aspirin substitute and plenty of cold drinks to relieve the discomfort. Recovery normally takes 7 to 10 days.

CALL YOUR PHYSICIAN NOW!
Meningitis, inflammation of the membranes surrounding the nervous system, may be the cause of such symptoms.
Treatment: Your child may be admitted to the hospital and he or she may be given fluids and possibly *antibiotics* through an intravenous drip. If your child has meningitis, a *lumbar puncture* (p. 52), to make an exact diagnosis, will be given.

Gastroenteritis, infection of the digestive tract, is the most likely cause of such symptoms, especially if your child is also vomiting.
Self-help: See *Treating your child's gastroenteritis,* p. 99. Consult your physician if your child is less than 2 years old, if he or she vomits repeatedly for more than 12 hours, or is dehydrated.

Pharyngitis and tonsillitis, infections of the throat and tonsils, respectively, are the most likely causes of a sore throat and fever.
Self-help: Give your child an aspirin substitute to relieve the discomfort and reduce fever. Do not force your child to eat if pain makes swallowing difficult. Plenty of cold drinks and ice cream will help to soothe the inflammation. Consult your physician if your child is no better in 48 hours or develops further symptoms, such as an earache. Call your physician at once if your child's breathing becomes noisy or difficult.

A urinary tract infection is a possible cause of fever and frequent or painful urination. Consult your physician.
Treatment: Your physician will probably ask for a mid-stream specimen of your child's urine (see *Collecting a mid-stream specimen,* p.103). If tests reveal an infection, your physician will probably prescribe *antibiotics* and advise you to give your child plenty to drink. (See also *Preventing urinary tract infections,* p.103.)

Overheating, leading to a rise in body temperature, can easily occur in such circumstances.
Self-help: Make your child lie down in a cool room with as little clothing on as possible. Sponge his or her body with tepid water and use a fan if available. Give plenty to drink along with the recommended dose of an aspirin substitute. Seek medical help if your child's temperature has not returned to normal within an hour.

Consult your physician if you are unable to make a diagnosis from this chart.

TAKING YOUR CHILD'S TEMPERATURE

The best way to see if your child has a fever is to take the temperature using a clinical thermometer. For children under 7 years old, place the thermometer under the arm (see *How to take your baby's temperature*, p. 33). Older children can have their temperature taken by mouth.

Taking a temperature by mouth
1 Shake the thermometer with firm downward flicks of the wrist so that the mercury runs down into the bulb and reads well below the "normal" mark.

2 Place the bulb of the thermometer inside your child's mouth under the tongue. Let it remain in place for 3 minutes.

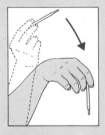

3 Remove the thermometer and turn it until you get a clear reading.

Using this method, you can consider your child feverish if his or her temperature is 100°F (38°C) or above. If your child's temperature rises above 102°F (39°C), whatever the suspected cause, call your physician at once.

36	37	38	39	40
Normal			Fever	
97	98	99	100	101	102	103	104

Temperature indicator strips
This alternative method for measuring body temperature is described on p. 33.

FOREIGN TRAVEL

If your child develops a fever soon after a visit to a hot climate, be sure to tell your physician. Your child may have caught a disease that is rare in this country, one that your physician might not otherwise suspect.

15 Swollen glands

The term "swollen glands" usually refers to swelling (sometimes with tenderness) of one or more of the lymph glands (below right). In babies under 1 year, this is an unusual symptom that is difficult for the parent to diagnose. Consult your physician. In older children, the glands, especially those in the neck, often swell noticeably as a result of minor infections and this is rarely cause for concern. Persistent or generalized swelling of the glands, particularly if your child's color seems off, should be reported to your physician.

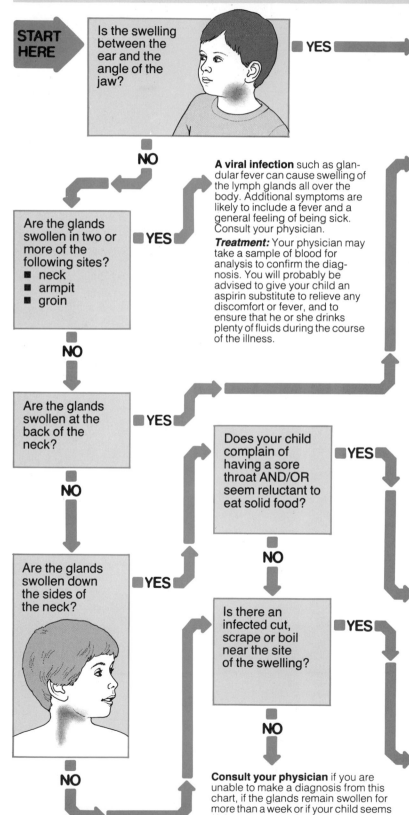

START HERE

Is the swelling between the ear and the angle of the jaw?

YES →

Mumps, a viral infection affecting the salivary glands, is a possibility, especially if your child has been in contact with the disease within the past 3 weeks (see *Comparison of childhood infectious diseases*, p. 75). Consult your physician.

Treatment: Your physician will probably advise you to keep your child at home and to give an aspirin substitute and plenty of cold drinks to relieve the discomfort. Recovery normally takes 7 to 10 days.

NO

Are the glands swollen in two or more of the following sites?
■ neck
■ armpit
■ groin

YES

A viral infection such as glandular fever can cause swelling of the lymph glands all over the body. Additional symptoms are likely to include a fever and a general feeling of being sick. Consult your physician.

Treatment: Your physician may take a sample of blood for analysis to confirm the diagnosis. You will probably be advised to give your child an aspirin substitute to relieve any discomfort or fever, and to ensure that he or she drinks plenty of fluids during the course of the illness.

German measles, or a similar viral infection, may cause these glands to swell. The appearance of a pink rash on the body within a couple of days would make a diagnosis of German measles more likely (see *Comparison of childhood infectious diseases,* p. 75).

Self-help: German measles is a mild illness and generally needs little treatment other than an aspirin substitute if your child seems feverish. It is important, however, to keep your child at home, to avoid infecting others, especially any woman who is pregnant, because of the damage the disease can do to the unborn child. If you want to consult your physician, telephone the office first. Your physician may want to visit your child at home.

NO

Are the glands swollen at the back of the neck?

YES →

Does your child complain of having a sore throat AND/OR seem reluctant to eat solid food?

YES →

LYMPH GLANDS

The lymphatic system consists of the lymph glands (or nodes) linked by vessels containing a watery fluid (lymph). The glands contain large numbers of lymphocytes, a type of white blood cell that fights infection. When large numbers of microbes are present, the lymph glands — especially those near the surface of the skin — become noticeably swollen.

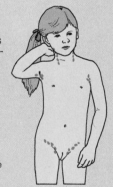

Glands near the skin surface
The illustration (right) shows the sites of the lymph glands that most often become obviously swollen as a result of infection in childhood.

NO

Are the glands swollen down the sides of the neck?

YES

Is there an infected cut, scrape or boil near the site of the swelling?

NO

YES →

Tonsillitis, inflammation of the tonsils as a result of viral or bacterial infection (see p. 44), often causes swelling of these glands.

Self-help: Do not force your child to eat if pain makes swallowing difficult. Follow the advice on treating a sore throat in the box on p. 85. Consult your physician if your child is no better in 48 hours or if he or she develops any of the danger signs listed in the box on p. 84. Your physician may prescribe *antibiotics*. An operation to remove the tonsils (see *Tonsils removal,* p. 85) is carried out only occasionally in cases of recurrent, severe tonsillitis.

NO

Localized infection may cause swelling of nearby lymph glands.

Self-help: Keep the wound or boil clean by bathing the area daily with a mild antiseptic solution and, if necessary, cover it with an adhesive bandage. Consult your physician if a wound is persistently painful, or if swelling persists for more than a week. *Antibiotic* treatment may be needed (see also *Warts and boils*, p. 73).

NO

Consult your physician if you are unable to make a diagnosis from this chart, if the glands remain swollen for more than a week or if your child seems sick.

16 Itching

This diagnostic chart deals with itching that affects either the whole body or a particular area, such as the scalp or anus. A variety of disorders including allergies, contact with certain plants or chemicals, and certain infectious parasites may cause such irritation. Your child is likely to scratch. If unchecked, this may lead to the development of sore, infected areas, so it is important to deal with any disorder that produces itching.

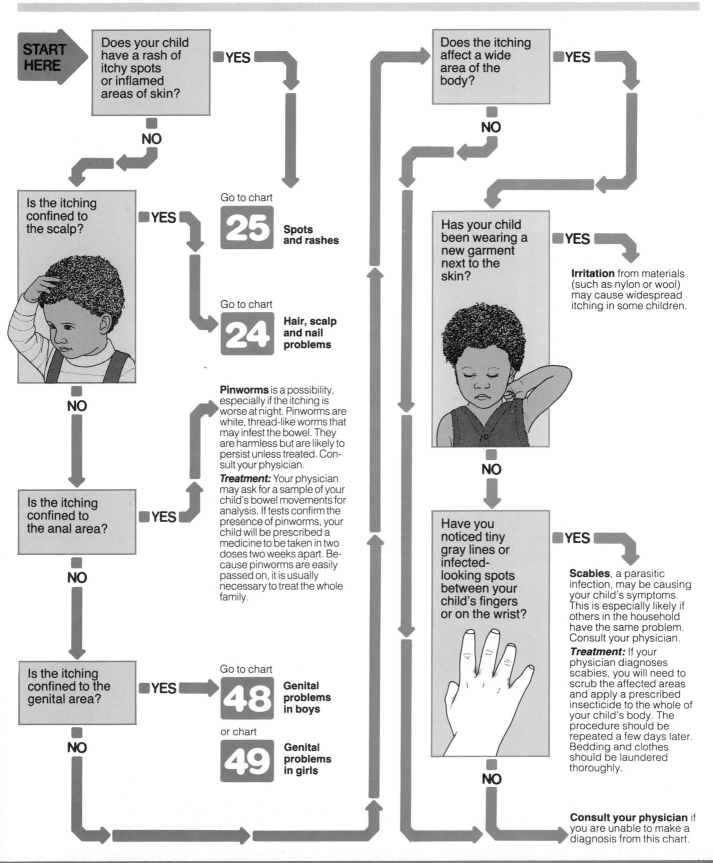

START HERE

Does your child have a rash of itchy spots or inflamed areas of skin?

YES — Go to chart **25** **Spots and rashes**

NO

Is the itching confined to the scalp?

YES — Go to chart **24** **Hair, scalp and nail problems**

NO

Is the itching confined to the anal area?

YES — **Pinworms** is a possibility, especially if the itching is worse at night. Pinworms are white, thread-like worms that may infest the bowel. They are harmless but are likely to persist unless treated. Consult your physician.
Treatment: Your physician may ask for a sample of your child's bowel movements for analysis. If tests confirm the presence of pinworms, your child will be prescribed a medicine to be taken in two doses two weeks apart. Because pinworms are easily passed on, it is usually necessary to treat the whole family.

NO

Is the itching confined to the genital area?

YES — Go to chart **48** **Genital problems in boys**
or chart **49** **Genital problems in girls**

NO

Does the itching affect a wide area of the body?

YES

NO

Has your child been wearing a new garment next to the skin?

YES — **Irritation** from materials (such as nylon or wool) may cause widespread itching in some children.

NO

Have you noticed tiny gray lines or infected-looking spots between your child's fingers or on the wrist?

YES — **Scabies**, a parasitic infection, may be causing your child's symptoms. This is especially likely if others in the household have the same problem. Consult your physician.
Treatment: If your physician diagnoses scabies, you will need to scrub the affected areas and apply a prescribed insecticide to the whole of your child's body. The procedure should be repeated a few days later. Bedding and clothes should be laundered thoroughly.

NO

Consult your physician if you are unable to make a diagnosis from this chart.

17 Fainting, dizzy spells and seizures

This chart deals with fainting, feelings of faintness and unsteadiness, dizzy spells and loss of consciousness including seizures and periods of "blankness." Many children feel faint from time to time and this is usually caused by anxiety or hunger, but frequent loss of consciousness or attacks during which a child suffers uncontrolled movements of the body or limbs is a sign of an underlying disorder.

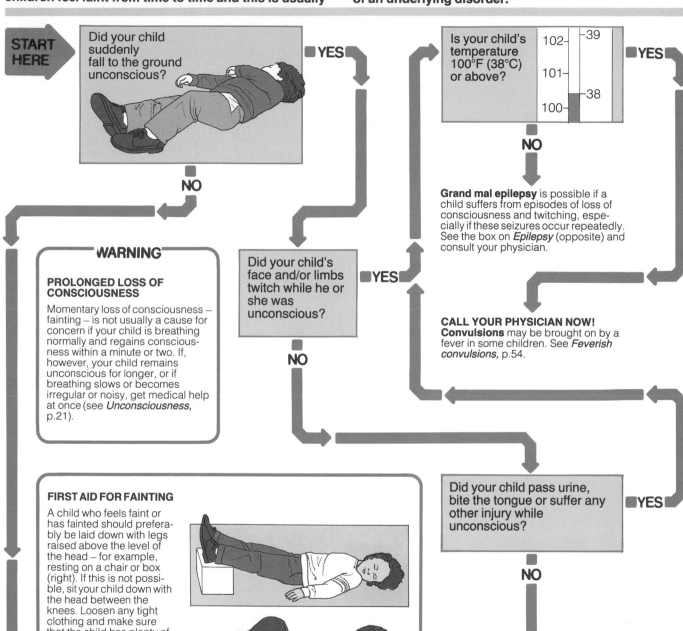

START HERE

Did your child suddenly fall to the ground unconscious? — **YES**

NO

Is your child's temperature 100°F (38°C) or above? — **YES**

102 — 39
101 —
100 — 38

NO

Grand mal epilepsy is possible if a child suffers from episodes of loss of consciousness and twitching, especially if these seizures occur repeatedly. See the box on *Epilepsy* (opposite) and consult your physician.

Did your child's face and/or limbs twitch while he or she was unconscious? — **YES**

NO

CALL YOUR PHYSICIAN NOW!
Convulsions may be brought on by a fever in some children. See *Feverish convulsions,* p.54.

WARNING

PROLONGED LOSS OF CONSCIOUSNESS

Momentary loss of consciousness – fainting – is not usually a cause for concern if your child is breathing normally and regains consciousness within a minute or two. If, however, your child remains unconscious for longer, or if breathing slows or becomes irregular or noisy, get medical help at once (see *Unconsciousness,* p.21).

Did your child pass urine, bite the tongue or suffer any other injury while unconscious? — **YES**

NO

FIRST AID FOR FAINTING

A child who feels faint or has fainted should preferably be laid down with legs raised above the level of the head – for example, resting on a chair or box (right). If this is not possible, sit your child down with the head between the knees. Loosen any tight clothing and make sure that the child has plenty of fresh air and is shaded from hot sunshine. When your child regains consciousness, do not allow him or her to get up for a few more minutes. A child who feels faint or has fainted may be suffering from low blood sugar as a result of not having eaten. When he or she has regained consciousness, offer a sweet drink such as orange juice and a light snack. Never try to give an unconscious child anything to eat or drink.

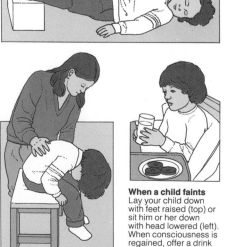

When a child faints
Lay your child down with feet raised (top) or sit him or her down with head lowered (left). When consciousness is regained, offer a drink and a snack (above).

Fainting (brief loss of consciousness, usually preceded by sudden pallor and a feeling of light-headedness or dizziness) is rarely any cause for concern in an otherwise healthy child. It is usually caused by a sudden drop in blood pressure as a result of anxiety, or by a low level of sugar in the blood as a result of not having eaten for some time.

Self-help: See *First aid for fainting,* left. Seek medical help at once if your child remains unconscious for more than a minute, or seems to have any difficulty breathing. Consult your physician if fainting spells recur.

Go to next page

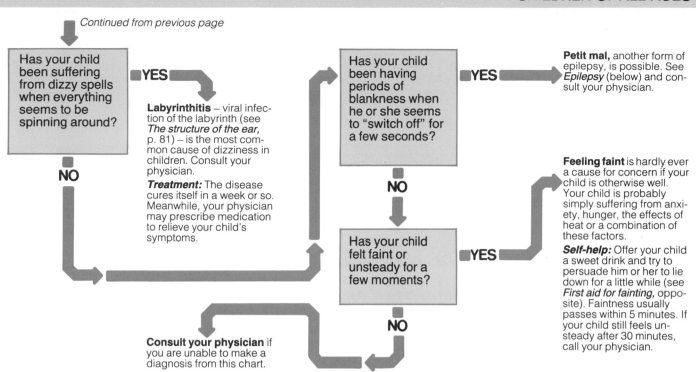

Continued from previous page

Has your child been suffering from dizzy spells when everything seems to be spinning around?

YES →

Labyrinthitis – viral infection of the labyrinth (see *The structure of the ear,* p. 81) – is the most common cause of dizziness in children. Consult your physician.

Treatment: The disease cures itself in a week or so. Meanwhile, your physician may prescribe medication to relieve your child's symptoms.

NO ↓

Has your child been having periods of blankness when he or she seems to "switch off" for a few seconds?

YES →

Petit mal, another form of epilepsy, is possible. See *Epilepsy* (below) and consult your physician.

NO ↓

Has your child felt faint or unsteady for a few moments?

YES →

Feeling faint is hardly ever a cause for concern if your child is otherwise well. Your child is probably simply suffering from anxiety, hunger, the effects of heat or a combination of these factors.

Self-help: Offer your child a sweet drink and try to persuade him or her to lie down for a little while (see *First aid for fainting,* opposite). Faintness usually passes within 5 minutes. If your child still feels unsteady after 30 minutes, call your physician.

NO ↓

Consult your physician if you are unable to make a diagnosis from this chart.

EPILEPSY

Epilepsy is the medical term for repeated loss of consciousness caused by abnormal electrical impulses in the brain. The underlying cause of the disorder is not known. The type and severity of symptoms may vary according to the nature of the abnormal impulses and the part of the brain affected. There are two main forms of the disease:

Grand mal

In the form of the disease known as grand mal, the child falls to the ground suddenly and may suffer injury during the fall. He or she remains unconscious for up to several minutes, often jerking the limbs or face uncontrollably. Gradually the movements stop and the child passes into normal sleep.

Petit mal

In petit mal epilepsy, the child loses full consciousness but does not fall to the ground. Attacks last for 10 to 15 seconds, during which the child's face becomes vacant, and he or she stops speaking and does not hear what people are saying. Petit mal attacks often cease after adolescence.

Treatment

If your child has seizures that lead your physician to suspect a form of epilepsy, your child will probably be referred to a specialist (neurologist) for diagnosis and treatment. Diagnosis of the precise form of the disease and decisions about the best treatment for a child are usually made following *electroencephalography* (above right). Most forms of epilepsy are effectively controlled by drug treatment. The neurologist will advise you about any special precautions you will need to take with your child in regard to swimming, cycling and other activities, and will explain how to deal with the seizures. You should tell your child's teachers, and anyone else who has regular care of your child, about the disease and explain to them what to do during seizures.

Dealing with seizures

During a grand mal seizure your priorities are to prevent your child from inhaling vomit and from suffering any injury. At the first sign of a seizure place the child on his or her stomach with the head to one side. Move nearby objects away from jerking arms and legs, but do not try to restrain the child from moving. Never try to place anything in the mouth of a child having an attack. Once the involuntary movements have ceased, allow him or her to sleep undisturbed.

A child having a petit mal seizure needs no special treatment and should be allowed to regain normal consciousness without interference.

Electroencephalography
Electroencephalography is a technique that enables physicians to monitor the electrical activity in the brain, and assists in the diagnosis of epilepsy and other conditions. A number of electrodes are placed on the scalp (right) and the signals that are picked up are recorded on paper. The procedure is not painful, but it may take some time and may therefore be tiresome for a young child.

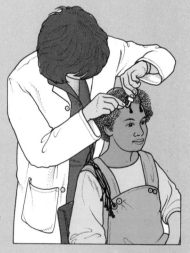

During a grand mal seizure
A child having a grand mal seizure should be gently turned on his or her stomach with the head to one side (below). Nearby objects likely to cause injury should be moved away.

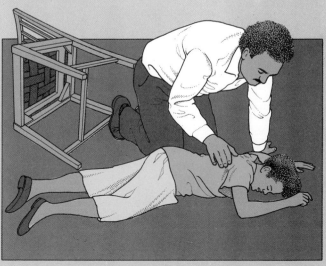

18 Headache

A headache can consist of pain on one or both sides of the head or forehead. It may vary from a dull ache to a sharp, stabbing pain. Children under the age of 3 are unlikely to complain of this symptom except as a direct result of injury. Headaches can be a symptom of a number of disorders, but they may also occur on their own, are most commonly due to muscle spasm and are usually easily cured by self-help measures.

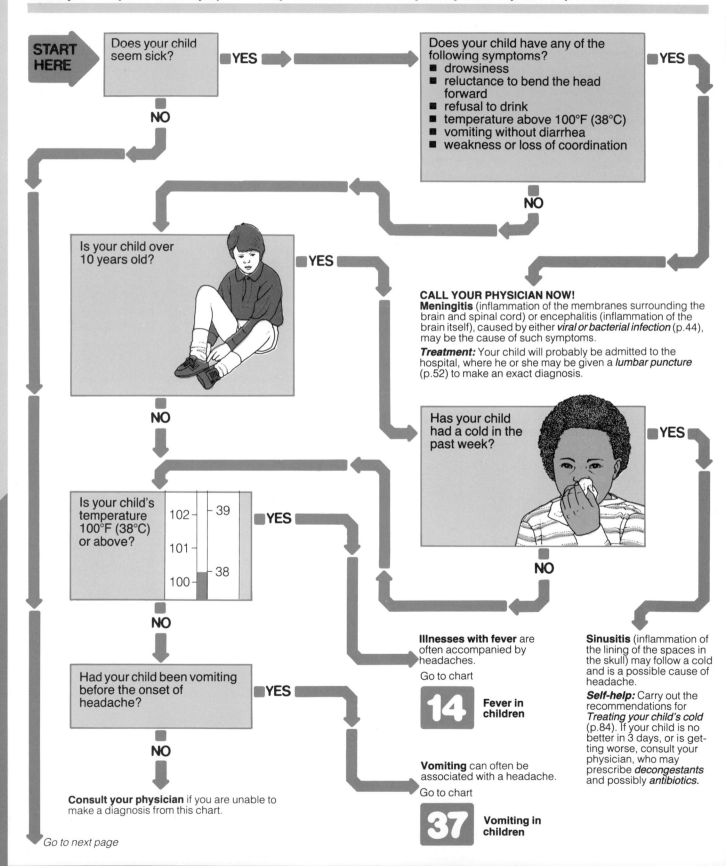

START HERE

Does your child seem sick? — **YES** →

Does your child have any of the following symptoms?
- drowsiness
- reluctance to bend the head forward
- refusal to drink
- temperature above 100°F (38°C)
- vomiting without diarrhea
- weakness or loss of coordination

— **YES** →

NO ↓

NO ↓

Is your child over 10 years old? — **YES** →

CALL YOUR PHYSICIAN NOW!
Meningitis (inflammation of the membranes surrounding the brain and spinal cord) or encephalitis (inflammation of the brain itself), caused by either *viral or bacterial infection* (p.44), may be the cause of such symptoms.

Treatment: Your child will probably be admitted to the hospital, where he or she may be given a *lumbar puncture* (p.52) to make an exact diagnosis.

NO ↓

Has your child had a cold in the past week? — **YES** →

Is your child's temperature 100°F (38°C) or above?

102	39
101	
100	38

— **YES** →

NO ↓

NO ↓

Had your child been vomiting before the onset of headache? — **YES** →

NO ↓

Illnesses with fever are often accompanied by headaches.
Go to chart

14 Fever in children

Vomiting can often be associated with a headache.
Go to chart

37 Vomiting in children

Sinusitis (inflammation of the lining of the spaces in the skull) may follow a cold and is a possible cause of headache.

Self-help: Carry out the recommendations for *Treating your child's cold* (p.84). If your child is no better in 3 days, or is getting worse, consult your physician, who may prescribe *decongestants* and possibly *antibiotics*.

Consult your physician if you are unable to make a diagnosis from this chart.

Go to next page

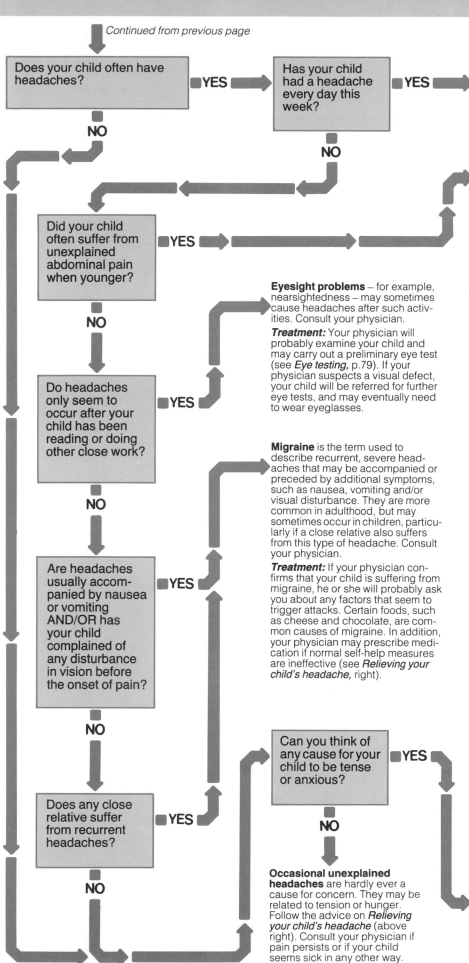

Continued from previous page

Does your child often have headaches? → **YES** → **Has your child had a headache every day this week?** → **YES** →

Frequent headaches in a child should be brought to your physician's attention. They may be *migraines* (see below left), especially if other members of the family suffer from them, but your physician may want to rule out the possibility of a more serious underlying disorder.

NO ↓ (from "Does your child often have headaches?")

NO ↓ (from "Has your child had a headache every day this week?")

The periodic syndrome is one term used to describe children's recurrent pains that may be of emotional origin.

Self-help: Although there may be no obvious physical cause for your child's headaches, the pain is nevertheless real. Follow the advice on *Relieving your child's headache* (below). Consult your physician if such measures fail to relieve the pain, if your child develops additional symptoms or if he or she seems sick. In addition, you should seek medical advice if the headaches start to occur increasingly often.

Did your child often suffer from unexplained abdominal pain when younger? → **YES** →

NO ↓

Do headaches only seem to occur after your child has been reading or doing other close work? → **YES** →

Eyesight problems – for example, nearsightedness – may sometimes cause headaches after such activities. Consult your physician.

Treatment: Your physician will probably examine your child and may carry out a preliminary eye test (see *Eye testing,* p.79). If your physician suspects a visual defect, your child will be referred for further eye tests, and may eventually need to wear eyeglasses.

NO ↓

Are headaches usually accompanied by nausea or vomiting AND/OR has your child complained of any disturbance in vision before the onset of pain? → **YES** →

Migraine is the term used to describe recurrent, severe headaches that may be accompanied or preceded by additional symptoms, such as nausea, vomiting and/or visual disturbance. They are more common in adulthood, but may sometimes occur in children, particularly if a close relative also suffers from this type of headache. Consult your physician.

Treatment: If your physician confirms that your child is suffering from migraine, he or she will probably ask you about any factors that seem to trigger attacks. Certain foods, such as cheese and chocolate, are common causes of migraine. In addition, your physician may prescribe medication if normal self-help measures are ineffective (see *Relieving your child's headache,* right).

NO ↓

Does any close relative suffer from recurrent headaches? → **YES** →

Can you think of any cause for your child to be tense or anxious? → **YES** →

NO ↓

NO ↓ (Does any close relative suffer...)

Occasional unexplained headaches are hardly ever a cause for concern. They may be related to tension or hunger. Follow the advice on *Relieving your child's headache* (above right). Consult your physician if pain persists or if your child seems sick in any other way.

RELIEVING YOUR CHILD'S HEADACHE

The vast majority of headaches in childhood can be treated simply at home in the following way:

- Give the recommended dose of an aspirin substitute.
- If your child is hungry, offer a light snack – for example, a glass of milk and a cookie.
- Allow your child to lie down in a cool, darkened room for a few hours.

The earlier treatment is offered, the greater its effectiveness. Consult your physician if these measures fail to relieve a headache within 4 hours, or if your child seems sick.

Tension headaches may be brought on by anxiety – for example, about schoolwork or family problems. Such headaches are generally no cause for concern.

Self-help: Follow the advice on *Relieving your child's headache* (above). Consult your physician if such measures fail to relieve the pain or if your child seems sick.

19 Clumsiness

Children differ greatly in their level of manual dexterity, physical coordination and agility. Some children naturally have more difficulty than others in carrying out delicate tasks (such as tying shoelaces) that require precise coordination between hand and eye. They may seem unable to prevent themselves from knocking things over. Such clumsiness is almost always present from birth and is most unlikely to be a sign of an underlying disorder. Occasionally, however, severe clumsiness or the sudden onset of clumsiness in a child who has previously been well coordinated may be the result of a nervous system or muscular disorder.

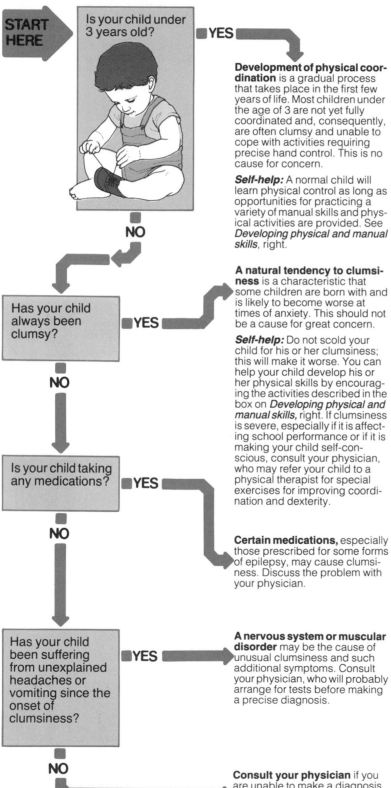

START HERE

Is your child under 3 years old? — **YES**

Development of physical coordination is a gradual process that takes place in the first few years of life. Most children under the age of 3 are not yet fully coordinated and, consequently, are often clumsy and unable to cope with activities requiring precise hand control. This is no cause for concern.

Self-help: A normal child will learn physical control as long as opportunities for practicing a variety of manual skills and physical activities are provided. See *Developing physical and manual skills*, right.

NO

Has your child always been clumsy? — **YES**

A natural tendency to clumsiness is a characteristic that some children are born with and is likely to become worse at times of anxiety. This should not be a cause for great concern.

Self-help: Do not scold your child for his or her clumsiness; this will make it worse. You can help your child develop his or her physical skills by encouraging the activities described in the box on *Developing physical and manual skills,* right. If clumsiness is severe, especially if it is affecting school performance or if it is making your child self-conscious, consult your physician, who may refer your child to a physical therapist for special exercises for improving coordination and dexterity.

NO

Is your child taking any medications? — **YES**

Certain medications, especially those prescribed for some forms of epilepsy, may cause clumsiness. Discuss the problem with your physician.

NO

Has your child been suffering from unexplained headaches or vomiting since the onset of clumsiness? — **YES**

A nervous system or muscular disorder may be the cause of unusual clumsiness and such additional symptoms. Consult your physician, who will probably arrange for tests before making a precise diagnosis.

NO

Consult your physician if you are unable to make a diagnosis from this chart.

DEVELOPING PHYSICAL AND MANUAL SKILLS

Children learn to control their bodies from the first weeks of life. They soon learn skills such as following a moving object with the eyes and grasping a toy that is held out to them. Some children learn these skills more easily than others and are naturally more agile than their peers. However, throughout childhood, you can help your child develop muscular coordination and manual dexterity to the best of his or her abilities by giving as many chances as possible for varied physical activities.

Athletic skills
A toddler who is running, hopping and jumping is learning physical skills that will help him or her to be good at sports and games. Swimming is a particularly good form of exercise for less coordinated children. Ball games will help improve hand-and-eye coordination (see right) as well as provide opportunities for strenuous physical activity.

Moving to music
Dancing is not only fun for young children but teaches them to coordinate their body's movements with the rhythms of music. Disciplined forms of dancing, such as ballet, can also improve balance, physical grace and agility.

Coordinating hand and eye
Banging pegs into a frame with a hammer is a game that most toddlers enjoy (below right). It also helps to teach coordination between the hand and eye and will help your child learn more sophisticated manual tasks such as sewing and woodworking later on. Similarly, scribbling on paper with crayons is an important stage in the development of the more delicate control needed for writing and drawing. Toys that are particularly good for hand-and-eye coordination include building blocks, puzzles with large pieces, and toy telephones.

20 Confusion

Confused children may talk nonsense, appear dazed or agitated, or see and hear things that are not real. An older child may mix up times, places and events. This is serious and requires medical attention.

START HERE

Has your child had a head injury within the past few days?

YES →

EMERGENCY
GET MEDICAL HELP NOW!

Pressure on the brain from slow bleeding within the skull is possible if a child who seemed to be all right at first becomes confused in the days following a head injury.

Treatment: Your child will be admitted to the hospital and will probably need to undergo tests such as a *CAT (computerized axial tomography) scan* (below) to determine the nature and extent of any damage to the brain or skull. An operation may be necessary.

NO

Is your child's temperature 100°F (38°C) or above?

102 — 39
101 —
100 — 38
— 38

YES →

CALL YOUR PHYSICIAN NOW!
Delirium may develop in a child with a fever, especially if his or her temperature rises above 102 °F (39°C). This may in turn lead to febrile convulsions (p.54).

Treatment: While waiting for medical help, carry out self-help measures (see *Lowering a raised temperature in a child,* p.14).

See also chart

14 Fever in children

NO

Does your child have one or more of the following symptoms?
- headache
- vomiting without diarrhea
- refusal to drink
- reluctance to bend the head forward
- drowsiness

YES →

CALL YOUR PHYSICIAN NOW!
Meningitis, inflammation of the membranes surrounding the brain and spinal cord, caused by either *viral or bacterial infection* (p.44), may be the cause of such symptoms.

Treatment: Your child may be admitted to the hospital where he or she will be given a *lumbar puncture* (p.52) to help make an exact diagnosis.

NO

Has your child been taking any prescribed or over-the-counter medication or has he or she had access to sedatives, tranquilizing medications or alcohol?

YES →

CALL YOUR PHYSICIAN NOW!
Certain medications, particularly some of those contained in travel sickness medicines, cough medicines and some medication used in the treatment of asthma, may cause confused behavior in some children.

NO

Consult your physician if you are unable to make a diagnosis from this chart.

CAT SCAN

A CAT (computerized axial tomography) scan is a painless and safe procedure that helps in the diagnosis of certain conditions. It involves many X-ray pictures being taken as a camera revolves around the body. The readings are fed into a computer, which assembles them into an accurate picture of the area. CAT scans can be taken of most parts of the body, but they are especially useful in diagnosing brain injury.

CAT scan of the head
For a CAT scan of the head, your child will lie on a movable table with his or her head resting inside the machine. Your child will be told not to make any movement so that the pictures are not blurred.

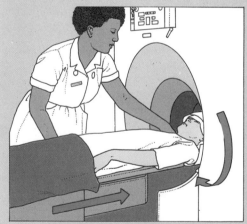

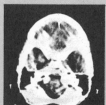

CAT scan at eye level
The scan (left) shows a cross section of a child's head at eye level. The front of the head is at the top. The white areas indicate bone; the gray areas, soft tissue; and the black areas, air spaces.

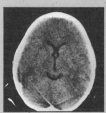

CAT scan at mid-forehead level
The scan (left) shows a cross section of the same head taken at mid-forehead level. The gray, central area is the brain.

21 Speech difficulties

Consult this chart if your child has any problem with his or her speech such as delay in starting to talk, lack of clarity, defects in pronunciation or stuttering. Most forms of speech difficulty resolve themselves in time without treatment. However, in some cases, a child's speech can be improved with therapy.

START HERE

Are you worried because your child seems late in starting to talk?

YES → **Is your child under 2 years old?**

YES → **Does your child seem to be developing normally in other ways – for example, in understanding and physical skills?**

NO (from first box)

Is your child able to say more than 5 words?

YES (from "spoken clearly")

Are all your child's words spoken clearly?

YES

NO

Unclear speech may be a sign of deafness. Consult your physician.
Treatment: Your physician will carry out a preliminary hearing test (p.83) and examine your child's ears (see *Ear examination,* p.81). If there seems to be any reason to suspect deafness, your child will be referred to a specialist for further tests and treatment.

See also chart

30 Deafness

NO

Delayed speech development may be the result of a number of factors, including normal late development, lack of stimulus and emotional stress. Occasionally it may be due to some form of hearing defect. Consult your physician.
Treatment: Your physician will examine your child, and will pay particular attention to the ears (see *Ear examination,* p.81). He or she will also discuss your child's general development with you. If no obvious cause for your child's late talking can be found, your physician will probably advise you to wait for your child to start talking in his or her own time, while creating plenty of opportunities for listening to adults and other children talking (see *How you can help your child's language development,* opposite). If your physician suspects the possibility of deafness, your child will be referred to a specialist so that further hearing tests can be carried out.

General delayed development may be the result of growth retardation, a physical abnormality or slow mental development. Consult your physician, who will probably arrange for tests so that a diagnosis can be made and appropriate treatment arranged.

Late speech development in a child of this age who is developing normally is unlikely to be a cause for concern. Many children, especially boys and only children, do not start to talk until late in the second year.
Self-help: Children learn to talk most readily when they are constantly in the company of other children and adults who are talking. Get into the habit of talking to your child about your daily activities. Joining a parent and toddler group may be helpful. See also *How you can help your child's language development,* opposite. If your child is not saying more than 2 words by 2 years of age, consult your physician.

Reluctance to speak when there is no difficulty in pronouncing words clearly is unlikely to be the result of a defect in the speech mechanism or of deafness. Consult your physician, who may arrange for your child to be assessed by a specialist.

Is your child under 5 years old?

YES

NO

Are you worried because your child stutters?

YES

NO

Go to next page

Stuttering in late childhood is usually a hangover from the normal hesitancy in speech that is common in younger children. It may be made worse by anxiety about the problem itself or about another unrelated worry. Consult your physician.
Treatment: Your physician may recommend that your child be referred for speech therapy. Children who are given such therapy at an early age usually overcome their difficulties.

Hesitancy in speaking is a phase that most young children go through. It may be because when they are excited their brain is working faster than they can talk. This is perfectly normal and nearly all children grow out of it.
Self-help: Do not draw attention to your child's stuttering by trying to finish his or her words; this may have the effect of creating anxiety that will prolong the stuttering phase. Consult your physician only if your child continues to stutter beyond the age of 5 years, or if the stutter is so severe that it seriously interferes with your child's speech.

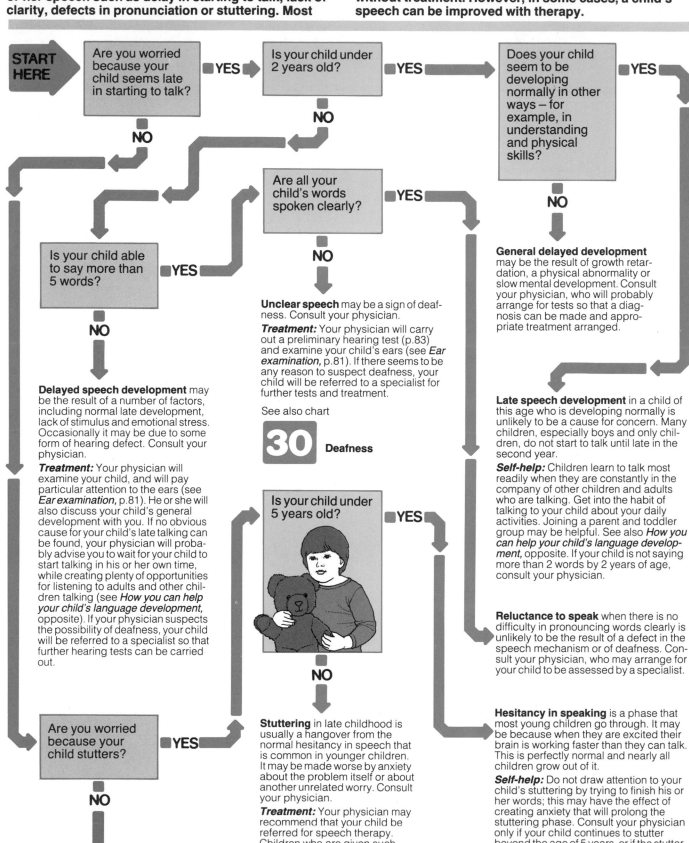

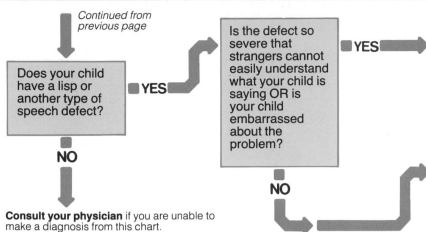

Continued from previous page

Does your child have a lisp or another type of speech defect?

▶ **YES** ▶

Is the defect so severe that strangers cannot easily understand what your child is saying OR is your child embarrassed about the problem?

YES ▶ **Serious defects** in pronunciation may be the result of a physical problem. Consult your physician.
Treatment: Your physician will examine your child, paying special attention to the mouth and ears, and may refer your child to a speech therapist for diagnosis and treatment. Many forms of speech defect can be corrected by speech therapy.

NO

NO

▶ **Minor speech defects** are common. In most cases children will gradually overcome their difficulties with various types of sound as they grow older. Trying to correct your child's speech is likely only to make your child anxious and self-conscious. Consult your physician if the speech defect starts to cause your child embarrassment or if it interferes with communication or school performance.

Consult your physician if you are unable to make a diagnosis from this chart.

SPEECH DEVELOPMENT

The first year
Children begin to communicate well before they are ready to talk. From birth they listen to and enjoy the sound of their parents' voices and learn to associate such sounds with comfort and security. From about 2 months they are learning to make a variety of their own noises, including grunting, gurgling and cooing sounds. Such noises develop during the second half of the first year into recognizable syllables such as "ma," "da" and "ga." These words gradually become more complex until your child is babbling in long strings of syllables. By the end of the first year most children are able to understand a few simple words, phrases and commands, and have usually learned to say at least one recognizable word in its proper context.

The second year
During the early part of the second year a child's vocabulary increases rapidly, although much of a child's conversation is still babbling. Gradually, phrases of linked words joining names of people or objects to actions or commands appear — for example, "mommy go" or "doggie eat." At this stage, understanding of things that you say is also developing rapidly. And even though it may not yet be apparent in your child's speech, a broad base of vocabulary and grammatical structure is being built up.

The third year
The third year is a time during which a child consolidates and builds on the basic knowledge of vocabulary and grammar that was learned in the second year. An apparently never-ending stream of questions about the names of objects and what they do enlarges vocabulary and increases a child's confidence in using words. By the end of this year the majority of children understand most of what an adult says as long as it is not too complex or abstract, and can communicate their wants and thoughts and hold simple conversations about everyday subjects that interest them.

HOW YOU CAN HELP YOUR CHILD'S LANGUAGE DEVELOPMENT

Children learn to talk most readily when constantly exposed to the sound of voices, in particular those of their parents, from an early age. The following specific suggestions will help you ensure that your child receives plenty of stimulation and encouragement to learn to talk when he or she is ready:

- Get into the habit of talking to your child from birth.
- Look directly at your child when you speak, so that the expression on your face gives clues to the meaning of what you are saying.
- Use actions to help your child associate particular words with objects and events.
- Use simple books and nursery rhymes to extend your child's vocabulary and to build confidence by the repetition of familiar words and phrases.
- Provide plenty of opportunities for your child to mix with other children and adults.
- Try not to interrupt your child constantly to correct errors in grammar or pronunciation; this may undermine confidence. Instead, concentrate on providing a good example in the way you speak.

Do not worry if your child seems to be a little late in uttering his or her first words. Your child will nevertheless be listening to you talking and building up the groundwork of language. Most children who are late-talkers catch up with their early-talking contemporaries very quickly once they start.

Talk and sing to encourage speech

Word association helps understanding

Repeated words in books build confidence

Playing with other children promotes communication skills

22 Behavior problems

Problems relating to your child's behavior can vary, and much depends on a parent's perception of what constitutes a problem. It is not possible to deal here with every aspect of childhood behavior problems. This chart covers some of the main areas that cause parents distress and worry. It will give you some idea when professional help, either from your family physician or from a child psychiatrist, may be advisable.

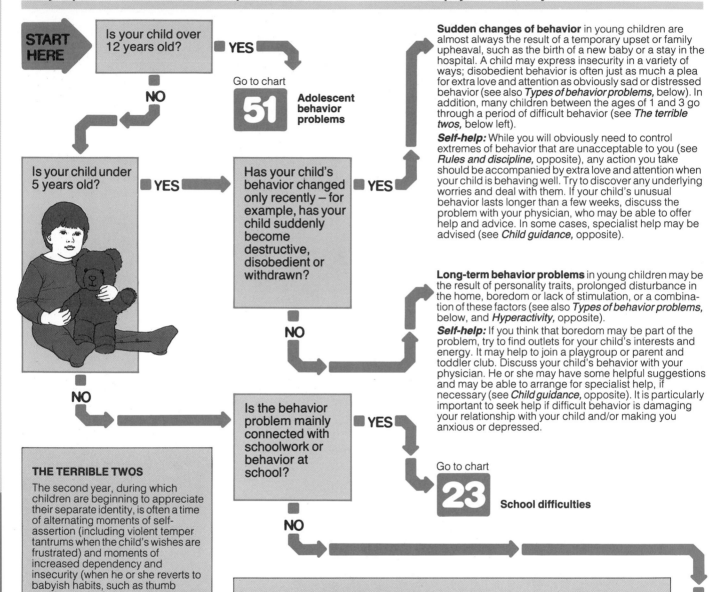

START HERE

Is your child over 12 years old? — **YES** → Go to chart **51** Adolescent behavior problems

NO ↓

Is your child under 5 years old? — **YES** → Has your child's behavior changed only recently – for example, has your child suddenly become destructive, disobedient or withdrawn? — **YES** →

NO ↓ (under question)

Sudden changes of behavior in young children are almost always the result of a temporary upset or family upheaval, such as the birth of a new baby or a stay in the hospital. A child may express insecurity in a variety of ways; disobedient behavior is often just as much a plea for extra love and attention as obviously sad or distressed behavior (see also *Types of behavior problems,* below). In addition, many children between the ages of 1 and 3 go through a period of difficult behavior (see *The terrible twos,* below left).

Self-help: While you will obviously need to control extremes of behavior that are unacceptable to you (see *Rules and discipline,* opposite), any action you take should be accompanied by extra love and attention when your child is behaving well. Try to discover any underlying worries and deal with them. If your child's unusual behavior lasts longer than a few weeks, discuss the problem with your physician, who may be able to offer help and advice. In some cases, specialist help may be advised (see *Child guidance,* opposite).

NO (from changed recently) ↓

Long-term behavior problems in young children may be the result of personality traits, prolonged disturbance in the home, boredom or lack of stimulation, or a combination of these factors (see also *Types of behavior problems,* below, and *Hyperactivity,* opposite).

Self-help: If you think that boredom may be part of the problem, try to find outlets for your child's interests and energy. It may help to join a playgroup or parent and toddler club. Discuss your child's behavior with your physician. He or she may have some helpful suggestions and may be able to arrange for specialist help, if necessary (see *Child guidance,* opposite). It is particularly important to seek help if difficult behavior is damaging your relationship with your child and/or making you anxious or depressed.

NO (child under 5) ↓

Is the behavior problem mainly connected with schoolwork or behavior at school? — **YES** → Go to chart **23** School difficulties

NO ↓

THE TERRIBLE TWOS

The second year, during which children are beginning to appreciate their separate identity, is often a time of alternating moments of self-assertion (including violent temper tantrums when the child's wishes are frustrated) and moments of increased dependency and insecurity (when he or she reverts to babyish habits, such as thumb sucking and refusal to be separated from the parents). This type of behavior can make the "terrible twos" a very trying time for parents.

Dealing with tantrums

If your child has tantrums, it is essential to keep calm. If you can remain unmoved by your screaming child, pick up your child and hold him or her closely until he or she has calmed down. But if you are upset by the tantrums, it is better to leave the room than to shout or display other signs of distress yourself. If frequent temper tantrums are making you feel anxious and unable to cope, consult your physician, who may be able to offer constructive help.

TYPES OF BEHAVIOR PROBLEMS

Aggressiveness
Assertiveness may be a natural part of a child's personality, but excessively aggressive or violent behavior may be a response to worry, boredom or lack of parental attention.

Stealing
A child who steals may simply want something very badly or may do it for a thrill and to gain the admiration of friends. It is common for a child to steal as a result of insecurity to gain attention. Occasionally, a child may repeatedly steal objects of little value. This may be a sign of an emotional disturbance. Seek professional help.

Disobedience and rudeness
If your child persistently defies you, it may be a sign that the rules you have set up are too rigid and your child is using disobedience as a means of expressing independence. Or it may be that your child has not fully understood the reasons for the rules. Children may also use deliberate defiance and the use of bad or insulting language as a means of gaining attention by provoking an angry reaction; such a response may be seen by them as preferable to no response at all (see also *Rules and discipline,* opposite).

Withdrawal
Sudden withdrawal from social contact in a child who previously has enjoyed the company of others could be a sign of anxiety or depression. If this type of behavior persists, try to find out the cause and seek medical advice.

Go to next page

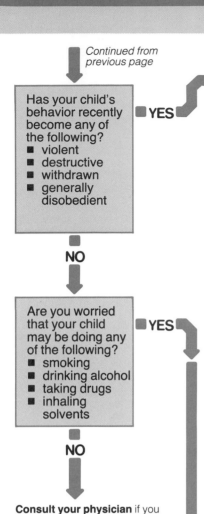

Continued from previous page

Has your child's behavior recently become any of the following?
■ violent
■ destructive
■ withdrawn
■ generally disobedient

NO

Are you worried that your child may be doing any of the following?
■ smoking
■ drinking alcohol
■ taking drugs
■ inhaling solvents

NO

Consult your physician if you are unable to find an explanation for your child's behavior on this chart, and if your child continues to behave in a worrisome way.

 YES

Has this change in behavior occurred following a family upset, such as the birth of a new baby or separation of the parents?

NO

Difficult behavior that starts for no obvious reason may have a variety of underlying causes. There may be problems at school about which you are unaware – for example, bullying. Your child may be worried about some future event, or he or she may sense tension in the home. Alternatively, your child may be bored as a result of insufficient stimulation at school (see *Gifted children,* p.69) or lack of constructive activities in the home. You will know best which explanation is most likely in your child's case (see also *Types of behavior problems,* opposite).

Self-help: Try to channel your child's energies into demanding activities that he or she enjoys. These may include sports, family outings or creative pastimes such as painting and crafts. Discuss the problem with your child's teacher, who may suggest ways of adjusting schoolwork to meet your child's needs more closely. If you suspect that your child is worrying about something, try to find out what the trouble is so that you can offer reassurance. If these suggestions do not work, and if you are unable to control your child's behavior in the usual ways (see *Rules and discipline,* below), consult your physician, who may, if needed, arrange for specialist help (see *Child guidance,* below right).

Such activities are discussed in the box on *Smoking, alcohol and drug abuse,* p.118.

YES

Insecurity and unhappiness can cause some children to misbehave. Bad behavior is a way for children to express anger with themselves or with others and is often a sign that a child needs extra reassurance and love (see *Types of behavior problems,* opposite).

Self-help: During this difficult time, you will need to be patient, but not overindulgent with your child. Continue to enforce your usual rules regarding behavior (see *Rules and discipline,* below left), but also make every effort to talk to your child about any underlying cause of insecurity. Offer plenty of reassurance. Try to set aside a regular time each day when you give your child your undivided attention. It is also a good idea to inform a child's teachers about any important changes in the home so that they will understand any temporary difficulties your child may have with schoolwork. If you find yourself unable to cope with your child's difficult behavior, or if you are worried that it seems to be persisting too long, consult your physician.

HYPERACTIVITY

Hyperactivity refers to excessively restless physical and mental activity in a child. A hyperactive child has a short attention span, is prone to temper tantrums, has apparently boundless energy and needs little sleep. Such behavior can be trying and requires patience and understanding.

Some physicians believe that hyperactivity is the result of brain damage so minimal that it cannot be detected by tests. The damage is thought to be the result of a difficult birth, an allergy to certain foods or chemical food additives, or a marginal vitamin deficiency. It is also thought that the consumption of refined carbohydrates may be related to hyperactivity. However, other physicians view hyperactivity as one end of the spectrum of normal behavior. Treatment will depend on your physician, and may consist of counseling to encourage greater awareness and tolerance among family members.

CHILD GUIDANCE

If your family physician feels that your child's persistent behavior problems could benefit from specialist help, he or she may suggest your child visit a child guidance clinic. This is a center specializing in the assessment of behavior problems in children so that the cause of the problem may be diagnosed accurately and appropriate treatment prescribed. Its staff may include a specialist in the treatment of emotional problems in childhood (child psychiatrist), specialists in child behavior and educational difficulties (educational psychologists) and, possibly, social workers to advise on practical difficulties that may contribute to, or arise out of, the child's problems.

Normally, on a first visit, the whole family will be asked to attend to discuss the problem with the clinic staff. On subsequent visits it may be necessary for the child to attend with only one parent. The child may participate in various activities such as play sessions or further discussions with the staff, depending on the child's age and the nature of the problem. This enables the staff to obtain a clear picture of the case and to advise on further action.

RULES AND DISCIPLINE

Most children benefit from a clearly understood system of rules setting out the bounds of acceptable behavior. Every family has its own standards of behavior and language; behavior that would not be tolerated in one family may be acceptable in another. As a parent you should be clear as to why you lay down certain rules; whether, for example, for reasons of safety or for consideration of the rights and feelings of others. And you should balance the advantages of adhering to certain rigid standards against the need for the occasional confrontation to enforce them. Wherever possible, try to allow your child scope for making independent decisions within the framework you lay down. Otherwise there is a danger of undermining initiative and self-confidence, or of provoking defiance to all your rules.

Punishment

Ideally, sanctions to enforce your wishes on your child should never be necessary. Your aim should be to avoid battles of will by using other, more positive, means of gaining your child's cooperation. Such means may include encouragement of good behavior through praise and reward, the use of example (particularly in relation to manners and language) and constant explanation of the reasons for any limitations you may want to impose. However, in the real world, every parent needs to use

punishment occasionally, and, on the whole, children accept and respect this. The effectiveness of punishment largely depends on how you use it. The following guidelines may help:

■ Always try to make the punishment appropriate to the seriousness of the misdemeanor. Where possible, make the punishment a form of reparation for the "crime."
■ Any punishment should immediately follow the offense and should not be delayed until later.
■ Never threaten a punishment that you know you will be unwilling to carry out; children can detect empty threats.
■ Make sure that it is understood that punishment for a specific offense is not a sign that you have ceased to love your child. For many children, your anger is punishment in itself. A peacemaking hug and words of reassurance afterward are a good idea.
■ Physical (corporal) punishment is generally an ineffective means of gaining a child's cooperation and can often lead to resentment that produces the opposite effect. However, the occasional spank is unlikely to do lasting damage. Seek advice from your physician if you find yourself unable to control your anger to the extent that you fear you may harm your child.

23 School difficulties

School difficulties fall into two main groups: those related principally to learning, whether of a specific subject or of schoolwork in general; and those more concerned with behavior, including classroom behavior and reluctance to go to school. Consult this chart if your child has any of these difficulties. Such problems may be the result of emotional difficulties, physical disorders or social factors, or they may arise out of a general problem of development. Most school difficulties benefit from discussions between parent and school staff, and it is often helpful to involve the family physician who has watched your child's development.

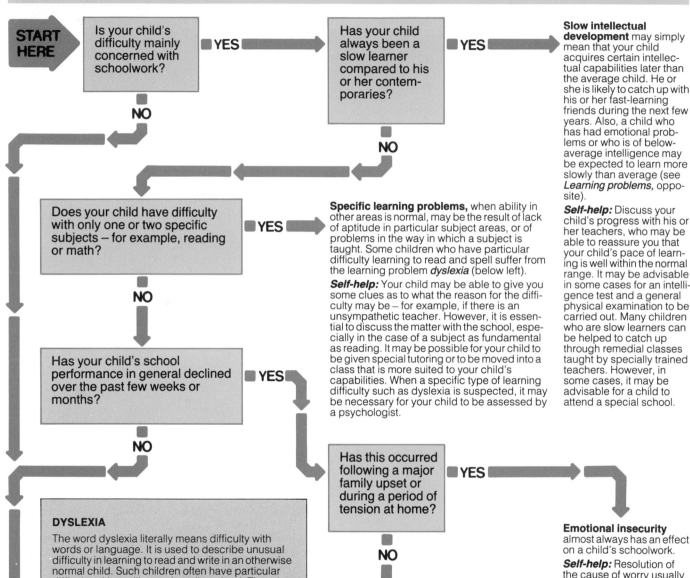

START HERE

Is your child's difficulty mainly concerned with schoolwork?

YES → **Has your child always been a slow learner compared to his or her contemporaries?**

YES → **Slow intellectual development** may simply mean that your child acquires certain intellectual capabilities later than the average child. He or she is likely to catch up with his or her fast-learning friends during the next few years. Also, a child who has had emotional problems or who is of below-average intelligence may be expected to learn more slowly than average (see *Learning problems,* opposite).

Self-help: Discuss your child's progress with his or her teachers, who may be able to reassure you that your child's pace of learning is well within the normal range. It may be advisable in some cases for an intelligence test and a general physical examination to be carried out. Many children who are slow learners can be helped to catch up through remedial classes taught by specially trained teachers. However, in some cases, it may be advisable for a child to attend a special school.

NO

Does your child have difficulty with only one or two specific subjects – for example, reading or math?

YES → **Specific learning problems,** when ability in other areas is normal, may be the result of lack of aptitude in particular subject areas, or of problems in the way in which a subject is taught. Some children who have particular difficulty learning to read and spell suffer from the learning problem *dyslexia* (below left).

Self-help: Your child may be able to give you some clues as to what the reason for the difficulty may be – for example, if there is an unsympathetic teacher. However, it is essential to discuss the matter with the school, especially in the case of a subject as fundamental as reading. It may be possible for your child to be given special tutoring or to be moved into a class that is more suited to your child's capabilities. When a specific type of learning difficulty such as dyslexia is suspected, it may be necessary for your child to be assessed by a psychologist.

NO

Has your child's school performance in general declined over the past few weeks or months?

YES → **Has this occurred following a major family upset or during a period of tension at home?**

YES → **Emotional insecurity** almost always has an effect on a child's schoolwork.

Self-help: Resolution of the cause of worry usually brings about an improvement. It is usually a good idea to inform teachers about any home problems that may affect a child's schoolwork so that allowances can be made and, where necessary, extra help given. If your child's work does not improve following resolution of the underlying difficulty, or if you are unable to resolve the problem, consult your physician, who will be able to advise you on whether further specialist help is necessary.

NO

A sudden decline in school performance, when there is no reason for anxiety, may be the result of an underlying physical problem – for example, a disorder of hearing or eyesight – or may be the result of social distractions or a hidden cause of anxiety. Consult your physician and discuss the problem with your child's teachers.

Treatment: Your physician will examine your child, paying particular attention to sight and hearing (see *Hearing tests for children,* p. 83, and *Eye testing,* p.79), and may arrange for your child to undergo further tests. If no physical disorder is found, your physician may advise further discussions with your child's school to find out if there is any other possible cause of the difficulties. It may be necessary to make adjustments in your child's schoolwork arrangements.

DYSLEXIA

The word dyslexia literally means difficulty with words or language. It is used to describe unusual difficulty in learning to read and write in an otherwise normal child. Such children often have particular difficulty with spelling and reading aloud. There is no agreement among physicians and psychologists about the cause of dyslexia. Some suggest that dyslexia is caused by abnormal nerve pathways in the brain, others that it is caused by certain forms of brain damage at birth or as a result of illness in infancy.

Diagnosing and treating dyslexia

You should consider the possibility of dyslexia if your child has greater difficulty learning to read and write than would be expected for a child of his or her level of intelligence. Your child's teachers will be able to advise you if your child's progress is not normal. If, after examining all aspects of your child's health and development (see *Learning problems,* opposite), school authorities agree that dyslexia could be the problem, remedial teaching, helpful for the majority of dyslexic children, can be arranged.

Go to next page

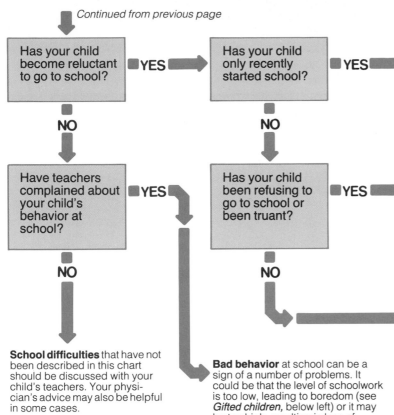

Continued from previous page

Has your child become reluctant to go to school? — YES →

Has your child only recently started school? — YES →

NO ↓

NO ↓

Have teachers complained about your child's behavior at school? — YES →

Has your child been refusing to go to school or been truant? — YES →

NO ↓

NO ↓

Fear of school is very common in children just starting a new school (especially when starting a nursery or primary school) if a child has not been used to being away from home and family for long periods.

Self-help: In most cases, increasing familiarity with the school surroundings and growing interest in school activities will help your child overcome his or her misgivings. During the period of adjustment, try to reassure your child that being left at school is not a form of abandonment. Most nursery classes will allow parents to stay with their children for the first week or so. Make sure that there is no special cause for anxiety such as awkward bathroom facilities and try never to be late in picking your child up from school. If fear of school persists, discuss the problem with the school faculty, who may recommend professional advice.

School difficulties that have not been described in this chart should be discussed with your child's teachers. Your physician's advice may also be helpful in some cases.

Bad behavior at school can be a sign of a number of problems. It could be that the level of schoolwork is too low, leading to boredom (see *Gifted children,* below left) or it may be too high, resulting in loss of interest and leading the child to use disruptive behavior to gain attention in class. It can also be the result of rejection of authority often linked to the emotional changes of adolescence (see chart 51, *Adolescent behavior problems*). In some cases, it may be the result of emotional disturbance.

Self-help: In cases of mild misbehavior it is often sufficient for your child to know that you are aware of the problem and invoke your usual forms of discipline (see *Rules and discipline,* p.67). However, it is also wise to discuss any possible causes of the problem with your child's teachers. Adjustments may need to be made in your child's schoolwork so that it meets your child's individual needs more closely. In cases of serious behavior problems, expert help through a *child guidance* professional (p.67) and, occasionally, special schools may be advisable.

Refusal to go to school is a sign that something is seriously wrong. It could be due to a problem at school such as bullying, a failure of the school to meet the child's individual needs, or it may be the result of the influence of friends at school. Occasionally, refusal to go to school is caused by anxiety about home life.

Self-help: To solve the problem of refusal to go to school, you are likely to need the help of the school authorities and possibly your physician, who may advise *child guidance* (p.67). The sooner the problem is tackled, the better. Make every effort to ensure that your child attends school and that the teachers concerned know that the problem exists so that unexplained absences from classes are not ignored. Meanwhile, try to discover the underlying cause of your child's refusal to go to school so that it can be dealt with as soon as possible.

Dislike of school can arise from a variety of factors. Your child may be having difficulties with schoolwork, or may be afraid of certain teachers or of other pupils.

Self-help: Dislike of school should be tackled promptly before it develops into the more serious problem of *refusal to go to school* (above). Try to find out from your child what the cause of the problem is and also discuss your child's feelings about school with his or her teachers so that they can look out for signs of a problem such as bullying or teasing. While you are trying to resolve the problem, do not keep your child at home unless advised to do so by the school; there is a danger that this may lead your child to stay away from school in the future. Depending on the underlying cause of the problem, it may be necessary for your child to change classes or to receive special tutoring.

GIFTED CHILDREN

Children who are unusually gifted, whether with an exceptional talent in one area or with a generally high level of intelligence, need special educational challenges from an early age. Without adequate stimulation, a gifted child may become unhappy, bored and/or disruptive.

You may suspect that your child is unusually gifted if he or she learns exceptionally quickly – especially if he or she reads voraciously and complains that school is boring. In this case you should discuss the matter with your child's teachers, who may arrange for your child to be assessed by an educational psychologist.

If your child is found to be exceptionally intelligent, the teachers may be able to devise a learning program that will challenge your child's intelligence adequately. Alternatively, education at a special school may be the best option. If your child has a special gift for music, for example, expert tutoring may be arranged.

Whatever educational program you choose for your child, you will need to remember that his or her emotional and social development is unlikely to be as advanced as his or her intellectual development. Your child should be encouraged to play with children of the same age and to join in sports and other recreational activities.

LEARNING PROBLEMS

In order to learn physical and intellectual skills at a normal rate, a child needs to have normal hearing, sight and intelligence. Impairment of any one of these faculties will lead to learning problems. In addition, a child's progress can be retarded by lack of sufficient stimulation in early childhood, by emotional upset, or by frequent absences from school.

Assessing the problem
Any child who is obviously having difficulty keeping pace with his or her contemporaries at school needs to be assessed by an educational psychologist. This can be arranged by the school authorities. The psychologist will carry out intelligence tests and may also arrange tests on hearing and vision. If a physi-cal problem such as deafness is found, it may be treated by your family physician. If an emotional cause for the learning difficulty is suspected, referral to a *child guidance* specialist (see p.67) will probably be recommended. A child who seems to be of normal intelligence, but who has learning problems not caused by physical illness or emotional upset, may be suffering from a specific learning difficulty known as *dyslexia* (opposite). Such children, as well as those whose difficulty is caused by lower-than-average intelligence, may be helped by special remedial classes in a regular school. When intelligence is severely subnormal, it may be best for the child to be taught at a special school.

24 Hair, scalp and nail problems

Consult this diagnostic chart if your child has any problem affecting hair growth, including hair thinning and bald patches, or if your child's scalp is affected by itching or flaking. The most common causes of such problems are infection or parasitic infestation that, although not serious, require treatment.

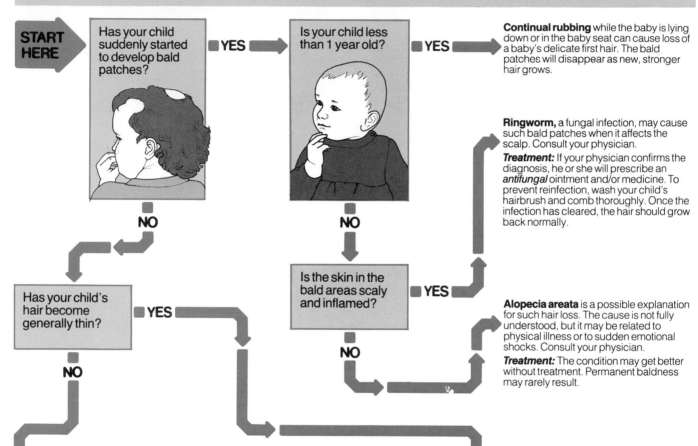

START HERE

Has your child suddenly started to develop bald patches? — **YES** → **Is your child less than 1 year old?** — **YES** → **Continual rubbing** while the baby is lying down or in the baby seat can cause loss of a baby's delicate first hair. The bald patches will disappear as new, stronger hair grows.

NO ↓ (from first box)

NO ↓ (from second box) → **Is the skin in the bald areas scaly and inflamed?** — **YES** →

Ringworm, a fungal infection, may cause such bald patches when it affects the scalp. Consult your physician.

Treatment: If your physician confirms the diagnosis, he or she will prescribe an ***antifungal*** ointment and/or medicine. To prevent reinfection, wash your child's hairbrush and comb thoroughly. Once the infection has cleared, the hair should grow back normally.

NO ↓ (from scaly box)

Has your child's hair become generally thin? — **YES** →

Alopecia areata is a possible explanation for such hair loss. The cause is not fully understood, but it may be related to physical illness or to sudden emotional shocks. Consult your physician.

Treatment: The condition may get better without treatment. Permanent baldness may rarely result.

NO ↓

WASHING YOUR CHILD'S HAIR

Children's hair should be washed regularly (about twice a week) and thoroughly. A very young baby's hair may be washed less often (perhaps once a week). Unless your child needs a special shampoo to control dandruff, almost any shampoo will do; expensive cosmetic shampoos are unlikely to improve a child's hair. However, for babies and young children, choose a mild baby shampoo that will not sting if it gets in the eyes. One application should be sufficient unless the hair is very dirty. Rinse the hair thoroughly afterward and towel dry. Allowing the hair to air dry is preferable to the use of a hot-air dryer.

Overcoming dislike of hair-washing
Many young children dislike having their hair washed, because they are frightened of getting water in their eyes. It may be helpful to encourage gentle water play in the bath (left). Spraying your child with a garden hose while playing in the yard is another way to ease your child's dislike of water in the face. Remember, though, never surprise your child.

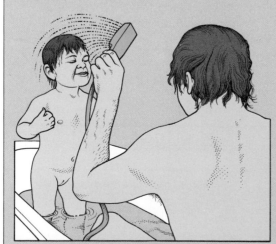

Is your child less than 1 year old? — **YES** →

NO ↓

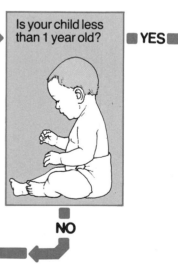

Loss of baby hair during the first year usually results in a noticeable thinning out of hair for a brief period. Over the next few months, new, stronger hair will grow that may be of a different color from that with which your baby was born.

1 *Go to next page column 1*

2 *Go to next page column 2*

1 *Continued from previous page column 1*

Is your child's scalp itchy? → **YES** →

NO ↓

Does your child have greasy, crusty patches on the scalp? → **YES** →

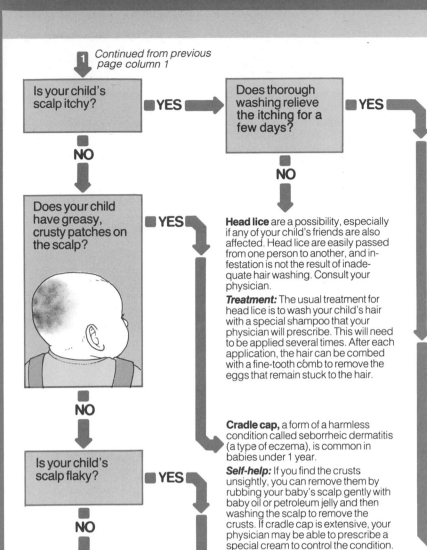

NO ↓

Is your child's scalp flaky? → **YES** →

NO ↓

Consult your physician if you are unable to make a diagnosis from this chart.

Does thorough washing relieve the itching for a few days? → **YES** →

NO ↓

Head lice are a possibility, especially if any of your child's friends are also affected. Head lice are easily passed from one person to another, and infestation is not the result of inadequate hair washing. Consult your physician.

Treatment: The usual treatment for head lice is to wash your child's hair with a special shampoo that your physician will prescribe. This will need to be applied several times. After each application, the hair can be combed with a fine-tooth comb to remove the eggs that remain stuck to the hair.

Cradle cap, a form of a harmless condition called seborrheic dermatitis (a type of eczema), is common in babies under 1 year.

Self-help: If you find the crusts unsightly, you can remove them by rubbing your baby's scalp gently with baby oil or petroleum jelly and then washing the scalp to remove the crusts. If cradle cap is extensive, your physician may be able to prescribe a special cream to control the condition.

Dandruff is the most likely cause of flaking of the scalp (see *Dandruff,* right).

---

2 *Continued from previous page column 2*

Has your child been taking any medications prescribed by your physician? → **YES** →

NO ↓

General thinning of the hair may be the result of illness in the past few months or may occur for no apparent reason.

Self-help: Other than ensuring that your child is otherwise healthy and is receiving an adequate diet (see *The components of a healthy diet,* p. 97), there is little you can do to encourage your child's hair to grow more thickly. If your child's hair is long, avoid tying it back tightly with elastic bands or pulling it into tight styles. Use a soft nylon or bristle brush because hard brushes may break the hair. Your child's hair may appear thicker if cut in a short style. If you are worried, consult your physician.

Certain medications may cause temporary hair loss. Discuss the problem with your physician.

Dandruff, which may sometimes be caused by seborrheic dermatitis, a form of eczema, is the most common cause of itching of the scalp. It is also likely to lead to flaking of the scalp.

Self-help: Dandruff is best controlled by frequent use of one of the many over-the-counter antidandruff shampoos. If this is not effective, consult your physician, who will prescribe another antidandruff shampoo, or a lotion to apply to the scalp.

NAIL CARE

The nails of babies and children should always be kept short. In babies this prevents accidental scratching and in older children helps to prevent nail-biting and the spread of infection from dirt under the fingernails. Always use blunt-ended scissors.

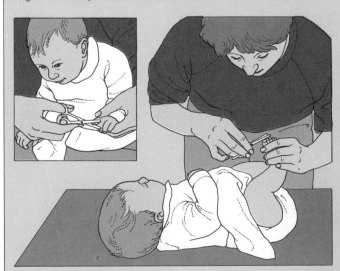

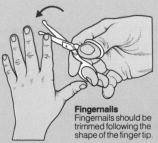

Fingernails
Fingernails should be trimmed following the shape of the finger tip.

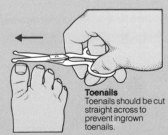

Toenails
Toenails should be cut straight across to prevent ingrown toenails.

Nail-biting
Nail-biting is a habit that often develops in children of primary school age. It may be copied from other children or arise as a nervous habit. It presents no risk to health, but bitten nails are unsightly and, if bitten down to the nail bed, may cause soreness.

If your child has a tendancy to bite his or her nails, try to keep them trimmed and smooth. Encourage your child to take pride in his or her appearance. Buying a manicure set and applying clear nail polish may help. Bitter-tasting paint for the nails is unlikely to have any effect and may simply make your child resentful. Most children stop biting their nails by the time they reach adolescence.

25 Spots and rashes

Spots and rashes in childhood are usually caused by inflammation of the skin as a result of infection, which may be localized, or part of a generalized illness or an allergic reaction. Most rashes that are not accompanied by a fever or a feeling of being sick are not a sign of serious illness but, if the rash is itchy or sore, you should consult your physician, who may be able to provide effective treatment.

For children under 1 year, see chart 4, Skin problems in babies

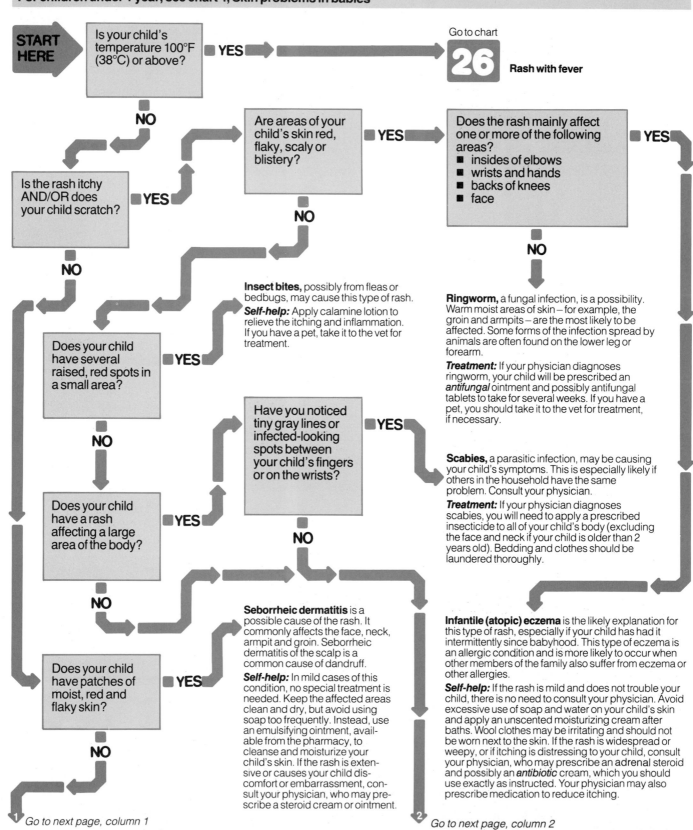

START HERE

Is your child's temperature 100°F (38°C) or above?

YES → Go to chart **26** Rash with fever

NO

Is the rash itchy AND/OR does your child scratch?

YES

Are areas of your child's skin red, flaky, scaly or blistery?

YES

Does the rash mainly affect one or more of the following areas?
- insides of elbows
- wrists and hands
- backs of knees
- face

YES

NO

NO

NO

Does your child have several raised, red spots in a small area?

NO

Does your child have a rash affecting a large area of the body?

YES

Have you noticed tiny gray lines or infected-looking spots between your child's fingers or on the wrists?

YES

NO

NO

Does your child have patches of moist, red and flaky skin?

YES

NO

Insect bites, possibly from fleas or bedbugs, may cause this type of rash.
Self-help: Apply calamine lotion to relieve the itching and inflammation. If you have a pet, take it to the vet for treatment.

Ringworm, a fungal infection, is a possibility. Warm moist areas of skin – for example, the groin and armpits – are the most likely to be affected. Some forms of the infection spread by animals are often found on the lower leg or forearm.
Treatment: If your physician diagnoses ringworm, your child will be prescribed an ***antifungal*** ointment and possibly antifungal tablets to take for several weeks. If you have a pet, you should take it to the vet for treatment, if necessary.

Scabies, a parasitic infection, may be causing your child's symptoms. This is especially likely if others in the household have the same problem. Consult your physician.
Treatment: If your physician diagnoses scabies, you will need to apply a prescribed insecticide to all of your child's body (excluding the face and neck if your child is older than 2 years old). Bedding and clothes should be laundered thoroughly.

Seborrheic dermatitis is a possible cause of the rash. It commonly affects the face, neck, armpit and groin. Seborrheic dermatitis of the scalp is a common cause of dandruff.
Self-help: In mild cases of this condition, no special treatment is needed. Keep the affected areas clean and dry, but avoid using soap too frequently. Instead, use an emulsifying ointment, available from the pharmacy, to cleanse and moisturize your child's skin. If the rash is extensive or causes your child discomfort or embarrassment, consult your physician, who may prescribe a steroid cream or ointment.

Infantile (atopic) eczema is the likely explanation for this type of rash, especially if your child has had it intermittently since babyhood. This type of eczema is an allergic condition and is more likely to occur when other members of the family also suffer from eczema or other allergies.
Self-help: If the rash is mild and does not trouble your child, there is no need to consult your physician. Avoid excessive use of soap and water on your child's skin and apply an unscented moisturizing cream after baths. Wool clothes may be irritating and should not be worn next to the skin. If the rash is widespread or weepy, or if itching is distressing to your child, consult your physician, who may prescribe an **adrenal** steroid and possibly an ***antibiotic*** cream, which you should use exactly as instructed. Your physician may also prescribe medication to reduce itching.

1 *Go to next page, column 1*

2 *Go to next page, column 2*

Does your child have a rash of pink spots that mainly affects the face and/or trunk?

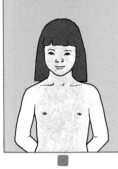

YES ▶

German measles (rubella) is possible. The disease is usually accompanied by swelling of the glands in the back of the neck and is unlikely to make your child feel very sick (see also *Comparison of childhood infectious diseases,* (p. 75).

Self-help: German measles is a mild illness and generally needs little treatment other than an aspirin substitute to reduce any fever. It is important, however, to keep your child at home to avoid infecting others, especially any woman who is pregnant, because of the damage the disease can do to the unborn child. If you want to consult your physician, telephone the office first. Your physician may want to visit your child at home.

NO ▼

Does your child have a blistery rash that dries up and forms a gold crust?

YES ▶

Impetigo, a bacterial skin infection that commonly affects the face, is possible. Consult your physician.

Treatment: If your physician confirms that your child has impetigo, you will probably be advised to wash the crusts away gently with salty water and to apply *antibiotic* cream to the affected areas. While the infection persists, you should make sure that your child keeps a separate towel and washcloth to avoid infecting the rest of the family. It may be necessary to use an antibiotic and keep your child away from school.

NO ▼

Is your child over 12 years old and suffering from one or more of the following?
- blackheads
- inflamed spots with white centers
- painful, red lumps under the skin

YES ▶

Acne is a common problem in adolescence and can occur with varying degrees of severity.

Go the chart

52 **Adolescent skin problems**

NO ▼

Does your child have several bright-red, slightly raised spots or patches with pale centers?

YES ▶

Urticaria (hives), an allergic reaction, produces this type of rash. It may occur as a reaction to certain foods – for example, shellfish or strawberries – or to medication. Sometimes it occurs when the skin is exposed to certain plants or to extremes of heat or cold. In many cases no cause for the rash can be found. Occasionally, the appearance of the rash is accompanied by swelling of the face and mouth. This can be dangerous and requires urgent medical treatment if difficult breathing occurs.

Self-help: An outbreak of urticaria normally subsides within a few hours without treatment. If your child suffers from repeated attacks, or if the rash persists for more than 4 hours, consult your physician, who may prescribe *antihistamines* and may carry out tests to determine the cause of the problem.

NO ▼

WARTS AND BOILS

Warts
A wart is a lump on the skin caused by virus infection. The most common type of wart is a hard, painless lump with a rough surface. Warts may occur singly, but more often several occur together. The hands are the most commonly affected area, but unraised warts called plantar warts often appear on the soles of the feet. Plantar warts may cause your child pain on walking.

Treatment
Warts need no treatment and will disappear on their own in time. However, if your child is embarrassed by unsightly warts, or has plantar warts, consult your physician, who may recommend treatment with a lotion painted onto the wart, or may refer your child to a clinic where the wart can be either burned or frozen off. Removal of warts by freezing does not cause scarring.

Boils
A boil occurs when a hair follicle (a pit in the skin from which a hair grows) becomes infected by bacteria, resulting in the collection of pus in the follicle. An inflamed lump with a white center develops under the skin. Eventually the boil bursts, releasing the pus, and the skin heals.

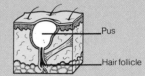

The formation of a boil
A boil forms when bacteria enter a hair follicle, causing pus to collect there.

Pus

Hair follicle

Treatment
A single boil usually heals without treatment. Adding a mild antiseptic to your child's bath water will help prevent the spread of infection. A warm, wet compress applied for 10 to 15 minutes twice a day will usually speed healing. When the boil bursts, carefully wipe away the pus with cotton soaked in an antiseptic solution and cover with an adhesive bandage. Consult your physician if your child has a large, painful boil, if several boils develop or if boils recur. Your physician may prescribe *antibiotics* or an antiseptic cream. Occasionally, a small cut is made in the center of a large boil to release the pus.

Certain medications may bring out a rash in susceptible children. Discuss the problem with your physician.

Is your child taking any medications?

YES ▶

NO ▼

Consult your physician if you are unable to make a diagnosis from this chart.

26 Rash with fever

Consult this chart if your child develops a rash while having a fever. This combination of symptoms usually indicates a common infectious disease of childhood. These diseases are caused by viruses (see *Viral and*

bacterial infections, p.44) and usually can be treated at home. In most cases, it is good for a child to get these infections out of the way. If your child is less than 1 year old, consult your physician to confirm the diagnosis.

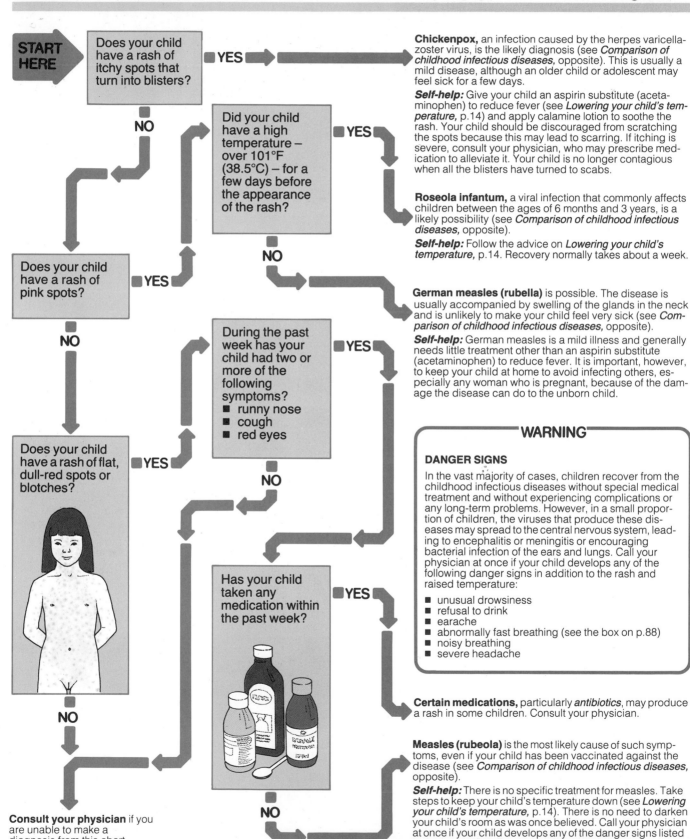

START HERE

Does your child have a rash of itchy spots that turn into blisters?

YES

NO

Did your child have a high temperature – over 101°F (38.5°C) – for a few days before the appearance of the rash?

YES

NO

Does your child have a rash of pink spots?

YES

NO

During the past week has your child had two or more of the following symptoms?
■ runny nose
■ cough
■ red eyes

YES

NO

Does your child have a rash of flat, dull-red spots or blotches?

YES

NO

Has your child taken any medication within the past week?

YES

NO

Consult your physician if you are unable to make a diagnosis from this chart.

Chickenpox, an infection caused by the herpes varicella-zoster virus, is the likely diagnosis (see *Comparison of childhood infectious diseases*, opposite). This is usually a mild disease, although an older child or adolescent may feel sick for a few days.

Self-help: Give your child an aspirin substitute (acetaminophen) to reduce fever (see *Lowering your child's temperature*, p.14) and apply calamine lotion to soothe the rash. Your child should be discouraged from scratching the spots because this may lead to scarring. If itching is severe, consult your physician, who may prescribe medication to alleviate it. Your child is no longer contagious when all the blisters have turned to scabs.

Roseola infantum, a viral infection that commonly affects children between the ages of 6 months and 3 years, is a likely possibility (see *Comparison of childhood infectious diseases*, opposite).

Self-help: Follow the advice on *Lowering your child's temperature*, p.14. Recovery normally takes about a week.

German measles (rubella) is possible. The disease is usually accompanied by swelling of the glands in the neck and is unlikely to make your child feel very sick (see *Comparison of childhood infectious diseases*, opposite).

Self-help: German measles is a mild illness and generally needs little treatment other than an aspirin substitute (acetaminophen) to reduce fever. It is important, however, to keep your child at home to avoid infecting others, especially any woman who is pregnant, because of the damage the disease can do to the unborn child.

WARNING

DANGER SIGNS

In the vast majority of cases, children recover from the childhood infectious diseases without special medical treatment and without experiencing complications or any long-term problems. However, in a small proportion of children, the viruses that produce these diseases may spread to the central nervous system, leading to encephalitis or meningitis or encouraging bacterial infection of the ears and lungs. Call your physician at once if your child develops any of the following danger signs in addition to the rash and raised temperature:

■ unusual drowsiness
■ refusal to drink
■ earache
■ abnormally fast breathing (see the box on p.88)
■ noisy breathing
■ severe headache

Certain medications, particularly *antibiotics*, may produce a rash in some children. Consult your physician.

Measles (rubeola) is the most likely cause of such symptoms, even if your child has been vaccinated against the disease (see *Comparison of childhood infectious diseases*, opposite).

Self-help: There is no specific treatment for measles. Take steps to keep your child's temperature down (see *Lowering your child's temperature*, p.14). There is no need to darken your child's room as was once believed. Call your physician at once if your child develops any of the danger signs listed in the box above. Recovery takes about 10 days.

COMPARISON OF CHILDHOOD INFECTIOUS DISEASES

Disease	Symptoms	Visual signs	Typical course of illness
Measles (incubation period* 10–14 days)	Fever; cough; runny nose; red eyes; flat, dull-red spots and blotches that first appear on the face and behind the ears and later spread to the trunk and upper limbs. Infectious from onset of first symptoms until 4 days after the appearance of the rash.	Rash distribution	Symptoms: Cough; Runny nose/sore eyes; Rash. Temperature 102, 101, 100. Days 1–9.
German measles (incubation period* 14–21 days)	Low fever; swollen glands in the neck; flat, pink spots that occur mainly on face and trunk at first. Infectious from 7 days before the rash appears until all the spots have scabs.	Rash distribution; Swollen glands	Symptoms: Rash; Swollen glands. Temperature 102, 101, 100. Days 1–9.
Chickenpox (incubation period* 7–21 days)	Fever; raised, red, itchy spots that turn into blisters and then scabs, mainly on face and trunk. Infectious from 5 days before the rash appears until all the spots have scabs.	Rash distribution	Symptoms: Spots/blisters; Scabs. Temperature 102, 101, 100. Days 1–9.
Roseola infantum (incubation period* Variable)	High fever; flat, light-red rash on the trunk; swollen glands in the neck. Infectious for 5 days after the onset of symptoms.	Rash distribution; Swollen glands	Symptoms: Rash; Swollen glands. Temperature 102, 101, 100. Days 1–9.
Mumps (incubation period* 14–28 days)	Swelling and tenderness of glands on one or both sides of the face; fever; sore throat. Infectious from 3 days before the glands swell until 7 days after the swelling has subsided.	Swollen glands	Symptoms: Swollen glands/sore throat. Temperature 102, 101, 100. Days 1–9.

* Time between contact with the disease and the development of symptoms.

IMMUNIZATION

Your child can be given highly effective immunity against various infectious diseases by vaccination. Some vaccines contain living microbes (in a harmless form) and these give lasting protection. Vaccines made from dead microbes or from the toxins they produce have to be given several times for best results. In each case, the body is stimulated to produce substances known as antibodies to fight the disease. Immunization during childhood not only protects your child from disease, but helps to reduce the spread of disease in the community. Most forms of immunization carry little risk. However, some vaccinations may be dangerous for children who have had convulsions or if anyone in the family has suffered from convulsions. In these cases, certain vaccinations (such as for whooping cough) may not be advisable. Discuss this with your physician. In addition, you should not have your child vaccinated when he or she is sick. The table (right) shows a typical immunization schedule.

TYPICAL IMMUNIZATION SCHEDULE

Age	Disease	Method of vaccination
2 months	Diphtheria, whooping cough, tetanus	Combined injection
2 months	Poliomyelitis	Oral
4 months	Diphtheria, whooping cough, tetanus	Combined injection
4 months	Poliomyelitis	Oral
6 months	Diphtheria, whooping cough, tetanus	Combined injection
15 months	Measles, mumps, German measles	Combined injection
18 months	Diphtheria, whooping cough, tetanus	Combined injection
18 months	Poliomyelitis	Oral
4–6 years	Diphtheria, whooping cough, tetanus	Combined injection
4–6 years	Poliomyelitis	Oral

27 Eye problems

This charts deals with pain, itching, redness and/or discharge from one or both eyes. In children, such symptoms are most commonly the result of infection or local irritation and can often be treated at home without consulting your physician. However, you should seek immediate medical advice about any obvious injury to the eye or any foreign body in the eye that cannot be removed by simple first-aid measures.

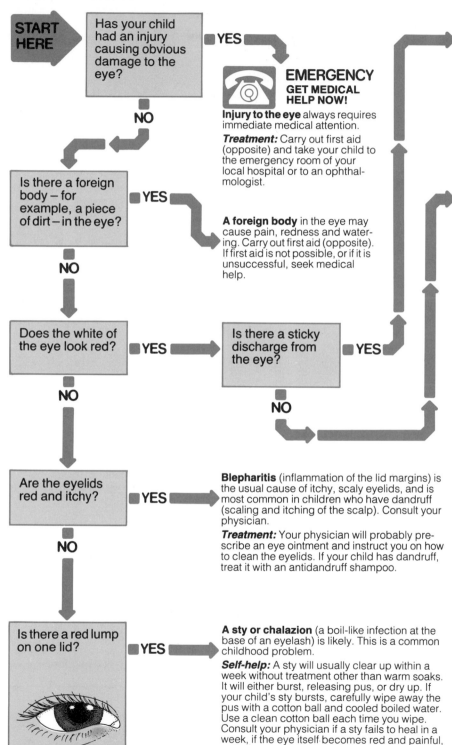

START HERE

Has your child had an injury causing obvious damage to the eye?

YES →

EMERGENCY GET MEDICAL HELP NOW!

Injury to the eye always requires immediate medical attention.
Treatment: Carry out first aid (opposite) and take your child to the emergency room of your local hospital or to an ophthalmologist.

NO ↓

Is there a foreign body – for example, a piece of dirt – in the eye?

YES →

A foreign body in the eye may cause pain, redness and watering. Carry out first aid (opposite). If first aid is not possible, or if it is unsuccessful, seek medical help.

NO ↓

Does the white of the eye look red?

YES →

Is there a sticky discharge from the eye?

YES →

NO ↓

Are the eyelids red and itchy?

YES →

Blepharitis (inflammation of the lid margins) is the usual cause of itchy, scaly eyelids, and is most common in children who have dandruff (scaling and itching of the scalp). Consult your physician.
Treatment: Your physician will probably prescribe an eye ointment and instruct you on how to clean the eyelids. If your child has dandruff, treat it with an antidandruff shampoo.

NO ↓

Is there a red lump on one lid?

YES →

A sty or chalazion (a boil-like infection at the base of an eyelash) is likely. This is a common childhood problem.
Self-help: A sty will usually clear up within a week without treatment other than warm soaks. It will either burst, releasing pus, or dry up. If your child's sty bursts, carefully wipe away the pus with a cotton ball and cooled boiled water. Use a clean cotton ball each time you wipe. Consult your physician if a sty fails to heal in a week, if the eye itself becomes red and painful, or if sties recur.

NO ↓ *Go to next page*

Conjunctivitis (inflammation of the membrane covering the eye and lining the eyelids) caused by infection is likely. Consult your physician.
Treatment: Your physician will probably prescribe *antibiotic* eye drops or ointment. The sticky discharge can be gently bathed away with comfortably warm boiled water. Make sure your child keeps the eyes closed after the drops have been administered, and use a clean cotton ball each time you wipe. Keep a separate towel and washcloth for your child to prevent the spread of infection.

Eye irritation caused by fumes or chemicals (for example, those in swimming-pool water) or an allergic reaction (for example, to pollen) is possible. However, if other children in your area also have this problem, it may be due to viral infection (viral conjunctivitis).
Self-help: If you suspect irritation from fumes or chemicals, no treatment is needed other than avoidance of the irritant. Similarly, irritation caused by allergy will subside as soon as the cause of the reaction is removed, but this is not always possible. Discuss this with your physician. Viral conjunctivitis will clear up on its own, but you will need to take steps to prevent the spread of infection (see *Conjunctivitis,* above). In any case, consult your physician if redness persists for more than a week, or if your child complains of pain.

DROOPING EYELID

Some children have a permanently drooping upper eyelid, a condition known as ptosis. This is often present from birth, and in such cases is usually the result of weakness of the muscles in the affected eyelid. Occasionally, ptosis may develop later in childhood as a result of a nerve or muscle disorder.

Risks
If ptosis is so severe that the vision in that eye is blocked, and the condition is untreated, it may cause deterioration in the vision in the "lazy" eye.

Treatment
If your child has a drooping eyelid, consult your physician. The condition may be treated by an operation to strengthen the muscles of the eyelid, or by special glasses. Ptosis that is caused by a nerve or muscle disorder may be cured by treating the underlying condition. If your child has developed a lazy eye, he or she may need to wear a patch over the good eye to force the lazy eye to work harder.

Drooping eyelid in a child

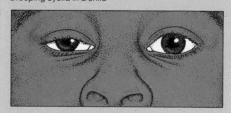

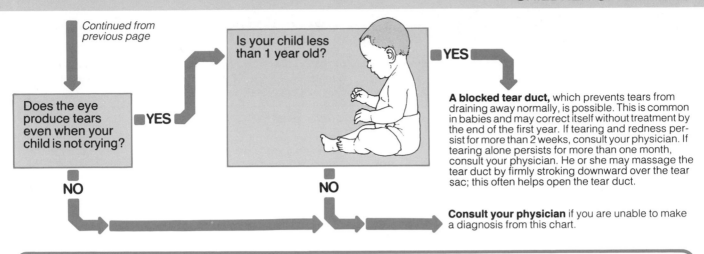

Continued from previous page

Does the eye produce tears even when your child is not crying?

YES →

Is your child less than 1 year old?

YES →

A blocked tear duct, which prevents tears from draining away normally, is possible. This is common in babies and may correct itself without treatment by the end of the first year. If tearing and redness persist for more than 2 weeks, consult your physician. If tearing alone persists for more than one month, consult your physician. He or she may massage the tear duct by firmly stroking downward over the tear sac; this often helps open the tear duct.

NO ↓   **NO** ↓

Consult your physician if you are unable to make a diagnosis from this chart.

FIRST AID FOR EYE INJURIES

If your child suffers an injury to the eye or eyelid, rapid action is essential (with the exception of a foreign body that has been successfully removed from the eye). As soon as you have carried out first aid, get your child to the emergency room of your local hospital or to an ophthalmologist by the fastest means possible.

Cuts to the eye or eyelid
Cover the injured eye with a clean pad (for example, a folded handkerchief) and hold the pad lightly in place with a bandage. Apply no pressure. Cover the other eye also to prevent movement of the eyeball. Seek medical help.

Blows to the eye area
Carry out first aid as for cuts to the eye or eyelid (above), but use a cold compress instead of a dry pad over the injured eye.

Corrosive chemicals in the eye
If your child spills any harsh chemical (for example, bleach) in the eye, immediately flood the eye with large quantities of cold, running water. Tilt your child's head with the injured eye downward so that the water runs from the inside outward. Keep the eyelids apart with your fingers (see below). When all traces of the chemical have been removed, lightly cover the eye with a clean pad and seek medical help.

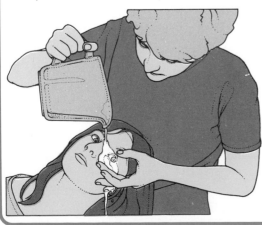

Foreign body in the eye
Never attempt to remove any of the following from your child's eye:

- an object that is embedded in the eyeball
- a chip of metal
- a particle over the colored part of the eye.

In any of these cases, cover both eyes as recommended for cuts to the eye or eyelid (left) and seek medical help.

Other foreign bodies – for example, specks of dirt or eyelashes floating on the white of the eye or inside the lids – may be removed as follows:

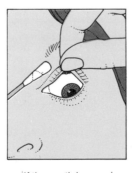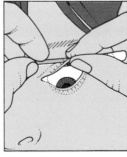

1 If you can see the particle on the white of the eye or inside the lower lid, pick it off using the moistened corner of a clean handkerchief or sterile cotton-tipped swab.

2 If you can see nothing, hold the lashes, pull the upper lid down over the lower lid and hold it for a moment. This may dislodge the particle.

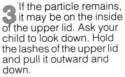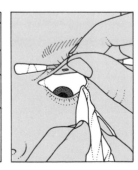

3 If the particle remains, it may be on the inside of the upper lid. Ask your child to look down. Hold the lashes of the upper lid and pull it outward and down.

4 Place a match or cotton-tipped swab over the upper lid and fold the lid back over it.

5 If the particle is now visible, pick it off with the corner of a handkerchief as in step 1.

If you do not succeed in removing the foreign body, lightly cover your child's injured eye and seek medical help at once.

28 Disturbed or impaired vision

Defects in vision in children are usually discovered at routine eye tests. But you may suspect that your child has a problem with his or her eyesight if he or she always holds books very close to the face. Or a teacher may notice that your child performs less well if he or she sits at the back of the classroom where it may be difficult to see the blackboard. Fortunately, disorders causing sudden or complete loss of vision are rare. Always consult your physician promptly about any problems with your child's eyesight.

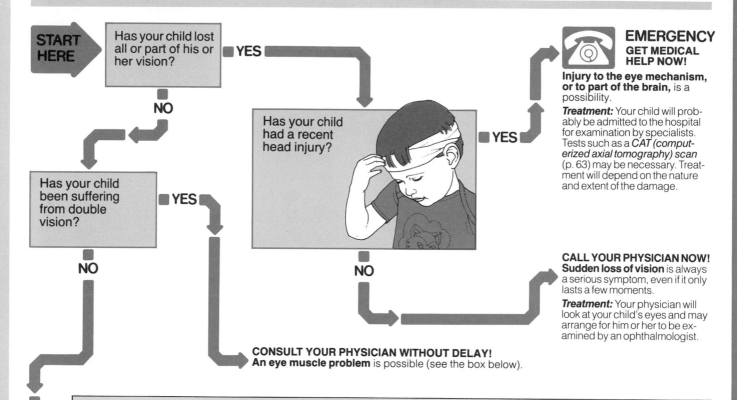

START HERE

Has your child lost all or part of his or her vision?

YES →

NO ↓

Has your child been suffering from double vision?

YES →

NO ↓

Has your child had a recent head injury?

YES →

NO ↓

EMERGENCY
GET MEDICAL HELP NOW!

Injury to the eye mechanism, or to part of the brain, is a possibility.

Treatment: Your child will probably be admitted to the hospital for examination by specialists. Tests such as a *CAT (computerized axial tomography) scan* (p. 63) may be necessary. Treatment will depend on the nature and extent of the damage.

CALL YOUR PHYSICIAN NOW!
Sudden loss of vision is always a serious symptom, even if it only lasts a few moments.

Treatment: Your physician will look at your child's eyes and may arrange for him or her to be examined by an ophthalmologist.

CONSULT YOUR PHYSICIAN WITHOUT DELAY!
An eye muscle problem is possible (see the box below).

STRABISMUS

Strabismus is when the eyes do not work together properly. When one eye focuses on any object, the other looks elsewhere, often inward, but sometimes outward, upward or downward (see below).

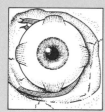

Eye muscles
Movement of the eyeball in the eye socket is controlled by 3 pairs of muscles (below). These are attached to the eyeball (left) and to the back of the eye socket (below left), and work together to produce the full range of eye movements.

1 Vertical muscles move the eyeball up and down.
2 Horizontal muscles move the eyeball from side to side.
3 Muscles encircling the eyeball enable it to rotate.

1 **2** **3**

Causes of squinting
In many babies under 3 months, the eyes may deviate occasionally as babies learn to focus, and this is no cause for concern. After 3 months, if the eyes are not coordinating properly, your child may have an eye muscle problem. Sometimes this is the result of one eye being more nearsighted or farsighted than the other eye. If untreated, this can result in deterioration of the vision in the wandering eye and cause amblyopia, or "lazy eye." Often strabismus appears for the first time later in childhood.

Treatment
Always consult your physician about a wandering eye or double vision in a child. The usual treatment is to prescribe eyeglasses if there is any abnormality. If one eye does not see adequately, even with eyeglasses, the better eye may have a patch put on it to force the child to use the "lazy" eye. This usually clears up the problem if it is detected and treated early. If the eye (or eyes) continues to wander after your child is fitted with appropriate eyeglasses, and after he or she has had a patch put on an eye, an operation on the eye muscles may be necessary.

A young child with strabismus may need to wear glasses with the lens over the good eye covered.

a   b

c   d

Types of squint
The illustrations (left) show different types of squint in which the eye on the right is not tracking correctly. The "lazy" eye may move inward (a), upward (b), outward (c), or downward (d).

Go to next page

Continued from previous page

Is your child's vision generally blurred?

YES →

Is either eye red and painful?

YES →

NO ↓

CONSULT YOUR PHYSICIAN WITHOUT DELAY!
Iritis (inflammation of the colored part of the eye) is possible, although uncommon in children. A less serious problem is more likely.
Treatment: If your physician diagnoses iritis, he or she will prescribe eye drops or ointment to reduce the inflammation and possibly medication to prevent damage to the lens. If your child has conjunctivitis, your physician may prescribe eye drops or ointment to counter infection. Your physician may perform a complete medical examination to find an underlying cause.

NO ↓

Could your child accidentally have taken medication prescribed for an adult?

YES →

CALL YOUR PHYSICIAN NOW!
Poisoning by certain drugs, in particular, quinine, may cause blurring of vision. See **Poisoning,** p. 21.

Is your child taking any medication?

YES →

Certain drugs may cause blurring of vision. Discuss the problem with your physician.

NO ↓

NO ↓

An error of refraction, which causes light to focus improperly, may cause blurred vision. The most common types of error in children are nearsightedness (difficulty in seeing far objects), farsightedness (difficulty in focusing on near objects) and astigmatism (distorted vision caused by uneven curvature of the front of the eye). Consult your physician.

Treatment: If your physician confirms the possibility of such a disorder, he or she will refer your child to an ophthalmologist for a full eye test. Your child may need to wear glasses.

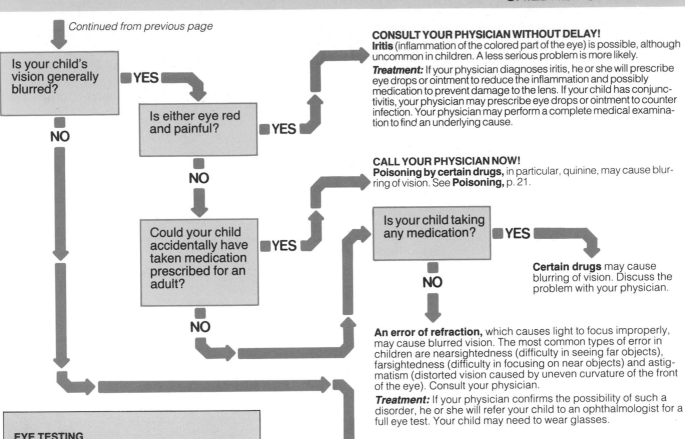

EYE TESTING

Your child's eyes and vision should be tested at regular intervals throughout childhood. In the preschool years your family physician will test your child's vision during routine visits.

When your child goes to school, his or her vision will be tested as part of a general medical examination. Most education authorities arrange for children to have several such examinations during their school years.

What happens

Your physician or ophthalmologist will test your child's ability to recognize objects at a distance. Each eye will be tested separately while the other is covered.

A child of school age will probably be asked to read letters of gradually diminishing size from a distance. Each eye will be tested separately with the other eye covered.

An eye examination by an ophthalmologist is recommended when a child is old enough to read or identify letters. If there is a family history of eye problems in childhood, an eye examination should be performed even earlier.

Does your child have difficulty seeing distant objects?

YES →

Nearsightedness is likely. This means that your child's eyes have difficulty focusing on distant objects. This type of defect is often inherited. Consult your physician.

Treatment: If your physician thinks that your child may be nearsighted, he or she will arrange for your child to have a full eye test by an ophthalmologist, who may prescribe glasses.

NO ↓

Has your child been seeing flashing lights or floating spots?

YES →

NO ↓

Has this happened on several past occasions AND does a severe headache normally follow?

YES →

Migraine headaches (recurrent severe headaches) may occasionally affect children. Consult your physician.

Treatment: If migraine is diagnosed, your physician may prescribe medication to take during attacks or to take (as a preventive measure) between attacks. Relaxing in a darkened room may also help your child's symptoms pass more quickly.

NO ↓

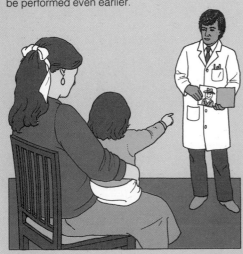

Consult your physician if you are unable to make a diagnosis from this chart.

29 Painful or irritated ear

Ear pain is common in babies and children (up to three attacks a year is usual) and can be distressing. A baby who is not old enough to tell you what the matter is may cry continuously or shriek loudly at intervals, and may pull at the affected ear. Earache is the most common explanation for waking at night in a baby who usually sleeps well. Most ear problems in childhood are due to infection and require medical attention.

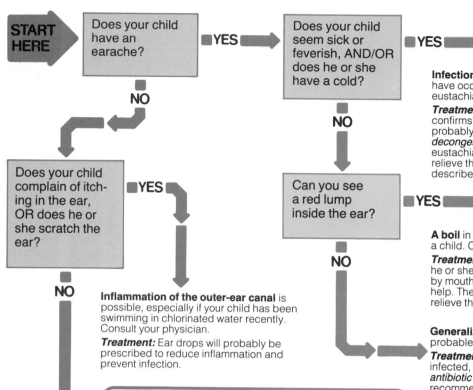

START HERE

Does your child have an earache?

→ **YES** → **Does your child seem sick or feverish, AND/OR does he or she have a cold?**

NO ↓

→ **YES** →

Infection of the middle ear is a possibility. This may have occurred as a result of germs traveling up the eustachian tube. Consult your physician.

Treatment: If, after examining your child, the physician confirms that the middle ear is inflamed, he or she will probably prescribe *antibiotics* and possibly some *decongestant* nose drops or spray to clear the eustachian tube. During this treatment you can help to relieve the pain by following the self-help suggestions described below.

Does your child complain of itching in the ear, OR does he or she scratch the ear?

NO ↓

→ **YES** →

Can you see a red lump inside the ear?

NO ↓

→ **YES** →

A boil in the outer-ear canal can cause severe pain in a child. Consult your physician.

Treatment: If your physician confirms this diagnosis, he or she may prescribe ear drops or *antibiotics* taken by mouth or by injection. Lancing the boil may also help. The self-help suggestions below should help relieve the pain in the meantime.

Inflammation of the outer-ear canal is possible, especially if your child has been swimming in chlorinated water recently. Consult your physician.

Treatment: Ear drops will probably be prescribed to reduce inflammation and prevent infection.

Generalized infection of the outer-ear canal is probable. Consult your physician.

Treatment: If your child's outer ear is found to be infected, your physician will probably prescribe *antibiotic* ear drops to treat the infection and will recommend that you give your child an aspirin substitute for the pain (see *How to relieve earache*, below).

FIRST AID FOR A FOREIGN BODY IN THE EAR

Young children often cause ear problems by poking small objects, such as beads or beans, into their ears. If this happens, do not try to remove the object yourself unless it is very close to the entrance of the outer-ear canal and you are sure that you will do no damage to the delicate lining of the outer-ear canal or to the eardrum. If you are in any doubt, consult your physician or go to the emergency room of your local hospital.

Insect in the ear
If an insect gets into your child's ear, you can safely try to remove it by pouring warm olive, baby or mineral oil into the ear so that it floats out. As you pour, pull the lobe of the ear gently backwards and upwards to straighten the canal. If these measures do not remove the insect, consult your physician.

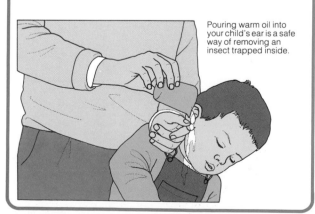

Pouring warm oil into your child's ear is a safe way of removing an insect trapped inside.

HOW TO RELIEVE EARACHE

Antibiotics may take up to 24 hours before helping to relieve the symptoms of an ear infection. During this time, you can help to relieve your child's earache by giving the recommended dose of syrup that contains an aspirin substitute or tablets (for an older child) every four hours, as needed. It may also be comforting to place a warm electric blanket or heating pad against the ear. Do not, however, put anything (a cotton ball, for example) inside the ear, as this may make the problem worse.

Remember, pain-relieving measures alone will not cure the underlying disorder. You should always seek your physician's advice about a persistent earache.

Go to next page

Continued from previous page

Is there a discharge from the affected ear?

YES ▶

Does the pain become worse when you gently pull on your child's earlobe?

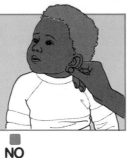

YES ▶

Infection of the outer-ear canal may cause pain and discharge. Consult your physician.

Treatment: If your physician finds that your child's outer-ear canal is infected, he or she will probably advise you to gently clean away any discharge from the outer ear and may prescribe *antibiotic* ear drops.

NO
▼

NO
▼

Infection of the middle ear may have caused your child's eardrum to rupture, producing pain and discharge. This is especially likely if your child has, or has recently had, a cold. Consult your physician.

Treatment: If your physician confirms this diagnosis, a course of *antibiotics* may be prescribed. Antibiotic ear drops to prevent infection of the outer-ear canal may also be prescribed and you will probably be advised to regularly clean away the discharge from the outer ear.

EAR EXAMINATION

Your child may need to have his or her ears examined because of ear problems or as part of a routine checkup. The physician uses an instrument called an otoscope to look inside the ear for abnormalities of the outer ear or of the eardrum. This is not usually painful, but a child with an ear infection may find the procedure uncomfortable. An older child can often be examined standing up, but a baby or young child can be examined sitting on your knee while you hold his or her head firmly against your chest to provide reassurance and to prevent the child from wriggling (below).

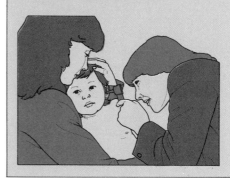

Did your child suddenly develop an earache during or immediately after air travel?

YES ▶

Barotrauma, in which the air pressure balance between the middle and outer ears is disrupted, is a possibility.

Self-help: To prevent barotrauma from occurring, encourage your child to suck and swallow during takeoff and landing. A baby can be fed by breast or bottle at these times and an older child can be offered hard candy to suck or gum to chew. Barotrauma is more likely to develop if your child has a stuffy nose, so it is best to avoid air travel, if possible, when your child has a cold. The symptoms of barotrauma normally clear up without treatment within a few hours. However, if the pain persists or your child seems otherwise sick, consult your physician.

NO
▼

THE STRUCTURE OF THE EAR

The ear is made up of three main parts:

The outer ear includes the external part of the ear, the pinna, which collects and funnels sound waves along the outer-ear canal to the eardrum, which then vibrates.

The middle ear contains the eardrum and three small bones that transmit the vibrations of the eardrum to the inner ear. Air pressure in the middle ear is kept normal by means of the eustachian tube that links the middle-ear cavity to the back of the throat. In children, this tube is shorter and straighter than in adults, allowing infection from the throat to travel more easily into the middle ear.

The inner ear is filled with fluid and contains the cochlea, which converts the vibrations from the middle ear into nerve impulses. These are passed to the brain by the auditory nerve. The inner ear also contains the labyrinth, which controls the body's balance.

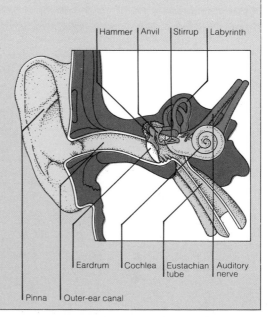

Hammer | Anvil | Stirrup | Labyrinth

Eardrum | Cochlea | Eustachian tube | Auditory nerve

Pinna | Outer-ear canal

Consult your physician if you are unable to make a diagnosis from this chart.

30 Deafness

Deafness is often overlooked in a child, particularly if only one ear is affected. If you find that you are having to repeat things you say to your child, if he or she always needs to have the television or radio louder than you think necessary or if there is a sudden deterioration in school performance, you may suspect deafness.

Hearing problems in babies are usually detected by the physician during developmental checks or at other routine consultations, but you may be the first to notice that your baby is not responding to sounds or learning to speak as quickly as you think he or she should. This should always be brought to your physician's attention.

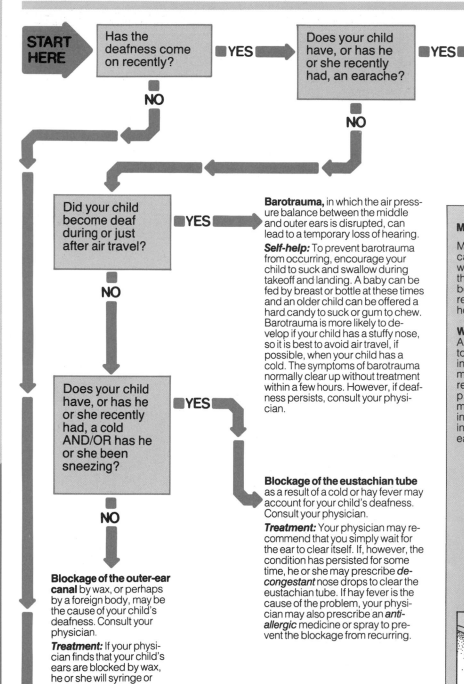

START HERE

Has the deafness come on recently?

→ **YES** → **Does your child have, or has he or she recently had, an earache?**

→ **YES** →

Infection of the middle ear or of the outer-ear canal can cause pain and temporary deafness that may persist after the infection has cleared. Consult your physician.

Treatment: Your physician will examine your child's ear (see *Ear examination*, p. 81) and if he or she finds signs of infection may prescribe *antibiotics*, either as syrup (for middle-ear infections) or as ear drops (for outer-ear infections). If the infection is in the middle ear, your physician may also prescribe *decongestant* nose drops to allow any accumulated fluid to drain away.

NO (from first question)

NO (from earache question)

Did your child become deaf during or just after air travel?

→ **YES** →

Barotrauma, in which the air pressure balance between the middle and outer ears is disrupted, can lead to a temporary loss of hearing.

Self-help: To prevent barotrauma from occurring, encourage your child to suck and swallow during takeoff and landing. A baby can be fed by breast or bottle at these times and an older child can be offered a hard candy to suck or gum to chew. Barotrauma is more likely to develop if your child has a stuffy nose, so it is best to avoid air travel, if possible, when your child has a cold. The symptoms of barotrauma normally clear up without treatment within a few hours. However, if deafness persists, consult your physician.

NO

Does your child have, or has he or she recently had, a cold AND/OR has he or she been sneezing?

→ **YES** →

Blockage of the eustachian tube as a result of a cold or hay fever may account for your child's deafness. Consult your physician.

Treatment: Your physician may recommend that you simply wait for the ear to clear itself. If, however, the condition has persisted for some time, he or she may prescribe *decongestant* nose drops to clear the eustachian tube. If hay fever is the cause of the problem, your physician may also prescribe an *anti-allergic* medicine or spray to prevent the blockage from recurring.

NO

Blockage of the outer-ear canal by wax, or perhaps by a foreign body, may be the cause of your child's deafness. Consult your physician.

Treatment: If your physician finds that your child's ears are blocked by wax, he or she will syringe or flush the wax out. The physician may first suggest you use wax-softening ear drops for a few days. If a foreign body is the cause of the trouble, your physician will remove it using the otoscope (see *Ear examination,* p. 81) or a syringe.

Go to next page

WARNING

INFECTIONS AND DEAFNESS

In rare cases, infections in childhood, such as measles, mumps or meningitis, may cause deafness. If your child shows any sign of loss of hearing following one of these illnesses, **consult your physician without delay.**

MYRINGOTOMY AND EAR TUBES

Myringotomy is a minor operation sometimes carried out in children when the eustachian tube, which runs between the middle ear and the back of the throat, may be blocked and the middle ear becomes filled with fluid. The operation may require a hospital stay but most often is done in a hospital or physician's office.

What happens
A small cut is made in the eardrum to allow the fluid to drain away. Usually a small plastic tube is then inserted into the hole to allow fluid to drain from the middle ear. In some cases, the adenoids may be removed at the same time (see *Adenoid removal*, p. 87). The tube usually stays in place for about six months, after which it drops out naturally. The hole in the eardrum then usually heals. While the tube is in place, it is important to avoid getting water in the ear canal.

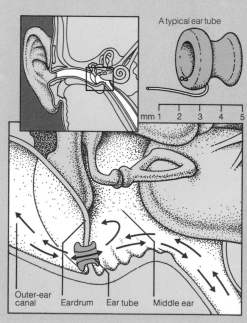

A typical ear tube

mm 1 2 3 4 5

Outer-ear canal   Eardrum   Ear tube   Middle ear

Continued from previous page

Did the onset of deafness follow an earache? ▶ **YES** ▶

Otitis media, accumulation of fluid in the middle ear, sometimes follows infection of the middle ear in children. Consult your physician.

Treatment: If your physician diagnoses middle-ear fluid, he or she may prescribe *decongestant* medicine or *antihistamines* to reduce swelling of the tissues and disperse the fluid. If this does not work, or if the congestion is severe, your physician may recommend a myringotomy (a small cut in the eardrum) and the insertion of an ear tube (see opposite). In most cases, hearing is restored to normal.

NO ▼

Are you worried that your child has never been able to hear properly? ▶ **YES** ▶

During pregnancy was there any possibility of contact or infection with German measles, OR was there any unexplained rash or fever? ▶ **YES**

German measles during pregnancy can cause deafness in the unborn child. Consult your physician.

Treatment: If your physician already knows that there was a possibility of German measles in pregnancy, it is likely that he or she is watching your child's progress carefully and would have noticed any hearing problems. However, if you are concerned about your child's hearing, explain your fears to your physician, who will be able to arrange for your child to have a hearing test. If your child is found to be deaf, you should receive advice from trained therapists on helping your child to talk and understand others.

Congenital hearing defects are rare without a history of German measles or a family history of deafness. However, if you are worried about your child's hearing, discuss the problem with your physician, explaining the basis for your fears.

Treatment: Your physician will probably want to know about your child's general health and about the pregnancy, particularly whether any drugs were taken. If, after examining your child, he or she thinks there may be grounds for concern or, if you are not satisfied by his or her reassurances, your physician can arrange for your child to have a full hearing test.

NO ▼

NO ▼

Consult your physician if you are unable to make a diagnosis from this chart. The problem may simply be the result of wax blockage (see *Blockage of the outer-ear canal*, opposite).

HEARING TESTS FOR CHILDREN

All children should have their hearing tested at regular intervals during early childhood, ideally at 8 to 9 months, at 3 years and at 5 years. Preliminary hearing tests are carried out by your family physician and depend on the age of your child.

Under 6 months (below): The physician will make a sudden sound and look for a startled reaction.

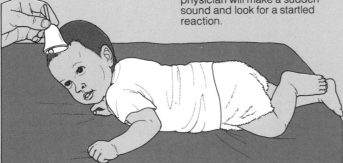

From 6 to 12 months (left): The best test is for one person to hold the baby's attention while another makes a soft sound (such as crinkling tissue paper) to distract the baby.

After 12 months: The physician will assess the child's reaction to quiet speech.

If the response to any of these tests gives your physician reason to suspect that your child may be deaf, he or she will be referred for special hearing tests, which can measure the response in the inner ear to sound, regardless of your child's age.

HEADPHONES AND LOUD MUSIC

Many older children and adolescents enjoy listening to loud music through headphones attached to a radio, stereo or portable tape player. However, parents should be aware of the potential danger to hearing that these present.

The risks
At normal volumes, headphones present no risk. But your child may be tempted to turn the volume up – for example, to exclude external noise – and could permanently damage his or her hearing. The sound need not be painfully loud to damage hearing, so the fact that your child insists that the volume is not uncomfortably high is not a reliable way of judging what level is safe. A useful guideline is that if others in the room can hear the music when your child is wearing headphones, it is likely that the volume is too high. Portable tape players with headphones may also increase the risk of road accidents if used when walking or cycling in traffic because they reduce awareness of what is going on around you.

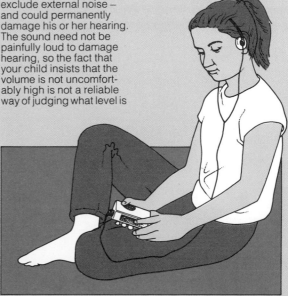

31 Runny or stuffed-up nose

Runny nose is probably the most common medical symptom in childhood. All children have a runny nose (usually accompanied by sneezing) at times, and, in most cases, the common cold, a virus, is responsible. A

runny nose can be irritating for the parents and child, and a stuffy nose can be distressing for a baby, making sucking difficult, but neither symptom on its own is likely to be a sign of serious disease.

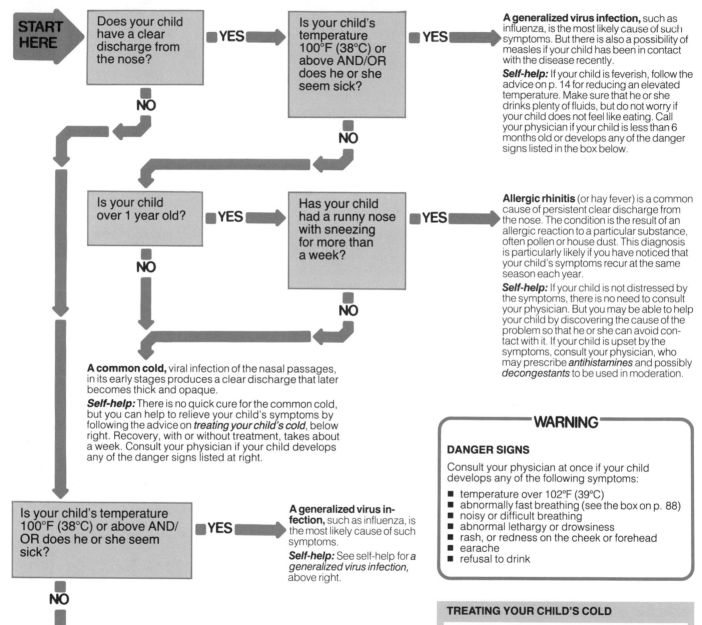

START HERE

Does your child have a clear discharge from the nose? — YES → **Is your child's temperature 100°F (38°C) or above AND/OR does he or she seem sick?** — YES →

A generalized virus infection, such as influenza, is the most likely cause of such symptoms. But there is also a possibility of measles if your child has been in contact with the disease recently.

Self-help: If your child is feverish, follow the advice on p. 14 for reducing an elevated temperature. Make sure that he or she drinks plenty of fluids, but do not worry if your child does not feel like eating. Call your physician if your child is less than 6 months old or develops any of the danger signs listed in the box below.

NO / NO →

Is your child over 1 year old? — YES → **Has your child had a runny nose with sneezing for more than a week?** — YES →

Allergic rhinitis (or hay fever) is a common cause of persistent clear discharge from the nose. The condition is the result of an allergic reaction to a particular substance, often pollen or house dust. This diagnosis is particularly likely if you have noticed that your child's symptoms recur at the same season each year.

Self-help: If your child is not distressed by the symptoms, there is no need to consult your physician. But you may be able to help your child by discovering the cause of the problem so that he or she can avoid contact with it. If your child is upset by the symptoms, consult your physician, who may prescribe *antihistamines* and possibly *decongestants* to be used in moderation.

NO / NO →

A common cold, viral infection of the nasal passages, in its early stages produces a clear discharge that later becomes thick and opaque.

Self-help: There is no quick cure for the common cold, but you can help to relieve your child's symptoms by following the advice on *treating your child's cold*, below right. Recovery, with or without treatment, takes about a week. Consult your physician if your child develops any of the danger signs listed at right.

Is your child's temperature 100°F (38°C) or above AND/OR does he or she seem sick? — YES →

A generalized virus infection, such as influenza, is the most likely cause of such symptoms.

Self-help: See self-help for *a generalized virus infection,* above right.

NO →

Does your child have a thick discharge from one nostril only? — YES →

A foreign body may be lodged in your child's nose. Consult your physician.

Treatment: Your physician may be able to remove the obstruction. But, if the foreign body is difficult to reach, admission to the hospital may be necessary to remove the obstruction.

NO →

A common cold, viral infection of the nasal passages, is the most likely cause of a thick discharge from both nostrils.

Self-help: See *Treating your child's cold,* right.

WARNING

DANGER SIGNS

Consult your physician at once if your child develops any of the following symptoms:

- temperature over 102°F (39°C)
- abnormally fast breathing (see the box on p. 88)
- noisy or difficult breathing
- abnormal lethargy or drowsiness
- rash, or redness on the cheek or forehead
- earache
- refusal to drink

TREATING YOUR CHILD'S COLD

When your child has a cold, you can reduce his or her discomfort in several ways. Whatever the age of your child, make sure he or she drinks plenty of fluids, including water and juices. If he or she is feverish, follow the advice on p. 18 for reducing an elevated temperature. Try to keep the atmosphere of your child's room warm and humid, as this helps to clear a stuffy nose (a room humidifier will moisten the air). If a young baby has difficulty sucking, you can use children's (pediatric) nose drops to clear the nose before feeding times. You must be careful not to exceed the recommended dose or to use them any longer than is necessary. An older child can be encouraged to inhale steam from a kettle or pan of hot water.

32 Sore throat

Sore throat is a common symptom in childhood. An older child will usually tell you that his or her throat hurts; in the case of a younger child, your attention is most likely to be drawn to your child's reluctance to eat because of the pain caused by swallowing. Most sore throats are due to bacteria or viruses and clear up within a few days, but, if you note any of the danger signs listed on the chart opposite, consult your physician.

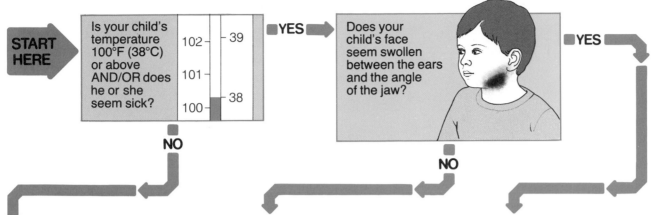

START HERE → Is your child's temperature 100°F (38°C) or above AND/OR does he or she seem sick?

YES → Does your child's face seem swollen between the ears and the angle of the jaw? → **YES**

NO

NO

TREATMENT OF A SORE THROAT

The following measures will give a child relief from most types of sore throat:

- Giving plenty of cold drinks (preferably milk, water or juices) and ice cream.
- Giving the recommended dose of an aspirin substitute.
- For older children (over 8), gargling with a mild antiseptic diluted with plain or salt water.

Pharyngitis or tonsillitis, infection of the throat or tonsils, respectively, is the likely cause of your child's sore throat. The infection may be caused by viruses or bacteria (see p.44).

Self-help: Give your child an aspirin substitute to relieve the discomfort and reduce any fever. Do not force your child to eat if pain makes swallowing difficult. Follow the advice on treating a sore throat. Consult your physician if your child is no better in 48 hours, or develops further symptoms, such as an earache. Your physician may prescribe *antibiotics* if the infection is found to be bacterial. An operation to remove the tonsils (below) is carried out only occasionally in cases of recurrent, severe tonsillitis.

Mumps, a viral infection affecting the salivary glands, is a possibility, especially if your child has been in contact with the disease within the past 3 weeks (see *Comparison of childhood infectious diseases*, p. 75). Consult your physician.

Treatment: Your physician will probably advise you to keep your child at home and give him or her an aspirin substitute to relieve the discomfort. Recovery normally takes 7 to 10 days.

A common cold, a viral infection of the nasal passages, is the most likely cause of your child's sore throat.

Self-help: There is no quick cure for the common cold but you can help to relieve the symptoms by following the advice on *treating your child's cold,* opposite. Recovery, with or without treatment, normally takes about a week. Consult your physician if your child develops any of the danger signs listed in the box opposite.

Has your child been sneezing AND/OR does he or she have a runny nose? → **YES**

NO

WHAT ARE TONSILS?

The tonsils are two glands at the back of the throat. They help guard against infection. They are very small at birth and enlarge gradually, reaching their maximum size when the child is 6 to 7 years old and is most at risk from infections of the nose, throat and lungs. After this age the tonsils become smaller again. The tonsils are normally noticeable only when they become inflamed and swollen as a result of infection, as shown in the illustration (right).

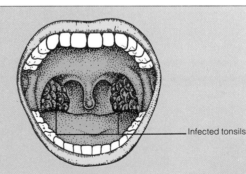

Infected tonsils

Inflammation of the throat, as a result of minor infection or local irritation, is the likely cause of a sore throat with no other symptoms.

Self-help: Give your child plenty of cold drinks to soothe the inflammation and, if necessary, give the recommended dose of an aspirin substitute. If his or her throat is no better in 48 hours, or if further symptoms (such as an earache) develop, consult your physician.

TONSILS REMOVAL (TONSILLECTOMY)

Occasionally, when a child has repeated and severe bacterial infections of the tonsils, an operation to remove the tonsils is recommended. This operation used to be carried out more frequently, but the increased effectiveness of *antibiotics* against bacterial infection has meant that this operation is now only necessary when there is a risk that recurrent illnesses may interfere with the child's general health or education.

The operation may require a hospital stay and can be carried out while the child is under a general or local anesthetic. The tonsils are cut away and sometimes the adenoids are removed at the same time (see *Adenoid removal*, p. 87). After the operation, your child's throat is likely to be very sore and there may be slight bleeding from the raw areas. Plenty of cold drinks and ice cream will help reduce the discomfort. Most children are back to normal within 2 weeks

33 Coughing

Coughing, a normal reaction to irritation and congestion in the throat and lungs, is a noisy expulsion of air from the lungs. It is an unusual symptom in babies under 6 months, and can be a sign of a serious lung infection. In older children, the vast majority of cases are due to minor infec-tions of the nose and throat. Occasionally, a sudden cough can be a sign of a more serious blockage in the respiratory tract. You should call your physician at once if your child's breathing seems in any way abnormal between bouts of coughing.

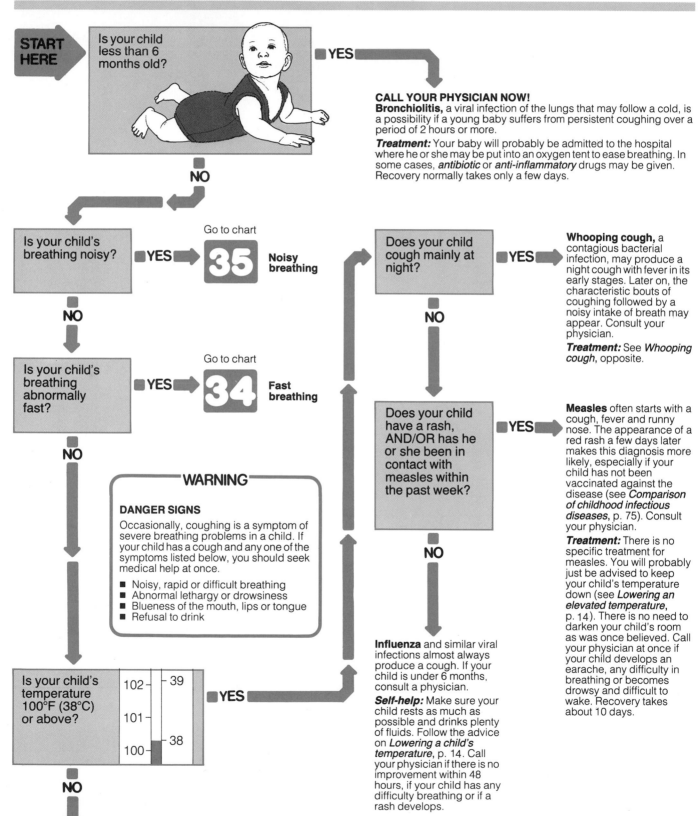

START HERE

Is your child less than 6 months old?

YES

CALL YOUR PHYSICIAN NOW!
Bronchiolitis, a viral infection of the lungs that may follow a cold, is a possibility if a young baby suffers from persistent coughing over a period of 2 hours or more.

Treatment: Your baby will probably be admitted to the hospital where he or she may be put into an oxygen tent to ease breathing. In some cases, *antibiotic* or *anti-inflammatory* drugs may be given. Recovery normally takes only a few days.

NO

Is your child's breathing noisy?

YES → Go to chart **35** **Noisy breathing**

NO

Is your child's breathing abnormally fast?

YES → Go to chart **34** **Fast breathing**

NO

WARNING

DANGER SIGNS

Occasionally, coughing is a symptom of severe breathing problems in a child. If your child has a cough and any one of the symptoms listed below, you should seek medical help at once.

- Noisy, rapid or difficult breathing
- Abnormal lethargy or drowsiness
- Blueness of the mouth, lips or tongue
- Refusal to drink

Is your child's temperature 100°F (38°C) or above?

102 — 39
101 —
100 — 38

YES

NO

Go to next page

Does your child cough mainly at night?

YES

Whooping cough, a contagious bacterial infection, may produce a night cough with fever in its early stages. Later on, the characteristic bouts of coughing followed by a noisy intake of breath may appear. Consult your physician.

Treatment: See *Whooping cough*, opposite.

NO

Does your child have a rash, AND/OR has he or she been in contact with measles within the past week?

YES

Measles often starts with a cough, fever and runny nose. The appearance of a red rash a few days later makes this diagnosis more likely, especially if your child has not been vaccinated against the disease (see *Comparison of childhood infectious diseases*, p. 75). Consult your physician.

Treatment: There is no specific treatment for measles. You will probably just be advised to keep your child's temperature down (see *Lowering an elevated temperature*, p. 14). There is no need to darken your child's room as was once believed. Call your physician at once if your child develops an earache, any difficulty in breathing or becomes drowsy and difficult to wake. Recovery takes about 10 days.

NO

Influenza and similar viral infections almost always produce a cough. If your child is under 6 months, consult a physician.

Self-help: Make sure your child rests as much as possible and drinks plenty of fluids. Follow the advice on *Lowering a child's temperature*, p. 14. Call your physician if there is no improvement within 48 hours, if your child has any difficulty breathing or if a rash develops.

Continued from previous page

Does your child have bouts of uncontrollable coughing followed by a noisy intake of breath, AND/OR is coughing often accompanied by vomiting?

YES →

Whooping cough, a contagious bacterial infection, produces this distinctive type of cough, often with a runny nose. Consult your physician.

Treatment: In most cases the illness can be treated at home with regular visits to the physician. Do not try to suppress the cough with cough medicines. If bouts of coughing are accompanied by vomiting, it is often helpful to give a light meal immediately after a coughing fit. Your physician may prescribe *antibiotics*, which can in some cases reduce the severity of the symptoms and may prevent other children from catching the disease. Call your physician at once if your child has severe difficulty in breathing or turns bluish during a bout of coughing.

NO ↓

Has the cough come on only within the past week or so?

YES →

Does your child have a runny or stuffy nose?

YES →

A cold is often accompanied by a cough, which is a natural reaction to mucus dripping down the back of the throat. Coughing prevents the lungs from becoming congested.

Self-help: For the first day or so of a cold, it is best to keep your child at home in a warm, but not dry, atmosphere. A stuffy nose in an older child can often be eased by inhaling steam from a basin of hot water. If a young child has a severely stuffy nose, your physician may prescribe *decongestant* nose drops. For further information on treating colds, see p. 84.

NO ↓

An inhaled foreign body is a possibility if a young child suddenly develops a cough, especially if he or she has recently been eating peanuts or playing with small objects. Even an older child may have breathed in a particle of food without realizing it. Consult your physician.

Treatment: If your physician suspects that your child has a foreign body in the lung, he or she may arrange for your child to go to the hospital for an examination of the lungs. If a foreign body is found, it will be removed and, if there is any sign of infection, *antibiotics* will be prescribed.

NO ↓

Does your child have a persistently runny nose?

YES →

Is your child's speech nasal, AND/OR does he or she suffer from recurrent ear infections?

YES →

Enlarged adenoids (glands at the back of the nasal passage) may be encouraging infection in your child's nose, ears and throat, creating an irritating discharge. Consult your physician.

Treatment: If the adenoids are enlarged, your physician will probably prescribe *antibiotics* to combat infection. However, if this treatment fails to cure the problem, an operation to remove the adenoids may be necessary (see *Adenoid removal*, below).

NO ↓

Has your child had whooping cough within the past few months?

YES →

NO ↓

Whooping cough, a contagious bacterial infection, can often leave a child with a persistent cough. If symptoms persist for more than 2 months after the original illness, or if your child seems sick or distressed, consult your physician.

Recurrent colds can produce an irritating mucous discharge that causes the child to cough. Such colds are the result of the child being exposed to viruses to which he or she has not yet built up an immunity.

Self-help: There is little you can do to prevent your child from getting colds, but you can help to alleviate the symptoms. For general advice on the treatment of colds, see p. 84. If coughing is disturbing your child's sleep, adjusting the pitch of the bed (raising the head of the bed to promote drainage) may help. A drink and a dose of cough mixture before bedtime may also soothe a troublesome cough. There is no need to consult your physician unless your child is distressed by the cough or seems quite sick.

Does anyone in the home smoke regularly OR could your child be smoking?

YES →

Smoke in the atmosphere and smoking itself can irritate a child's throat and lungs, causing a persistent cough and increasing the likelihood of chest infections. Giving up smoking will benefit your own and your child's health. A child who is smoking should be discouraged from this habit.

Go to chart

22 **Behavior problems.**

NO ↓

Consult your physician if you are unable to make a diagnosis from this chart.

ADENOID REMOVAL (ADENOIDECTOMY)

The adenoids are lymph-gland swellings at the back of the nose, near the tonsils. If they become so enlarged that they cause recurrent ear or throat infections, they can be removed surgically, sometimes together with the tonsils, usually when the child is 3 to 4 years old. The child may have a sore throat for a few days after the operation. Since the adenoids are part of a child's immunodefense system, they should be removed only after careful consideration, which may include a second opinion.

Adenoids

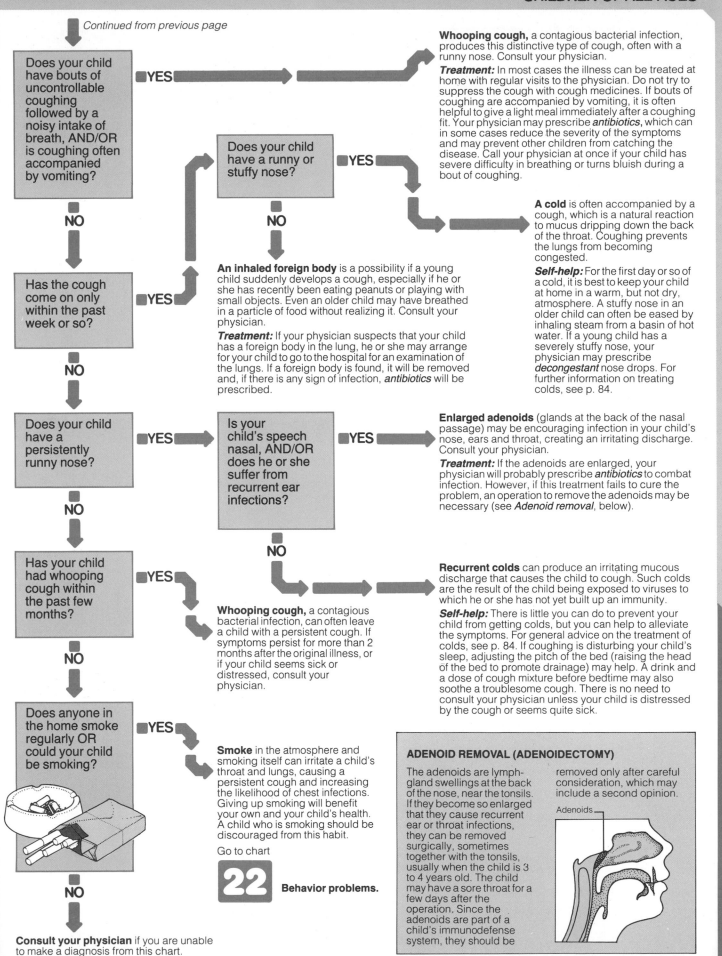

34 Fast breathing

A child's breathing is an important indicator for determining the seriousness of any problems affecting the windpipe or lungs. If your child's breathing is faster than the normal rate shown in the box below, there may be some cause for concern, especially if he or she is under 1 year or has additional symptoms, such as blueness of the tongue or excessive drowsiness, in which case you should get medical help at once.

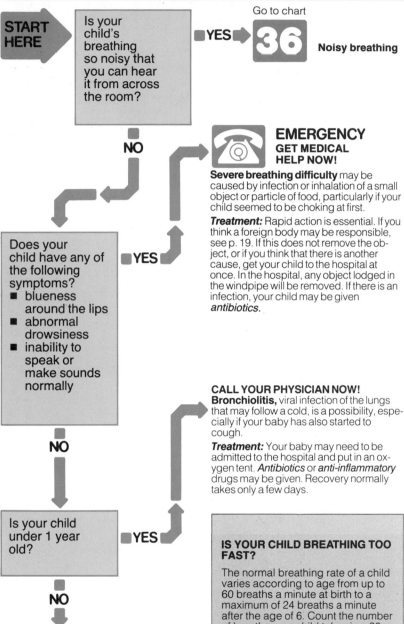

START HERE

Is your child's breathing so noisy that you can hear it from across the room?

YES → Go to chart **36** **Noisy breathing**

NO

Does your child have any of the following symptoms?
- blueness around the lips
- abnormal drowsiness
- inability to speak or make sounds normally

NO

Is your child under 1 year old?

NO

YES

YES

EMERGENCY
GET MEDICAL HELP NOW!

Severe breathing difficulty may be caused by infection or inhalation of a small object or particle of food, particularly if your child seemed to be choking at first.

Treatment: Rapid action is essential. If you think a foreign body may be responsible, see p. 19. If this does not remove the object, or if you think that there is another cause, get your child to the hospital at once. In the hospital, any object lodged in the windpipe will be removed. If there is an infection, your child may be given *antibiotics*.

CALL YOUR PHYSICIAN NOW!
Bronchiolitis, viral infection of the lungs that may follow a cold, is a possibility, especially if your baby has also started to cough.

Treatment: Your baby may need to be admitted to the hospital and put in an oxygen tent. *Antibiotics* or *anti-inflammatory* drugs may be given. Recovery normally takes only a few days.

CALL YOUR PHYSICIAN NOW!
A chest infection is possible, especially if your child has had a cold within the last week.

Treatment: Your physician may decide that your child can be treated at home with frequent visits to the office, but in some cases he or she may recommend that your child be admitted to the hospital. In either case, treatment will probably consist of an aspirin substitute to reduce any fever and ease discomfort, and possibly *antibiotics* to fight the infection. If you are looking after your child at home; make sure that he or she drinks plenty of fluids. Keeping the air moist, by using a room humidifier, for example, may help to ease your child's breathing.

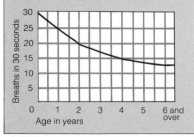

IS YOUR CHILD BREATHING TOO FAST?
The normal breathing rate of a child varies according to age from up to 60 breaths a minute at birth to a maximum of 24 breaths a minute after the age of 6. Count the number of breaths your child takes in a 30-second period while he or she is sitting quietly. Then check the result against the graph below. If your child is taking more breaths than is normal, he or she is likely to need medical attention.

Breaths in 30 seconds (vertical axis: 5, 10, 15, 20, 25, 30)
Age in years (horizontal axis: 0, 1, 2, 3, 4, 5, 6 and over)

ALL ABOUT ASTHMA
In asthma the small airways in the lungs sometimes become narrowed by swelling of their walls and production of mucus. This partially obstructs the airflow in the lungs, causing difficulty in breathing. Asthma attacks can be triggered by an allergic reaction to a particular substance, such as house-dust mites, pollen or animal fur. However, attacks may also be triggered by infection, inhaling irritant substances or by physical or psychological distress.

Susceptibility to asthma often runs in families, and children who suffer from hay fever (allergic rhinitis) or eczema are more likely to develop asthma. Attacks of asthma are unusual in children under the age of 4 and often cease after puberty.

Symptoms
The main symptoms of asthma are attacks of wheezing and difficulty in breathing. The severity of these attacks can vary from slight wheezing to severe and distressing shortness of breath. Some children are rarely free from wheezing, while others may go many months in normal health between attacks. Severe attacks may be life-threatening and should always be taken seriously.

Treatment
Treatment will depend on the frequency and severity of the attacks. If your child has only occasional breathless attacks, your physician may prescribe a *bronchodilator* to use when the attacks occur or before exercise. However, if your child suffers from frequent attacks of asthma or often coughs at night, your physician may also prescribe medications to be taken regularly to prevent attacks.

An inhalant that sprays a bronchodilator drug into the lungs is prescribed for most asthmatic children.

Nowadays there is no need for the asthmatic child to be treated as an invalid. In fact, it has been shown that physical activity is beneficial, even if you have to increase the drug treatment to prevent attacks after exercise. Encourage your child to participate in sports such as swimming.

Preventing asthma attacks
If your child is asthmatic, you may be able to reduce the frequency of attacks by identifying, and then helping your child to avoid, the triggering factors. In many cases, however, there is no obvious cause. Your physician may help you by arranging skin tests in which a solution of the suspected allergen is put on or injected into the skin to see if it produces an allergic response. It may also be helpful to keep a diary of your child's activities, including what food he or she ate, or if, for example, he or she has attacks in the house, but not in the open country, or when staying with some friends, but not with others. All this information can give valuable clues to the cause of your child's asthma.

35 Noisy breathing

Many children wheeze slightly when they have a chest cold. This is no cause for concern, providing the child is not distressed and is able to breathe easily. This chart deals only with breathing that is loud enough to be heard about 10 feet away. The sound produced may vary from loud wheezing and grunting to a harsh crowing noise that gets louder when the child breathes in. Except when a child has already been diagnosed as having asthma and has home treatment available, such noisy breathing is always a serious symptom requiring swift, expert attention. In all cases you should be alert to any of the danger signs listed in the box below.

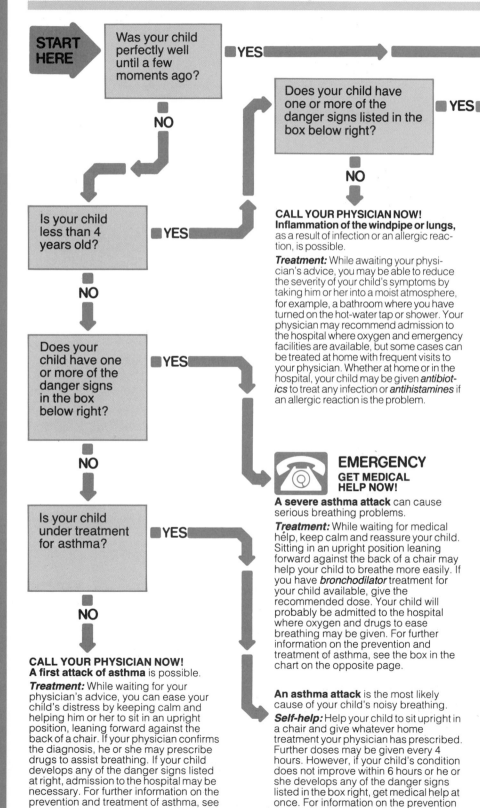

START HERE

Was your child perfectly well until a few moments ago? — **YES** →

NO ↓

Is your child less than 4 years old?

YES →

NO ↓

Does your child have one or more of the danger signs in the box below right?

YES →

NO ↓

Is your child under treatment for asthma?

YES →

NO ↓

Does your child have one or more of the danger signs listed in the box below right? — **YES** →

NO ↓

EMERGENCY
GET MEDICAL HELP NOW!

A foreign body may be lodged in your child's windpipe. See *First aid for choking,* p. 19. If the treatment described does not remove the object at once, call an ambulance or get your child to the hospital yourself as fast as you can.

Treatment: If you succeed in removing the foreign body yourself, no further treatment is needed and your child should quickly return to normal. However, if your child develops a cough or fever within the next few days, it may be a sign of a lung infection and you should consult your physician at once. In the hospital, treatment of a foreign body in the windpipe may consist of an emergency operation to remove the object and allow your child to breathe freely.

EMERGENCY
GET MEDICAL HELP NOW!

Narrowing of the air passages caused by an infection such as croup or epiglottitis is a possibility. Another cause for an emergency would be an allergic reaction.

Treatment: While you are waiting for medical help to arrive, you may be able to ease your child's breathing by moistening the air with steam. Taking your child into a bathroom where you have turned on the hot-water tap or shower is often effective. Be prepared to carry out artificial respiration (p. 18) if your child stops breathing. Your child will probably need to be admitted to the hospital where he or she may be given oxygen and intravenous fluids. If a bacterial infection is diagnosed, *antibiotics* may be given.

CALL YOUR PHYSICIAN NOW!
Inflammation of the windpipe or lungs, as a result of infection or an allergic reaction, is possible.

Treatment: While awaiting your physician's advice, you may be able to reduce the severity of your child's symptoms by taking him or her into a moist atmosphere, for example, a bathroom where you have turned on the hot-water tap or shower. Your physician may recommend admission to the hospital where oxygen and emergency facilities are available, but some cases can be treated at home with frequent visits to your physician. Whether at home or in the hospital, your child may be given *antibiotics* to treat any infection or *antihistamines* if an allergic reaction is the problem.

EMERGENCY
GET MEDICAL HELP NOW!

A severe asthma attack can cause serious breathing problems.

Treatment: While waiting for medical help, keep calm and reassure your child. Sitting in an upright position leaning forward against the back of a chair may help your child to breathe more easily. If you have *bronchodilator* treatment for your child available, give the recommended dose. Your child will probably be admitted to the hospital where oxygen and drugs to ease breathing may be given. For further information on the prevention and treatment of asthma, see the box in the chart on the opposite page.

An asthma attack is the most likely cause of your child's noisy breathing.

Self-help: Help your child to sit upright in a chair and give whatever home treatment your physician has prescribed. Further doses may be given every 4 hours. However, if your child's condition does not improve within 6 hours or he or she develops any of the danger signs listed in the box right, get medical help at once. For information on the prevention and treatment of asthma, see opposite.

CALL YOUR PHYSICIAN NOW!
A first attack of asthma is possible.

Treatment: While waiting for your physician's advice, you can ease your child's distress by keeping calm and helping him or her to sit in an upright position, leaning forward against the back of a chair. If your physician confirms the diagnosis, he or she may prescribe drugs to assist breathing. If your child develops any of the danger signs listed at right, admission to the hospital may be necessary. For further information on the prevention and treatment of asthma, see opposite.

WARNING

DANGER SIGNS

If your child's noisy breathing is accompanied by any one of the following symptoms, it is a sign that he or she has severe breathing problems. This is an EMERGENCY and you should seek medical help at once.

- Blueness of the tongue
- Abnormal drowsiness
- Inability to speak or make sounds normally
- Abnormally fast breathing (see chart 34, Fast breathing)

36 Toothache

Your child's teeth are just as much living structures as any other part of the body, despite their tough appearance. They are constantly under threat from our Western diet because of the high level of sugar we consume. Bacteria act on sugar to produce acids that attack enamel, the tooth's protective layer. When this happens, it is not long before bacterial destruction (decay) spreads down the root canal to the nerve, causing inflammation and pain. Any pain coming from your child's tooth, or from the teeth and gums in general, whether it is a dull throb or a sharp twinge, should be brought to your dentist's attention for investigation and treatment.

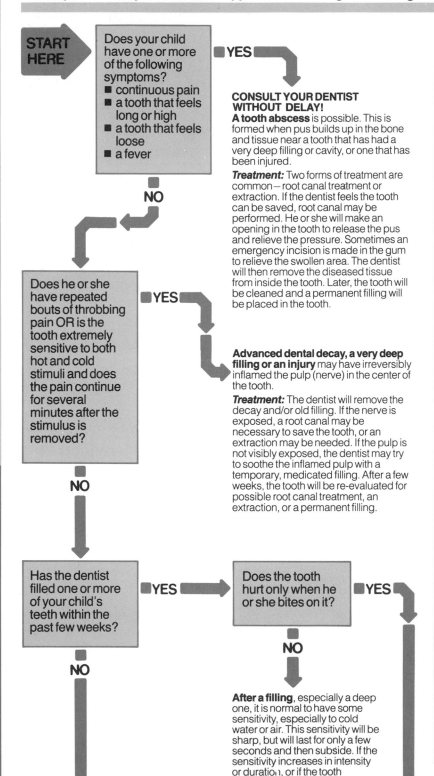

START HERE

Does your child have one or more of the following symptoms?
■ continuous pain
■ a tooth that feels long or high
■ a tooth that feels loose
■ a fever

YES →

NO ↓

CONSULT YOUR DENTIST WITHOUT DELAY!
A tooth abscess is possible. This is formed when pus builds up in the bone and tissue near a tooth that has had a very deep filling or cavity, or one that has been injured.

Treatment: Two forms of treatment are common—root canal treatment or extraction. If the dentist feels the tooth can be saved, root canal may be performed. He or she will make an opening in the tooth to release the pus and relieve the pressure. Sometimes an emergency incision is made in the gum to relieve the swollen area. The dentist will then remove the diseased tissue from inside the tooth. Later, the tooth will be cleaned and a permanent filling will be placed in the tooth.

Does he or she have repeated bouts of throbbing pain OR is the tooth extremely sensitive to both hot and cold stimuli and does the pain continue for several minutes after the stimulus is removed?

YES →

NO ↓

Advanced dental decay, a very deep filling or an injury may have irreversibly inflamed the pulp (nerve) in the center of the tooth.

Treatment: The dentist will remove the decay and/or old filling. If the nerve is exposed, a root canal may be necessary to save the tooth, or an extraction may be needed. If the pulp is not visibly exposed, the dentist may try to soothe the inflamed pulp with a temporary, medicated filling. After a few weeks, the tooth will be re-evaluated for possible root canal treatment, an extraction, or a permanent filling.

Has the dentist filled one or more of your child's teeth within the past few weeks?

YES →

Does the tooth hurt only when he or she bites on it?

YES →

NO ↓

NO ↓

After a filling, especially a deep one, it is normal to have some sensitivity, especially to cold water or air. This sensitivity will be sharp, but will last for only a few seconds and then subside. If the sensitivity increases in intensity or duration, or if the tooth becomes sensitive to heat, consult your dentist for the possibility of irreversible pulp (nerve) damage.

Go to next page

An uneven or "high" filling can cause discomfort. Your dentist will adjust the filling if necessary.

THE ORDER IN WHICH TEETH APPEAR

The ages at which teeth appear vary considerably from child to child, so the ages given here are only a rough guide. A few children have one or more teeth at birth, while others still have none at a year old. The sequence or order in which teeth erupt is more important than the age of eruption. Neither early nor late teething is cause for worry.

With the exception of the permanent (adult) molars (which do not replace primary [baby] molars), the remaining permanent teeth should appear soon after their corresponding primary teeth fall out. The first permanent molar should be the first adult tooth to appear at 6 or 7 years of age. Many parents may mistake this tooth for a baby tooth since it erupts so early and appears just behind the second primary molar. Next, the incisors (front teeth) appear, with the lowers usually preceding the uppers. Occasionally, the primary teeth must be extracted early to allow the permanent teeth to grow into the correct position. The order in which the primary cuspids (canines) and molars are lost varies considerably.

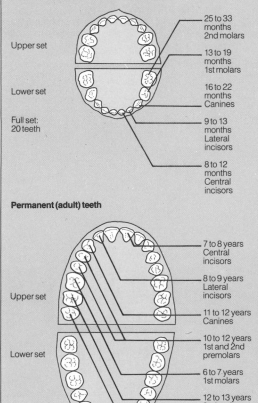

Primary (baby) teeth

Upper set

Lower set

Full set: 20 teeth

- 25 to 33 months 2nd molars
- 13 to 19 months 1st molars
- 16 to 22 months Canines
- 9 to 13 months Lateral incisors
- 8 to 12 months Central incisors

Permanent (adult) teeth

Upper set

Lower set

Full set: 32 teeth

- 7 to 8 years Central incisors
- 8 to 9 years Lateral incisors
- 11 to 12 years Canines
- 10 to 12 years 1st and 2nd premolars
- 6 to 7 years 1st molars
- 12 to 13 years 2nd molars
- Over 17 years 3rd molars (wisdom teeth)

Continued from previous page

Does the pain occur only when your child is eating something cold or sweet (ice cream or chocolate) AND does the pain go away after a few seconds?

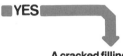**YES**

Decay under an old filling, a cracked tooth or filling, or exposure of the root surface due to improper toothbrushing or gum disease may be the cause of the pain. Consult your dentist.

Treatment: Your dentist may recommend replacing an old filling or remove any decay. If the problem is sensitivity, the dentist may recommend a special desensitizing toothpaste, protective fluoride applications or bonding to seal over the sensitive root area.

**NO**

Does the tooth hurt only when your child bites or chews on it?

YES

A cracked filling or a cracked or fractured tooth is probably the cause of the pain. Consult your dentist.

Treatment: Your child may need to have the affected tooth crowned (capped) or have a root canal if the pain becomes more severe. The tooth may need to be extracted if the crack is too deep into the tooth. Pain may also be caused by acute sinus problems that make the upper back teeth ache and tender to bite on. If this is the case, your child may need to see a physician for further treatment.

NO

Dental decay may have caused a hole (or cavity) in the tooth. Consult your dentist.

Treatment: Your dentist will probably clean out the affected tooth and put in a filling.

HOW TO RELIEVE YOUR CHILD'S TOOTHACHE

If the toothache is not too severe, a few home remedies may be helpful temporarily while you are waiting for professional help. Aspirin or an aspirin substitute should only be swallowed. Never place a tablet in the cheek next to a bothersome tooth. This can cause a "chemical burn" to the gum tissues. Oil of cloves applied to the aching tooth may also help.

OTHER DISEASES THAT CAUSE TOOTHACHES

Sinus problems
Often, since the roots of the upper back teeth are very near a sinus cavity, pressure on these roots from a sinus condition can simulate a dull toothache. Usually, several of these upper back teeth will hurt (not just one) when your child bites, and often he or she will experience an increased sensitivity to cold things (e.g., air or liquids). Your child may have a runny nose or congestion. When the condition clears up, the pain should subside. Consult your physician.

Periodontal disease
Periodontal disease is a common disease of the gums and other structures that support the teeth. The gums are usually red and swollen and bleed easily (especially with brushing). Pain does not frequently occur in the early stages of the disease. Treatment for early periodontal disease can range from calculus (tartar) removal by scaling the teeth to gum surgery. Young children may have early periodontal disease, which can be cleared up with thorough brushing and flossing each day.

PREVENTING DECAY

Fluoride
Fluoride is a naturally occurring mineral that has been shown to increase the tooth's resistance to acid attack, thereby lowering the risk of tooth decay. In many areas of the country, fluoride is added to the water supply. If you have a well or the amount of fluoride in your local water supply is low, your dentist may suggest that you give your child additional fluoride in the form of tablets or drops. Once the tooth erupts and appears in the mouth, giving fluoride in the form of toothpastes, rinses or topical applications can also be beneficial.

Diet
Sugar in the diet is the principal cause of tooth decay. Minimizing the amount, reducing the frequency and controlling the types of sweets (sticky sugars are worse than liquids) that your child eats are important steps in preventing tooth decay.

Nursing-bottle mouth
Never put an infant or young child to bed with a bottle filled with sweet liquids (juice, sugar water, milk or formula). These liquids pool around teeth and can cause serious decay, called "nursing-bottle mouth." If you feel you must give your child a bottle, fill it only with plain water or use a clean pacifier (one that is *not* dipped in any sweet liquid).

Cleaning your child's teeth
The goal of cleaning teeth is to remove the bacterial plaque (a sticky, colorless film that constantly forms, especially near the junction of the tooth and gum). Without plaque, there is no decay or periodontal disease.

You should ensure that your child's teeth are brushed and flossed thoroughly at least once a day. At first, clean your baby's teeth and gums using a clean, damp piece of gauze. You may find the best position to do this is with your baby sitting on your lap, held securely against your chest. Later on, develop your child's habit of brushing by encouraging the young child to help using a small toothbrush and a dab of toothpaste. But make sure that you follow this procedure with a thorough cleaning and rinsing. As for an infant, the proper position for cleaning a young child's teeth is from behind. When a child is 6 years old, he or she should be able to brush the teeth under supervision. Flossing can be done by the child, without supervision, when he or she is about 8 years old. A parent can check the effectiveness of the child's cleaning by using disclosing tablets or solutions to detect the remaining plaque.

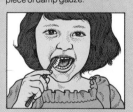

A baby should be held against your chest (left) while you clean the teeth and gums using toothpaste on cotton swabs or a piece of damp gauze.

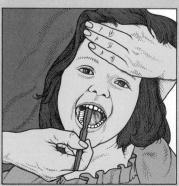

Using the toothbrush Teach your child to brush both the outer and inner surfaces of all the teeth, as well as the chewing surfaces. The brush should be angled 45° against the gums.

Sealants
Your child has natural deep grooves (pits or fissures) on the top surfaces of his or her back teeth. Your dentist may want to place a plastic resin in these grooves to help prevent decay.

37 Vomiting in children

Vomiting is the forceful throwing up of the contents of the stomach as a result of sudden contraction of the muscles around the stomach. In children, vomiting can be caused by almost any physical or emotional upset, but is most likely to be caused by an infection of the digestive tract. In rare cases, vomiting can be a symptom of a serious condition needing urgent medical attention, so you must always be on the lookout for the danger signs listed in the box below. Any child who is vomiting persistently needs to be given plenty of fluids to avoid dehydration (see What to do when your child vomits, opposite).

For children under 1 year, consult chart 7, Vomiting in babies

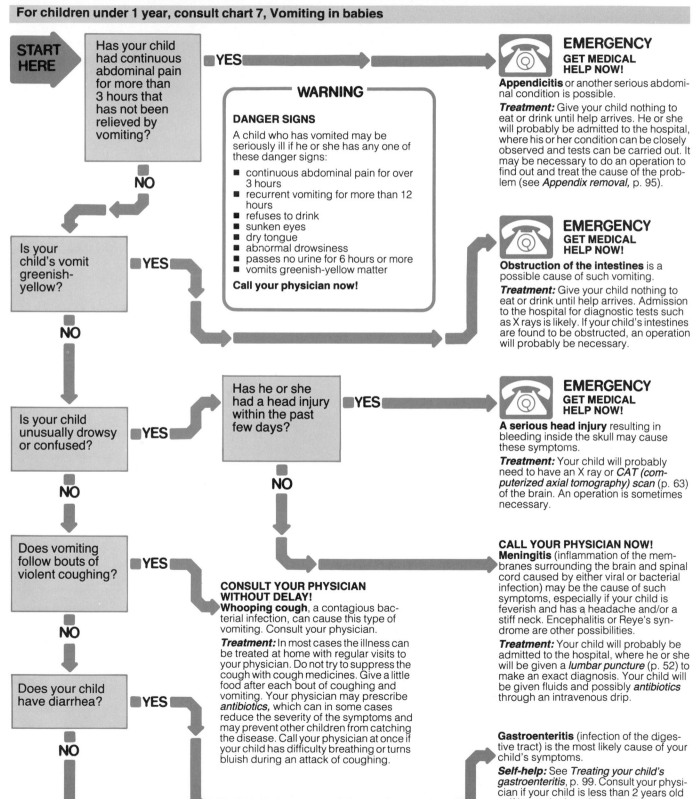

START HERE

Has your child had continuous abdominal pain for more than 3 hours that has not been relieved by vomiting? — **YES** →

EMERGENCY GET MEDICAL HELP NOW!
Appendicitis or another serious abdominal condition is possible.
Treatment: Give your child nothing to eat or drink until help arrives. He or she will probably be admitted to the hospital, where his or her condition can be closely observed and tests can be carried out. It may be necessary to do an operation to find out and treat the cause of the problem (see *Appendix removal,* p. 95).

NO ↓

WARNING

DANGER SIGNS

A child who has vomited may be seriously ill if he or she has any one of these danger signs:

- continuous abdominal pain for over 3 hours
- recurrent vomiting for more than 12 hours
- refuses to drink
- sunken eyes
- dry tongue
- abnormal drowsiness
- passes no urine for 6 hours or more
- vomits greenish-yellow matter

Call your physician now!

Is your child's vomit greenish-yellow? — **YES** →

EMERGENCY GET MEDICAL HELP NOW!
Obstruction of the intestines is a possible cause of such vomiting.
Treatment: Give your child nothing to eat or drink until help arrives. Admission to the hospital for diagnostic tests such as X rays is likely. If your child's intestines are found to be obstructed, an operation will probably be necessary.

NO ↓

Is your child unusually drowsy or confused? — **YES** → Has he or she had a head injury within the past few days? — **YES** →

EMERGENCY GET MEDICAL HELP NOW!
A serious head injury resulting in bleeding inside the skull may cause these symptoms.
Treatment: Your child will probably need to have an X ray or *CAT (computerized axial tomography) scan* (p. 63) of the brain. An operation is sometimes necessary.

NO ↓

NO ↓

Does vomiting follow bouts of violent coughing? — **YES** →

CALL YOUR PHYSICIAN NOW!
Meningitis (inflammation of the membranes surrounding the brain and spinal cord caused by either viral or bacterial infection) may be the cause of such symptoms, especially if your child is feverish and has a headache and/or a stiff neck. Encephalitis or Reye's syndrome are other possibilities.
Treatment: Your child will probably be admitted to the hospital, where he or she will be given a *lumbar puncture* (p. 52) to make an exact diagnosis. Your child will be given fluids and possibly *antibiotics* through an intravenous drip.

CONSULT YOUR PHYSICIAN WITHOUT DELAY!
Whooping cough, a contagious bacterial infection, can cause this type of vomiting. Consult your physician.
Treatment: In most cases the illness can be treated at home with regular visits to your physician. Do not try to suppress the cough with cough medicines. Give a little food after each bout of coughing and vomiting. Your physician may prescribe *antibiotics,* which can in some cases reduce the severity of the symptoms and may prevent other children from catching the disease. Call your physician at once if your child has difficulty breathing or turns bluish during an attack of coughing.

NO ↓

Does your child have diarrhea? — **YES** →

Gastroenteritis (infection of the digestive tract) is the most likely cause of your child's symptoms.
Self-help: See *Treating your child's gastroenteritis,* p. 99. Consult your physician if your child is less than 2 years old or if he or she is no better in 24 hours.

NO ↓

Go to next page

Continued from previous page

Does your child have two
or more of these symptoms?
■ fever
■ pain below the waist
■ bed-wetting (when
previously dry at night)
■ pain on urination
■ frequent urination
■ foul-smelling urine

YES

Urinary tract infection may be the cause of
your child's vomiting. This diagnosis is more
likely if your child is a girl (see *Structure of the
urinary tract*, p. 103). Consult your physician.
Treatment: If your physician suspects a urinary tract infection, he or she will probably ask
you to provide a sample of your child's urine for
analysis (see *Collecting a mid-stream specimen*, p. 103). If tests confirm the diagnosis, the
usual treatment is a course of *antibiotics*.

NO

Did the vomiting
occur while your
child was very
excited or before
a possibly
stressful event –
for example, the
first day at
school?

YES

Vomiting at times of emotional stress is
common among children, and most parents
learn to distinguish between this type of vomiting and a physical illness.
Self-help: Treat the vomiting sympathetically;
your child is likely to be upset by it (see *What to
do when your child vomits*, below). If you think
that worry about a particular event has caused
the vomiting, do not force your child to participate if you can avoid it. However, if the problem
is related to school, you will need patience to
help your child overcome his or her fears.
Discussing the problem with the teacher or
your physician may be useful.

See also chart

23 School difficulties

NO

Is your child
passing white
stools and
unusually dark
urine?

YES

Hepatitis (viral infection of the liver) is possible.
Consult your physician.
Treatment: Your physician will probably advise
you to give nothing to eat while vomiting and
nausea persist. Instead, give frequent drinks of
glucose solution (see *Treating gastroenteritis in
babies*, p. 41), possibly flavored with a little fruit
juice. To prevent infection from spreading, you will
need to keep your child's eating utensils and towels
separate from those of the rest of the family. Your
physician may recommend that other members of
the family be immunized against the disease.

NO

Occasional bouts of vomiting are normal
during childhood and may often have no
obvious physical cause.
Self-help: See *What to do when your child
vomits*, below.

TRAVEL SICKNESS

Nausea and vomiting while traveling by car,
sea or air are caused by disturbance to the
balance mechanism of the inner ear by motion.
Children's ears are particularly sensitive and
this may be why they are especially prone to
travel sickness. Most children become less
susceptible to it as they get older. If your child
is often travel sick, some of the following
suggestions may help to prevent problems.

■ Don't give heavy meals before or while
traveling.
■ Discourage your child from looking out of
the car windows.
■ Provide plenty of distractions, such as toys
and games.
■ Try to prevent your child from becoming
overexcited.
■ Keep at least one window of the car open.
■ Allow frequent stops for your child to stretch
his or her legs and get some fresh air.
■ Travel at night when your child is more likely
to sleep.
■ Learn to recognize the signs of travel sickness (sudden pallor and quietness) and be
prepared to stop.

WHAT TO DO WHEN YOUR CHILD VOMITS

A child who is vomiting may be frightened and upset and, above all,
needs you to be calm and sympathetic. Your child may find it reassur-
ing if you hold his or her forehead while he or she vomits. After vomiting give your child some water to rinse out the mouth and sponge his
or her face. Give a change of clothes, if necessary. Then encourage
him or her to lie down and sleep. If you think that your child may vomit
again, have a bowl ready nearby.

If your child is vomiting persistently, you must make sure that he or
she drinks plenty of fluids, especially if he or she has diarrhea as well
(as in gastroenteritis). He or she should drink at least 1 quart (2 pints)
a day of cold, clear fluids. This should preferably be a glucose solution (see *Treating gastroenteritis in babies*, p. 41). It is better if this is
taken in frequent, small sips, rather than in large quantities less often.
While your child is feeling ill, give no solids or milk products.

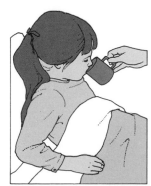

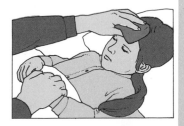

A hand held against the forehead while
your child vomits (far left) is often comforting. After vomiting, a drink (left) and a
face-wash (above) will make your child
feel better.

38 Abdominal pain

Pain between the bottom of the rib cage and the groin in a child may have a wide variety of causes, both physical and emotional. Most stomachaches disappear on their own without treatment from a physician, but occasionally there is a serious physical cause, and you should be aware of the symptoms that may indicate such an illness so that you can feel confident in handling the far more likely minor conditions. The questions in this chart mainly concern children over the age of 2 because babies and toddlers are unlikely to complain of stomachache. However, if you suspect that your child under 2 has abdominal pain, consult your physician.

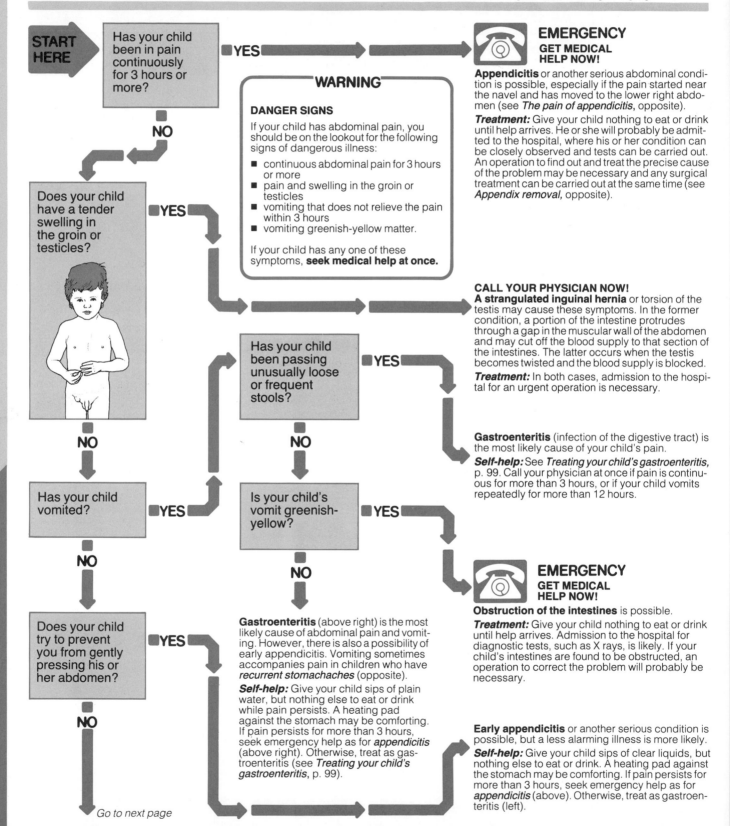

START HERE

Has your child been in pain continuously for 3 hours or more?

YES →

NO ↓

Does your child have a tender swelling in the groin or testicles?

YES →

NO ↓

Has your child vomited?

NO ↓

Does your child try to prevent you from gently pressing his or her abdomen?

YES →

NO ↓

Go to next page

YES ← **Has your child been passing unusually loose or frequent stools?**

NO ↓

Is your child's vomit greenish-yellow?

YES →

NO ↓

← YES

WARNING

DANGER SIGNS

If your child has abdominal pain, you should be on the lookout for the following signs of dangerous illness:

- continuous abdominal pain for 3 hours or more
- pain and swelling in the groin or testicles
- vomiting that does not relieve the pain within 3 hours
- vomiting greenish-yellow matter.

If your child has any one of these symptoms, **seek medical help at once.**

EMERGENCY
GET MEDICAL HELP NOW!

Appendicitis or another serious abdominal condition is possible, especially if the pain started near the navel and has moved to the lower right abdomen (see *The pain of appendicitis*, opposite).

Treatment: Give your child nothing to eat or drink until help arrives. He or she will probably be admitted to the hospital, where his or her condition can be closely observed and tests can be carried out. An operation to find out and treat the precise cause of the problem may be necessary and any surgical treatment can be carried out at the same time (see *Appendix removal,* opposite).

CALL YOUR PHYSICIAN NOW!
A strangulated inguinal hernia or torsion of the testis may cause these symptoms. In the former condition, a portion of the intestine protrudes through a gap in the muscular wall of the abdomen and may cut off the blood supply to that section of the intestines. The latter occurs when the testis becomes twisted and the blood supply is blocked.

Treatment: In both cases, admission to the hospital for an urgent operation is necessary.

Gastroenteritis (infection of the digestive tract) is the most likely cause of your child's pain.

Self-help: See *Treating your child's gastroenteritis,* p. 99. Call your physician at once if pain is continuous for more than 3 hours, or if your child vomits repeatedly for more than 12 hours.

EMERGENCY
GET MEDICAL HELP NOW!

Obstruction of the intestines is possible.

Treatment: Give your child nothing to eat or drink until help arrives. Admission to the hospital for diagnostic tests, such as X rays, is likely. If your child's intestines are found to be obstructed, an operation to correct the problem will probably be necessary.

Gastroenteritis (above right) is the most likely cause of abdominal pain and vomiting. However, there is also a possibility of early appendicitis. Vomiting sometimes accompanies pain in children who have *recurrent stomachaches* (opposite).

Self-help: Give your child sips of plain water, but nothing else to eat or drink while pain persists. A heating pad against the stomach may be comforting. If pain persists for more than 3 hours, seek emergency help as for *appendicitis* (above right). Otherwise, treat as gastroenteritis (see *Treating your child's gastroenteritis,* p. 99).

Early appendicitis or another serious condition is possible, but a less alarming illness is more likely.

Self-help: Give your child sips of clear liquids, but nothing else to eat or drink. A heating pad against the stomach may be comforting. If pain persists for more than 3 hours, seek emergency help as for *appendicitis* (above). Otherwise, treat as gastroenteritis (left).

Continued from previous page

Does your child have pain below the waist AND two or more of the following symptoms?
- fever of 100°F (38°C) or above
- bed-wetting (when previously dry at night)
- pain on urination
- frequent urination
- foul-smelling urine

YES

Urinary tract infection may be the cause of your child's pain. This diagnosis is more likely if your child is a girl (see *Structure of the urinary tract*, p. 103). Consult your physician.

Treatment: If your physician suspects a urinary tract infection, he or she will probably want a sample of your child's urine for analysis (see *Collecting a mid-stream specimen*, p. 103). If tests confirm the diagnosis, the usual treatment is a course of *antibiotics*.

NO

Does your child have a cold or sore throat?

YES

Upper respiratory tract infections in children are often accompanied by abdominal pain. Look for any of the danger signs listed in the box opposite, but treat the cold or sore throat in the usual way (see *Treating your child's cold*, p. 84, and *How to relieve a sore throat*, p. 85).

NO

Did your child seem well before the onset of pain?

YES

Has your child had similar bouts of pain in the past few months?

YES

NO

NO

THE PAIN OF APPENDICITIS
Symptoms of appendicitis in children can vary considerably. But typically the pain starts in the center of the abdomen, near the navel, and moves toward the lower-right abdomen. If your child has this type of pain, you should be especially alert for any of the danger signs listed in the box opposite.

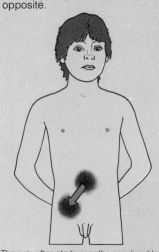

The pain often starts near the navel and later moves toward the lower-right abdomen.

Recurrent stomachaches are common in children. They may be the result of stress or insecurity, but often there is no obvious explanation.

Self-help: Take the symptoms seriously; although there is unlikely to be a physical cause, your child's pain is nevertheless real. Allow him or her to rest in bed with a heating pad. Do not force food on your child but make sure he or she drinks plenty of clear fluids. Remember that a child with recurrent stomachaches is just as likely to get a serious disease, such as appendicitis, as any other child, so be on the lookout for any of the danger signs listed in the box opposite. Call your physician if your child's symptoms differ from his or her usual stomachaches. If you have not already done so, discuss the problem with your physician, who will rule out the possibility of a physical disorder and try to help you discover any underlying emotional problems.

Unexplained abdominal pain is common in childhood. Give your child clear fluids only. A heating pad on the stomach may ease the pain. Look out for any of the danger signs in the box opposite and consult your physician if further symptoms develop, or if your child is still sick the following day.

APPENDIX REMOVAL
Appendix removal (or appendectomy) is carried out in cases of appendicitis, when there is infection or inflammation of the appendix, a worm-shaped pouch that protrudes from the large intestine near where it meets the small intestine. The operation needs to be done as soon as symptoms suggest the possibility of appendicitis, because there is a danger that an inflamed appendix will burst, creating a dangerous generalized infection in the abdomen (peritonitis).

The operation itself is straightforward. Your child will be given a general anesthetic and an incision will be made in the abdomen. The appendix will then be removed. In most cases recovery is rapid and there are no aftereffects.

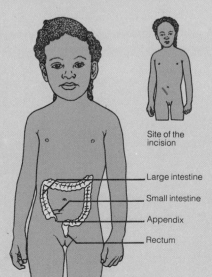

Site of the incision

Large intestine

Small intestine

Appendix

Rectum

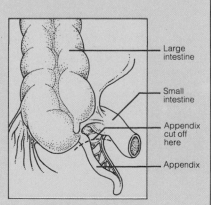

Large intestine

Small intestine

Appendix cut off here

Appendix

The incision is made in the lower-right abdomen (above). The appendix is cut off at its base and removed (right).

39 Loss of appetite

Children's appetites are more closely governed by the body's energy requirements than are adult appetites. During active times children may consume large amounts, but when they use little energy they may have no appetite. A child who is growing rapidly is likely to eat much more than a child who is going through a phase of little growth. Some children naturally burn less energy than others. Fluctuations in appetite are normal as long as your child is active and growing normally. Do not try to override the natural appetite-regulating mechanism by forcing your child to eat. However, be concerned if a child who has no appetite seems sick or is failing to grow at the expected rate (see Growth patterns in childhood, p. 47).

For children under 1 year, go to chart 6, Feeding problems

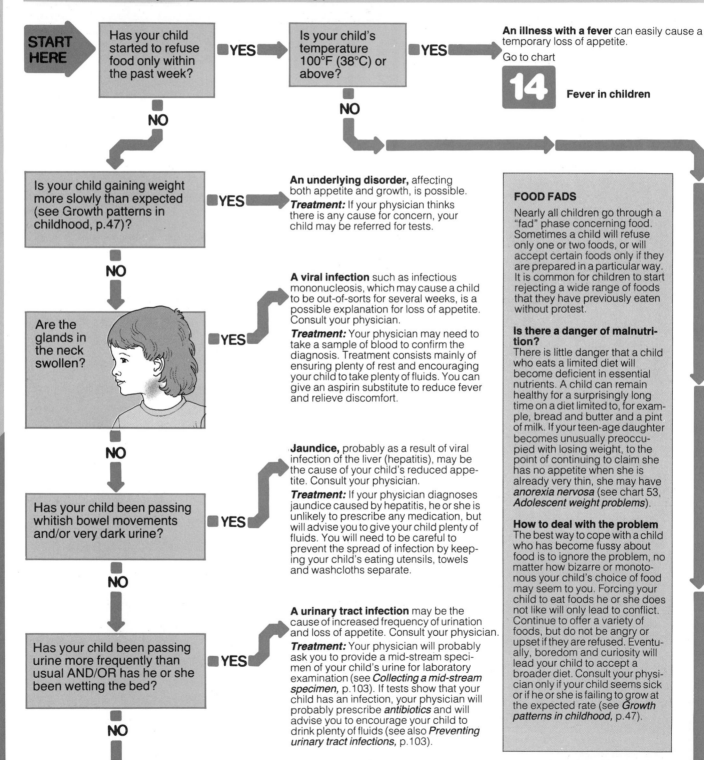

START HERE

Has your child started to refuse food only within the past week?

YES → Is your child's temperature 100°F (38°C) or above?

YES → **An illness with a fever** can easily cause a temporary loss of appetite.

Go to chart **14** **Fever in children**

NO

NO

Is your child gaining weight more slowly than expected (see Growth patterns in childhood, p.47)?

YES → **An underlying disorder,** affecting both appetite and growth, is possible.
Treatment: If your physician thinks there is any cause for concern, your child may be referred for tests.

NO

Are the glands in the neck swollen?

YES → **A viral infection** such as infectious mononucleosis, which may cause a child to be out-of-sorts for several weeks, is a possible explanation for loss of appetite. Consult your physician.
Treatment: Your physician may need to take a sample of blood to confirm the diagnosis. Treatment consists mainly of ensuring plenty of rest and encouraging your child to take plenty of fluids. You can give an aspirin substitute to reduce fever and relieve discomfort.

NO

Has your child been passing whitish bowel movements and/or very dark urine?

YES → **Jaundice,** probably as a result of viral infection of the liver (hepatitis), may be the cause of your child's reduced appetite. Consult your physician.
Treatment: If your physician diagnoses jaundice caused by hepatitis, he or she is unlikely to prescribe any medication, but will advise you to give your child plenty of fluids. You will need to be careful to prevent the spread of infection by keeping your child's eating utensils, towels and washcloths separate.

NO

Has your child been passing urine more frequently than usual AND/OR has he or she been wetting the bed?

YES → **A urinary tract infection** may be the cause of increased frequency of urination and loss of appetite. Consult your physician.
Treatment: Your physician will probably ask you to provide a mid-stream specimen of your child's urine for laboratory examination (see *Collecting a mid-stream specimen,* p.103). If tests show that your child has an infection, your physician will probably prescribe *antibiotics* and will advise you to encourage your child to drink plenty of fluids (see also *Preventing urinary tract infections,* p.103).

NO

Go to next page, column 1

FOOD FADS

Nearly all children go through a "fad" phase concerning food. Sometimes a child will refuse only one or two foods, or will accept certain foods only if they are prepared in a particular way. It is common for children to start rejecting a wide range of foods that they have previously eaten without protest.

Is there a danger of malnutrition?
There is little danger that a child who eats a limited diet will become deficient in essential nutrients. A child can remain healthy for a surprisingly long time on a diet limited to, for example, bread and butter and a pint of milk. If your teen-age daughter becomes unusually preoccupied with losing weight, to the point of continuing to claim she has no appetite when she is already very thin, she may have *anorexia nervosa* (see chart 53, *Adolescent weight problems*).

How to deal with the problem
The best way to cope with a child who has become fussy about food is to ignore the problem, no matter how bizarre or monotonous your child's choice of food may seem to you. Forcing your child to eat foods he or she does not like will only lead to conflict. Continue to offer a variety of foods, but do not be angry or upset if they are refused. Eventually, boredom and curiosity will lead your child to accept a broader diet. Consult your physician only if your child seems sick or if he or she is failing to grow at the expected rate (see *Growth patterns in childhood,* p.47).

Go to next page, column 2

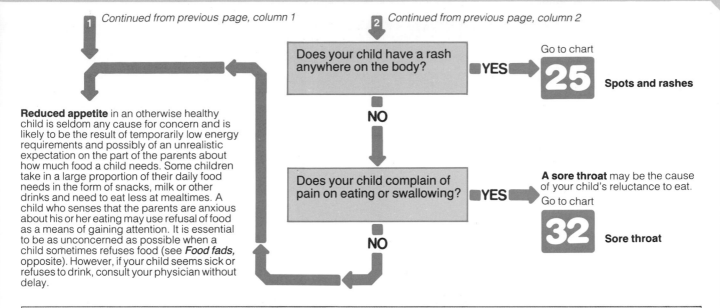

1 Continued from previous page, column 1

2 Continued from previous page, column 2

Does your child have a rash anywhere on the body?

YES → Go to chart **25** Spots and rashes

NO

Does your child complain of pain on eating or swallowing?

YES → **A sore throat** may be the cause of your child's reluctance to eat. Go to chart **32** Sore throat

NO

Reduced appetite in an otherwise healthy child is seldom any cause for concern and is likely to be the result of temporarily low energy requirements and possibly of an unrealistic expectation on the part of the parents about how much food a child needs. Some children take in a large proportion of their daily food needs in the form of snacks, milk or other drinks and need to eat less at mealtimes. A child who senses that the parents are anxious about his or her eating may use refusal of food as a means of gaining attention. It is essential to be as unconcerned as possible when a child sometimes refuses food (see *Food fads,* opposite). However, if your child seems sick or refuses to drink, consult your physician without delay.

THE COMPONENTS OF A HEALTHY DIET

A healthy diet is one that contains adequate amounts of each of the various nutrients that the body requires to function efficiently, to repair itself and, in the case of children, to grow. The main food categories and their nutritional values are listed in the table below. In western societies, dietary deficiencies in children are rare; the main risk is overnutrition, either in total calorie intake (see below), leading to obesity, or in consumption of unnecessarily large amounts of certain types of food such as fats and refined carbohydrates (for example, sugar or white flour). Providing a variety of different types of food will almost certainly ensure that your child is amply nourished. Even if your child becomes fussy about eating, malnutrition is most unlikely (see *Food fads,* opposite).

Food category	Diet advice
Proteins are used for growth, repair and replacement of body tissues. Animal products such as meat, fish, eggs, cheese and other milk products are high in protein, as are peas, beans and lentils.	Many animal products are also high in fat, so make a point of offering nonanimal sources of protein fairly often.
Carbohydrates are used for energy but when eaten in excess are stored in the body as fat. Foods containing a high proportion of carbohydrates include sugar, grain products and root vegetables.	When selecting carbohydrate foods, choose unrefined products such as whole-grain breads, which also contain fiber and other nutrients, in preference to sugar and refined cereals, which only provide energy or fat.
Fats (sometimes known as lipids) are a concentrated source of energy and provide more calories than any other food. They are found in animal products such as meat, eggs and butter, and also in certain plant products such as nuts, olives and vegetable oils.	Nutritionists recommend that intake of fats of all kinds be kept to a minimum.
Fiber is the indigestible residue of plant products that passes through the digestive system. While it contains no energy value or nutrients, it is essential for healthy bowel action.	To ensure adequate fiber intake, choose whole-grain products and serve plenty of fruit and vegetables.
Vitamins are complex chemical compounds that are needed by the body in tiny quantities. A child receiving a normal diet is unlikely to become deficient in any vitamin.	Vitamins may sometimes be destroyed by lengthy cooking, so offer uncooked vegetables and fruit regularly. Some physicians recommend vitamins for children under 5. While they are often unnecessary, they will do no harm and may reassure parents who are worried about whether their child is receiving an adequate diet.
Minerals and certain salts are needed in minute quantities. These include iron, potassium, calcium and sodium (found in table salt). A normal child is unlikely to suffer from shortages of such substances.	Too much salt in the diet may be harmful, so use as little as possible.
Calories are the units used to measure the amount of energy provided by food. If a child's diet contains more calories than necessary, the excess will be stored as fat. Conversely, if a child consumes fewer calories than are being burned up, he or she will use up fat reserves and become thin. Foods containing a high proportion of fats or carbohydrates are generally high in calories.	It is important that a child's diet contain enough, but not too many, calories. A child's natural appetite-regulating mechanism normally ensures that the correct amount of calories is eaten.

40 Diarrhea in children

Diarrhea is the passing of unusually runny bowel movements more frequently than is normal for your child. In older children diarrhea is unlikely to have a serious cause or to present any risk to health as long as you ensure that your child drinks plenty of fluids while diarrhea persists. The most common cause of diarrhea is infection of the digestive tract (gastroenteritis). In most cases, drugs are not effective; the best treatment is to allow the body to rid itself of the infection (see Treating your child's gastroenteritis, opposite).

For children under 1 year, see chart 8, Diarrhea in babies

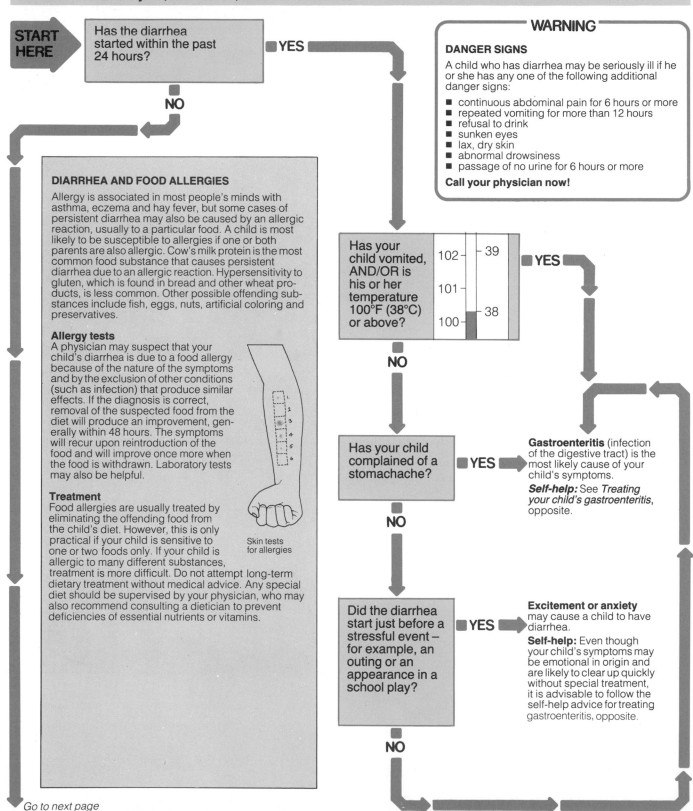

START HERE

Has the diarrhea started within the past 24 hours? **YES** / **NO**

WARNING

DANGER SIGNS

A child who has diarrhea may be seriously ill if he or she has any one of the following additional danger signs:

- continuous abdominal pain for 6 hours or more
- repeated vomiting for more than 12 hours
- refusal to drink
- sunken eyes
- lax, dry skin
- abnormal drowsiness
- passage of no urine for 6 hours or more

Call your physician now!

DIARRHEA AND FOOD ALLERGIES

Allergy is associated in most people's minds with asthma, eczema and hay fever, but some cases of persistent diarrhea may also be caused by an allergic reaction, usually to a particular food. A child is most likely to be susceptible to allergies if one or both parents are also allergic. Cow's milk protein is the most common food substance that causes persistent diarrhea due to an allergic reaction. Hypersensitivity to gluten, which is found in bread and other wheat products, is less common. Other possible offending substances include fish, eggs, nuts, artificial coloring and preservatives.

Allergy tests
A physician may suspect that your child's diarrhea is due to a food allergy because of the nature of the symptoms and by the exclusion of other conditions (such as infection) that produce similar effects. If the diagnosis is correct, removal of the suspected food from the diet will produce an improvement, generally within 48 hours. The symptoms will recur upon reintroduction of the food and will improve once more when the food is withdrawn. Laboratory tests may also be helpful.

Skin tests for allergies

Treatment
Food allergies are usually treated by eliminating the offending food from the child's diet. However, this is only practical if your child is sensitive to one or two foods only. If your child is allergic to many different substances, treatment is more difficult. Do not attempt long-term dietary treatment without medical advice. Any special diet should be supervised by your physician, who may also recommend consulting a dietician to prevent deficiencies of essential nutrients or vitamins.

Has your child vomited, AND/OR is his or her temperature 100°F (38°C) or above?

102 — 39
101 —
100 — 38

YES / **NO**

Has your child complained of a stomachache? **YES** / **NO**

Gastroenteritis (infection of the digestive tract) is the most likely cause of your child's symptoms.

Self-help: See *Treating your child's gastroenteritis,* opposite.

Did the diarrhea start just before a stressful event — for example, an outing or an appearance in a school play? **YES** / **NO**

Excitement or anxiety may cause a child to have diarrhea.

Self-help: Even though your child's symptoms may be emotional in origin and are likely to clear up quickly without special treatment, it is advisable to follow the self-help advice for treating gastroenteritis, opposite.

Go to next page

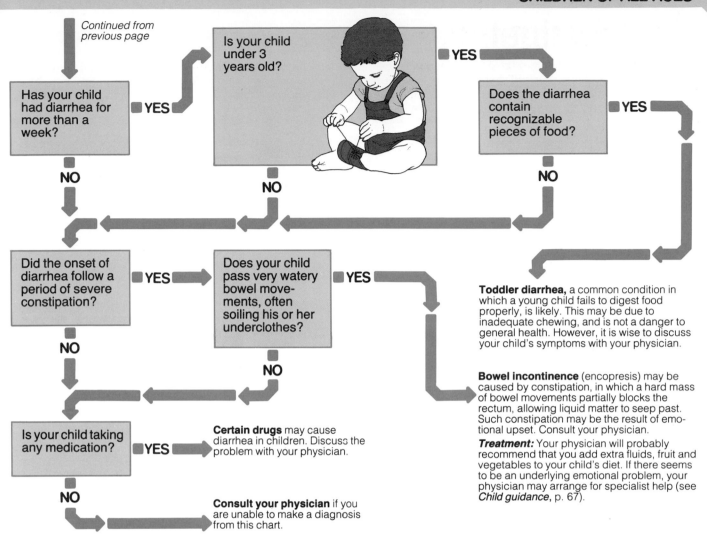

Continued from previous page

Has your child had diarrhea for more than a week? → **YES** → **Is your child under 3 years old?** → **YES** → **Does the diarrhea contain recognizable pieces of food?** → **YES**

NO (from "Has your child had diarrhea for more than a week?")

NO (from "Is your child under 3 years old?")

NO (from "Does the diarrhea contain recognizable pieces of food?")

Did the onset of diarrhea follow a period of severe constipation? → **YES** → **Does your child pass very watery bowel movements, often soiling his or her underclothes?** → **YES**

NO (from "Did the onset of diarrhea follow a period of severe constipation?")

NO (from "Does your child pass very watery bowel movements...")

Is your child taking any medication? → **YES** → **Certain drugs** may cause diarrhea in children. Discuss the problem with your physician.

NO → **Consult your physician** if you are unable to make a diagnosis from this chart.

Toddler diarrhea, a common condition in which a young child fails to digest food properly, is likely. This may be due to inadequate chewing, and is not a danger to general health. However, it is wise to discuss your child's symptoms with your physician.

Bowel incontinence (encopresis) may be caused by constipation, in which a hard mass of bowel movements partially blocks the rectum, allowing liquid matter to seep past. Such constipation may be the result of emotional upset. Consult your physician.
Treatment: Your physician will probably recommend that you add extra fluids, fruit and vegetables to your child's diet. If there seems to be an underlying emotional problem, your physician may arrange for specialist help (see *Child guidance*, p. 67).

TREATING YOUR CHILD'S GASTROENTERITIS

If you suspect that your child has gastroenteritis or a similar disorder and is not dehydrated, try the following home treatment. It allows the body to get rid of the infection while preventing dehydration. The treatment should reduce the frequency of bowel movements within 24 hours. But the bowel movements may remain runny for 5 to 7 days.

General points
- Give plenty of clear fluids – 1 to 1½ quarts (2 to 3 pints) a day. A glucose and mineral solution (see *Treating gastroenteritis*, p. 41) is best for small babies, otherwise give clear liquids such as apple juice or gelatins.
- If your child is vomiting, give drinks in frequent small sips – 1 to 2 fl.oz (30 to 60 ml) every hour.
- Give no milk products (milk, yogurt or cheese) for a week.
- If your older child has crampy diarrhea, a heating pad on the abdomen may be comforting.

Day-by-day treatment plan

Day 1
Give only clear fluids (see *General points*, left).

Day 2
Offer, in addition, vegetable and unsweetened fruit purees or gelatins (e.g., mashed potatoes or bananas or apple sauce).

Day 3
Offer, in addition, chicken and/or soups.

Day 4
Offer, in addition, white bread (spread with margarine, not butter), crackers, eggs, meat and/or fish.

Day 5
Resume a normal diet, but continue to exclude milk products for 2 more days.

When to call your physician
Consult your physician if your child is under 2 years old or if symptoms do not start to subside within 48 hours. Call your physician at once if your child shows any of the danger signs listed in the box opposite.

Preventing the spread of infection
If anyone in the house has gastroenteritis, it is important to prevent the spread of infection.

- Wash your hands thoroughly after going to the toilet and before preparing food.

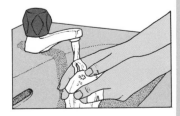

- Do not share towels, sponges or washcloths.

41 Constipation

There is no rule that says a child should have a bowel movement every day. Some children defecate a few times a day, others only once every three days. Both extremes are normal as long as your child is well and provided that the bowel movements are not so hard that they cause discomfort or straining. Temporary alterations in your child's normal bowel rhythms may be caused by a change in diet, minor illness or emotional stress.

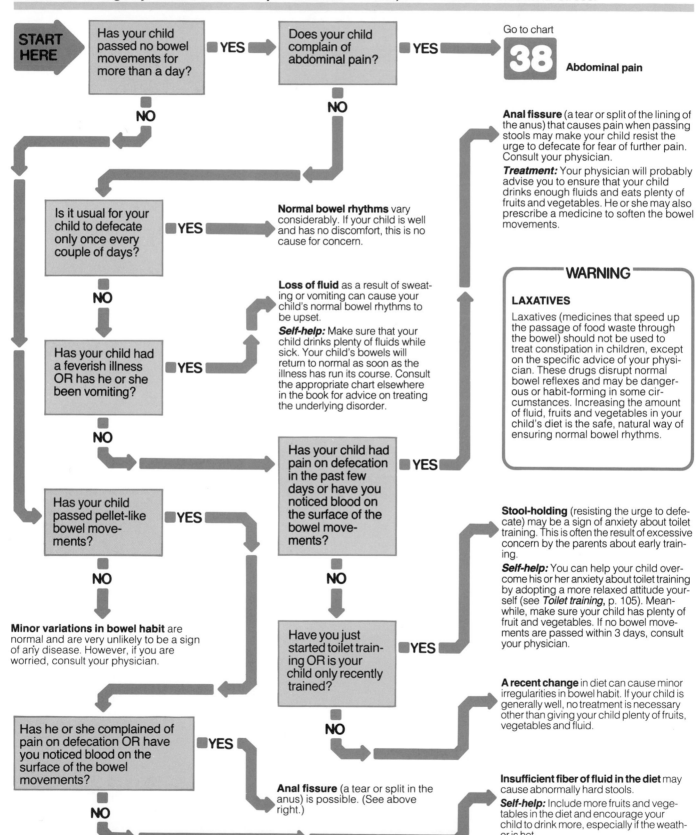

START HERE

Has your child passed no bowel movements for more than a day?
YES → **Does your child complain of abdominal pain?**
YES → Go to chart **38** **Abdominal pain**

NO ↓ / NO ↓

Is it usual for your child to defecate only once every couple of days?
YES → **Normal bowel rhythms** vary considerably. If your child is well and has no discomfort, this is no cause for concern.

NO ↓

Has your child had a feverish illness OR has he or she been vomiting?
YES → **Loss of fluid** as a result of sweating or vomiting can cause your child's normal bowel rhythms to be upset.
Self-help: Make sure that your child drinks plenty of fluids while sick. Your child's bowels will return to normal as soon as the illness has run its course. Consult the appropriate chart elsewhere in the book for advice on treating the underlying disorder.

NO ↓

Has your child passed pellet-like bowel movements?
YES → **Has your child had pain on defecation in the past few days or have you noticed blood on the surface of the bowel movements?**
YES → **Anal fissure** (a tear or split of the lining of the anus) that causes pain when passing stools may make your child resist the urge to defecate for fear of further pain. Consult your physician.
Treatment: Your physician will probably advise you to ensure that your child drinks enough fluids and eats plenty of fruits and vegetables. He or she may also prescribe a medicine to soften the bowel movements.

NO ↓

Minor variations in bowel habit are normal and are very unlikely to be a sign of any disease. However, if you are worried, consult your physician.

Has your child had pain on defecation in the past few days or have you noticed blood on the surface of the bowel movements?
NO ↓
Have you just started toilet training OR is your child only recently trained?
YES → **Stool-holding** (resisting the urge to defecate) may be a sign of anxiety about toilet training. This is often the result of excessive concern by the parents about early training.
Self-help: You can help your child overcome his or her anxiety about toilet training by adopting a more relaxed attitude yourself (see *Toilet training*, p. 105). Meanwhile, make sure your child has plenty of fruit and vegetables. If no bowel movements are passed within 3 days, consult your physician.

NO ↓

A recent change in diet can cause minor irregularities in bowel habit. If your child is generally well, no treatment is necessary other than giving your child plenty of fruits, vegetables and fluid.

Has he or she complained of pain on defecation OR have you noticed blood on the surface of the bowel movements?
YES → **Anal fissure** (a tear or split in the anus) is possible. (See above right.)

NO ↓

Insufficient fiber of fluid in the diet may cause abnormally hard stools.
Self-help: Include more fruits and vegetables in the diet and encourage your child to drink more, especially if the weather is hot.

WARNING

LAXATIVES

Laxatives (medicines that speed up the passage of food waste through the bowel) should not be used to treat constipation in children, except on the specific advice of your physician. These drugs disrupt normal bowel reflexes and may be dangerous or habit-forming in some circumstances. Increasing the amount of fluid, fruits and vegetables in your child's diet is the safe, natural way of ensuring normal bowel rhythms.

42 Abnormal-looking bowel movements

Minor variations in the color of bowel movements are normal and are usually caused by a change in diet. Consult this chart only if there is a marked change in the appearance of your child's bowel movements. In most cases, the cause of the trouble is something that the child has eaten but, occasionally, there may be an underlying disorder that your physician should investigate. A sample of your child's bowel movements will assist in the diagnosis. Blood in the stools or on toilet paper should not be ignored.

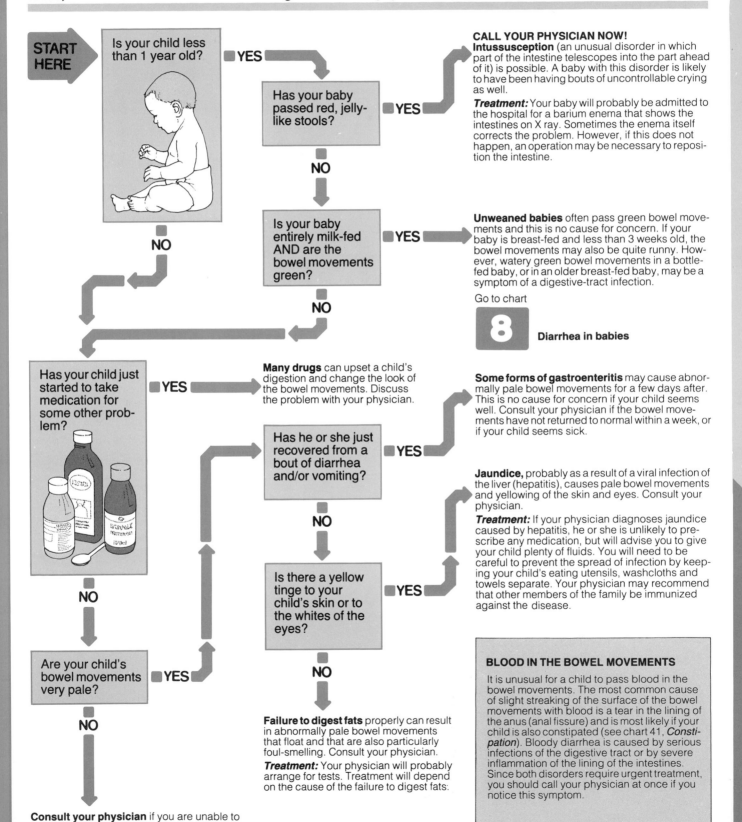

START HERE

Is your child less than 1 year old?

YES → Has your baby passed red, jelly-like stools?

YES →

CALL YOUR PHYSICIAN NOW!
Intussusception (an unusual disorder in which part of the intestine telescopes into the part ahead of it) is possible. A baby with this disorder is likely to have been having bouts of uncontrollable crying as well.

Treatment: Your baby will probably be admitted to the hospital for a barium enema that shows the intestines on X ray. Sometimes the enema itself corrects the problem. However, if this does not happen, an operation may be necessary to reposition the intestine.

NO

Is your baby entirely milk-fed AND are the bowel movements green?

YES →

Unweaned babies often pass green bowel movements and this is no cause for concern. If your baby is breast-fed and less than 3 weeks old, the bowel movements may also be quite runny. However, watery green bowel movements in a bottle-fed baby, or in an older breast-fed baby, may be a symptom of a digestive-tract infection.

Go to chart

8 Diarrhea in babies

NO

NO

Has your child just started to take medication for some other problem?

YES → **Many drugs** can upset a child's digestion and change the look of the bowel movements. Discuss the problem with your physician.

NO

Has he or she just recovered from a bout of diarrhea and/or vomiting?

YES → **Some forms of gastroenteritis** may cause abnormally pale bowel movements for a few days after. This is no cause for concern if your child seems well. Consult your physician if the bowel movements have not returned to normal within a week, or if your child seems sick.

NO

Is there a yellow tinge to your child's skin or to the whites of the eyes?

YES →

Jaundice, probably as a result of a viral infection of the liver (hepatitis), causes pale bowel movements and yellowing of the skin and eyes. Consult your physician.

Treatment: If your physician diagnoses jaundice caused by hepatitis, he or she is unlikely to prescribe any medication, but will advise you to give your child plenty of fluids. You will need to be careful to prevent the spread of infection by keeping your child's eating utensils, washcloths and towels separate. Your physician may recommend that other members of the family be immunized against the disease.

NO

Are your child's bowel movements very pale?

YES →

NO

Failure to digest fats properly can result in abnormally pale bowel movements that float and that are also particularly foul-smelling. Consult your physician.

Treatment: Your physician will probably arrange for tests. Treatment will depend on the cause of the failure to digest fats:

BLOOD IN THE BOWEL MOVEMENTS

It is unusual for a child to pass blood in the bowel movements. The most common cause of slight streaking of the surface of the bowel movements with blood is a tear in the lining of the anus (anal fissure) and is most likely if your child is also constipated (see chart 41, *Constipation*). Bloody diarrhea is caused by serious infections of the digestive tract or by severe inflammation of the lining of the intestines. Since both disorders require urgent treatment, you should call your physician at once if you notice this symptom.

Consult your physician if you are unable to make a diagnosis from this chart.

43 Urinary problems

Most children need to urinate more frequently than adults. This is because a child's bladder is smaller than that of an adult, and muscular control may be less well developed. In addition, children who drink large amounts are likely to need to pass urine more often than average. Consult this chart if your child has any pain when passing urine, if your child starts to urinate more frequently than usual without a noticeable increase in fluid intake, if your child needs to pass urine more than once an hour, if your child is passing small amounts of urine frequently or if your child has been waking several times during the night to pass urine.

For problems of bladder or bowel control, see chart 44, Toilet-training problems

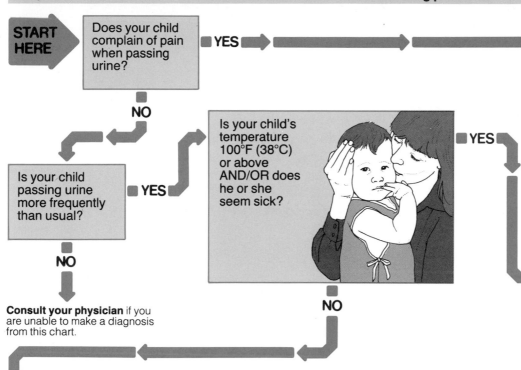

START HERE

Does your child complain of pain when passing urine? → **YES** →

An infection of the urinary tract may cause painful urination. Consult your physician.

Treatment: Your physician will probably need a specimen of your child's urine for analysis and culture (see *Collecting a mid-stream specimen,* opposite). If your child is found to have a urinary-tract infection, he or she will probably be given *antibiotics.* You will probably be advised to ensure that your child drinks plenty of fluids during this treatment. (See also *Preventing urinary tract infections,* opposite.)

NO ↓

Is your child passing urine more frequently than usual? → **YES** →

Is your child's temperature 100°F (38°C) or above AND/OR does he or she seem sick? → **YES** →

An infection of the urinary tract is the most likely explanation for your child's frequency of urination. Consult your physician.

Treatment: Your physician will probably have the child undergo some tests (see above). If the tests reveal an infection, it will be treated as described above.

NO ↓

Consult your physician if you are unable to make a diagnosis from this chart.

NO ↓

ABNORMAL-LOOKING URINE

Color of urine	Possible causes	What action is necessary
Pink, red or smoky	There is a chance that there may be blood in the urine, possibly caused by infection or another disorder of the urinary tract. However, natural or artificial red food colorings can also pass into the urine.	Consult your physician without delay. He or she may need to take samples of urine and blood for analysis in order to make a firm diagnosis. Treatment will depend on the underlying problem.
Dark yellow or orange	Concentration of urine caused by low fluid intake, fever, diarrhea or vomiting can darken the urine.	This is no cause for concern. Your child's urine will return to its normal color as soon as the fluid intake is increased.
Clear and dark brown	Jaundice caused by hepatitis (liver infection) is a possibility, especially if your child's bowel movements are very pale, and the skin or eyes look yellow.	Consult your physician. He or she will take samples of urine and blood for analysis in order to make a firm diagnosis. Treatment will depend on the underlying problem.
Green or blue	Artificial coloring in food or medication is almost certainly the cause of this.	This is no cause for concern; the coloring will pass through without harmful effects.

Go to next page

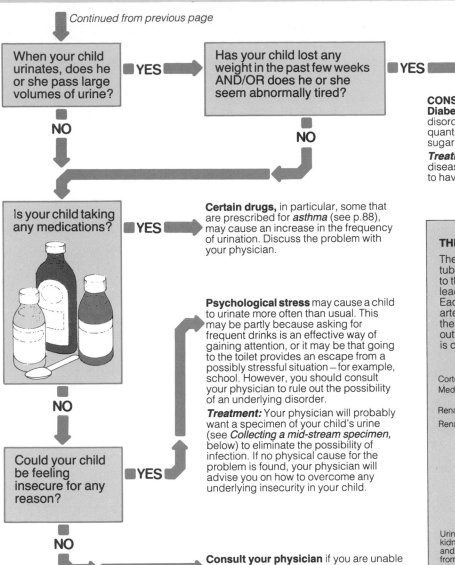

Continued from previous page

When your child urinates, does he or she pass large volumes of urine? ▶ **YES** ▶ **Has your child lost any weight in the past few weeks AND/OR does he or she seem abnormally tired?** ▶ **YES**

NO

NO

CONSULT YOUR PHYSICIAN WITHOUT DELAY!
Diabetes may cause an increase in urination. This disorder occurs when the body fails to make sufficient quantities of the hormone insulin, which helps convert sugar into energy.
Treatment: Tests will reveal the presence of this disease. If diabetes is confirmed, your child may need to have regular injections of insulin for life.

Is your child taking any medications? ▶ **YES** ▶ **Certain drugs,** in particular, some that are prescribed for *asthma* (see p.88), may cause an increase in the frequency of urination. Discuss the problem with your physician.

NO

Psychological stress may cause a child to urinate more often than usual. This may be partly because asking for frequent drinks is an effective way of gaining attention, or it may be that going to the toilet provides an escape from a possibly stressful situation – for example, school. However, you should consult your physician to rule out the possibility of an underlying disorder.

Treatment: Your physician will probably want a specimen of your child's urine (see *Collecting a mid-stream specimen,* below) to eliminate the possibility of infection. If no physical cause for the problem is found, your physician will advise you on how to overcome any underlying insecurity in your child.

Could your child be feeling insecure for any reason? ▶ **YES**

NO

Consult your physician if you are unable to make a diagnosis from this chart.

THE STRUCTURE OF THE URINARY TRACT

The urinary tract consists of the 2 kidneys; the 2 tubes, called the ureters, leading from the kidneys to the bladder; the bladder itself; and the tube leading from the bladder to the outside, the urethra. Each kidney is supplied with blood from the renal artery. As blood passes through the tiny tubes in the cortex and medulla, waste products are filtered out in the form of urine. The filtered, purified blood is carried away via the renal vein.

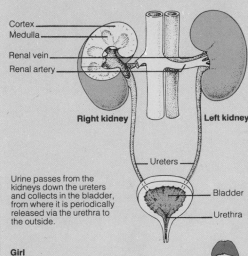

Cortex
Medulla
Renal vein
Renal artery

Right kidney   **Left kidney**

Urine passes from the kidneys down the ureters and collects in the bladder, from where it is periodically released via the urethra to the outside.

Ureters
Bladder
Urethra

Girl

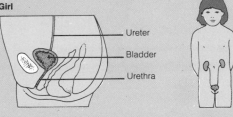

Ureter
Bladder
Urethra

Boy

Ureter
Bladder
Urethra

The female urethra is much shorter than the male urethra, allowing germs to travel up a girl's urinary tract more easily.

Preventing urinary tract infections
Most urinary tract infections are caused by germs from the bowel entering the urethra. To reduce the chances of infection, girls should be taught always to wipe from front to back after going to the toilet.

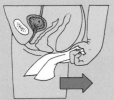

COLLECTING A MID-STREAM SPECIMEN

If your physician suspects that your child has a urinary tract infection, you will probably be asked to provide a mid-stream specimen of the child's urine for analysis. A mid-stream specimen is a sample of urine that has been collected after some urine has already been passed.

Collecting the urine
Your physician will give you a clean container in which to collect the urine. Urine should be passed directly into this, after starting to urinate into the toilet or another container. The accuracy of the test depends on the specimen being free from contamination by germs from the outside of the opening of the urethra. Your child will need to have his or her urethral opening (where the urine comes out) cleaned before starting to urinate.

Girls
The urine of a young girl is best collected by placing the container in the bottom of a pot (see right) before she starts to urinate. It may be easier for an older girl to hold the container under the stream while she sits well back on the toilet.

Boys
A boy's urine can be collected by holding the container in the stream after a little urine has been passed.

Boys

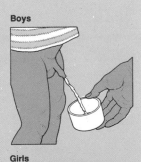

Girls

The method you use to collect the urine sample depends on whether your child is a boy or girl.

44 Toilet~training problems

The neuromuscular function that results in gaining control over both the bladder and the bowels takes place over a span of about 3 years between the second and the fifth year. Few children have reliable control before the age of 2 years, and most do not have any problems apart from the occasional "accident" after the age of 5. Within this range, there are great variations in the order and in the timing at which an individual child masters the different skills of toilet training. Serious disorders causing delay or disruption of the development of bladder or bowel control are rare in normal children; most such problems resolve with time and patience. Consult this chart if you are concerned about your child's ability to control bladder or bowels.

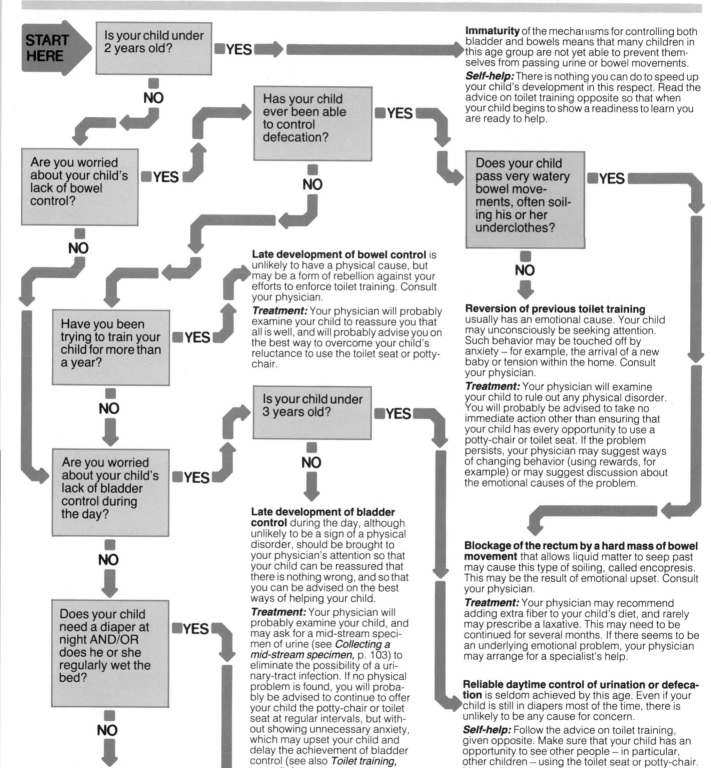

START HERE

Is your child under 2 years old? — **YES**

Immaturity of the mechanisms for controlling both bladder and bowels means that many children in this age group are not yet able to prevent themselves from passing urine or bowel movements.

Self-help: There is nothing you can do to speed up your child's development in this respect. Read the advice on toilet training opposite so that when your child begins to show a readiness to learn you are ready to help.

NO

Has your child ever been able to control defecation? — **YES**

NO

Are you worried about your child's lack of bowel control? — **YES**

NO

Does your child pass very watery bowel movements, often soiling his or her underclothes? — **YES**

NO

Late development of bowel control is unlikely to have a physical cause, but may be a form of rebellion against your efforts to enforce toilet training. Consult your physician.

Treatment: Your physician will probably examine your child to reassure you that all is well, and will probably advise you on the best way to overcome your child's reluctance to use the toilet seat or potty-chair.

Reversion of previous toilet training usually has an emotional cause. Your child may unconsciously be seeking attention. Such behavior may be touched off by anxiety – for example, the arrival of a new baby or tension within the home. Consult your physician.

Treatment: Your physician will examine your child to rule out any physical disorder. You will probably be advised to take no immediate action other than ensuring that your child has every opportunity to use a potty-chair or toilet seat. If the problem persists, your physician may suggest ways of changing behavior (using rewards, for example) or may suggest discussion about the emotional causes of the problem.

Have you been trying to train your child for more than a year? — **YES**

NO

Are you worried about your child's lack of bladder control during the day? — **YES**

Is your child under 3 years old? — **YES**

NO

Late development of bladder control during the day, although unlikely to be a sign of a physical disorder, should be brought to your physician's attention so that your child can be reassured that there is nothing wrong, and so that you can be advised on the best ways of helping your child.

Treatment: Your physician will probably examine your child, and may ask for a mid-stream specimen of urine (see *Collecting a mid-stream specimen*, p. 103) to eliminate the possibility of a urinary-tract infection. If no physical problem is found, you will probably be advised to continue to offer your child the potty-chair or toilet seat at regular intervals, but without showing unnecessary anxiety, which may upset your child and delay the achievement of bladder control (see also *Toilet training*, opposite).

Blockage of the rectum by a hard mass of bowel movement that allows liquid matter to seep past may cause this type of soiling, called encopresis. This may be the result of emotional upset. Consult your physician.

Treatment: Your physician may recommend adding extra fiber to your child's diet, and rarely may prescribe a laxative. This may need to be continued for several months. If there seems to be an underlying emotional problem, your physician may arrange for a specialist's help.

Reliable daytime control of urination or defecation is seldom achieved by this age. Even if your child is still in diapers most of the time, there is unlikely to be any cause for concern.

Self-help: Follow the advice on toilet training, given opposite. Make sure that your child has an opportunity to see other people – in particular, other children – using the toilet seat or potty-chair. Most children learn quickest by imitation.

NO

Does your child need a diaper at night AND/OR does he or she regularly wet the bed? — **YES**

NO

Consult your physician if you are unable to make a diagnosis from this chart.

Go to next page

Continued from previous page

Has your child ever been dry at night for more than a week? → **YES** → A **urinary tract infection** may cause a child who has previously been reliably dry at night to start bed-wetting. Consult your physician.

Treatment: Your physician will probably ask you to provide a specimen of your child's urine for analysis and culture (see *Collecting a midstream specimen,* p.103). If the tests reveal an infection, your child will probably be prescribed a course of *antibiotics.* You will probably be advised to ensure that your child has plenty of fluids during this treatment. If no infection is found, your physician will help you look into any possible emotional cause for the bed-wetting.

NO ↓

Is your child under 5 years old? → **YES** → **Lack of bladder control at night** is common in children under 5, and is hardly ever a cause for concern. Even after this age, many children continue to wet their beds occasionally.

Self-help: The best way to help your child is to prevent yourself from showing anxiety. If you are still putting your child in diapers, continue to do so until they are often dry in the morning. If your child is out of diapers, but regularly wets the bed, try lifting your child onto the toilet seat before you go to bed at night. When accidents do occur, do not reprimand your child, but deal with the wet nightclothes and bedclothes without comment. Your child is probably as anxious as you to achieve night-time control, and will do so when ready.

NO ↓

Regular bed-wetting in an older child seldom has a physical cause. However, you should discuss the problem with your physician, who may be able to offer helpful advice.

Treatment: Most children are worried by their bed-wetting and need plenty of reassurance that they will soon learn to be dry at night. Try some of the suggestions for overcoming bed-wetting outlined in the box below.

THE DEVELOPMENT OF BLADDER AND BOWEL CONTROL

Control over passing urine and bowel movements depends on a child recognizing the sensation of a full bladder or rectum and then being able to hold onto or release the contents at will. Most children do not develop the capacity to do this until well into their second year. Most children learn reliable daytime control of bladder and bowel functions between the ages of 18 months and 3 years, although accidents, especially accidental urination, may occur from time to time. Control over urination at night usually develops between about 2½ and 3½ years of age, but regular bed-wetting is common up to age 5, and may happen occasionally until a child is older.

Age in years	Bladder control		Bowel control
	Night	Day	
1			
2			
3			
4			
5			

■ Time when reliable control is learned   □ Time when "accidents" are still likely

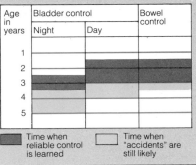
A child seat that fits inside the adult toilet seat and a step to help your child get up onto the toilet are useful aids when a child is graduating from potty-chair to adult toilet.

TOILET TRAINING

There is no single correct way of introducing your child to the use of the potty-chair or toilet. Much will depend on your child's level of development and personality, and on your family routine. The main thing for parents to remember is not to make the use of the toilet a cause for conflict or tension. Your child will master control of bladder and bowels when he or she is physiologically and mentally ready. Your job is simply to provide the conditions that will make the process of learning as relaxed and easy as possible.

The guide to toilet training below provides a basic structure. Use your own judgment to adapt it to your child's needs.

Gaining control by stages
1 Introductions
Buy a child's potty-chair when your child is about 18 months old. Explain what it is for, but don't expect your child to use it for some time. Allow your child to go without diapers during the day as often as possible so that he or she gets used to being without them. When your child has reached the stage of being able to control urination and bowel movements for several hours, you can start to suggest (but never insist) that he or she use the potty-chair occasionally. Once your child has started, move on to stage 2.

2 Becoming confident
Continue to encourage your child to use the potty-chair whenever he or she shows the need to urinate or defecate, but do not be upset when accidents occur. Conversely, do not be too effusive in your praise when your child succeeds in using the potty-chair properly. Gradually phase out the use of diapers until you are using them only at night.

3 Adult toilets and night-time control
Once your child is confident with the use of a potty-chair, you can introduce use of the toilet. Buy a special child seat that fits inside the toilet seat to make your child feel more secure. Explain that the toilet can be used in the same way as a potty-chair. Alternate use of the potty-chair and toilet seat until your child feels equally at ease with both.

During this time look out for signs that your child is ready to go through the night without a diaper. Dry diapers on several mornings is probably the best indicator. When you decide to start leaving diapers off at night, prepare yourself mentally for the inevitable occasional wet beds. If your child's bed does not have a waterproof mattress, use a plastic undersheet. This will help you to be less concerned when your child does wet the bed. Some children can be helped to be dry at night by being lifted onto the toilet a few hours after bedtime. However, if this disturbs your child so that getting back to sleep after-

ward is difficult, it may not be worth the trouble. Restricting fluids in the evening is not usually an effective way of preventing bed-wetting.

Bed-wetting in an older child
Many children continue to wet their beds occasionally throughout childhood. This is seldom a cause for medical concern but, if a child frequently wets the bed, it can be distressing for parents and child. You may be able to help in the following ways:

■ **Recording dry nights** Give your child a calendar and encourage him or her to record (for example, by using a stick-on star) any dry nights. You can try offering a reward after an agreed number of stars (for example, 5 dry nights in a row). Wet nights should be ignored. Increasing numbers of stars will build up your child's confidence and increase the incentive to master night time bladder control.

■ **Bed-wetting alarms** If record-keeping fails to help the problem, your physician may suggest the use of an alarm. This is a device fitted to a child's bed that causes an alarm to ring as soon as any urine is passed. This wakes the child so that he or she can get up to finish urinating in the potty-chair or toilet. This method has a high success rate.

45 Painful arm or leg

As soon as children start to walk, they become subject to frequent minor injuries as a result of falls, collisions and the straining of muscles. Pain in the arm or leg in childhood is usually the result of such injuries and is seldom serious enough to warrant medical attention.

Occasionally, however, an injury may result in a broken bone (or fracture) and this requires immediate medical treatment. Pain that occurs without obvious signs of injury should always be brought to your physician's attention if it lasts more than a day or so.

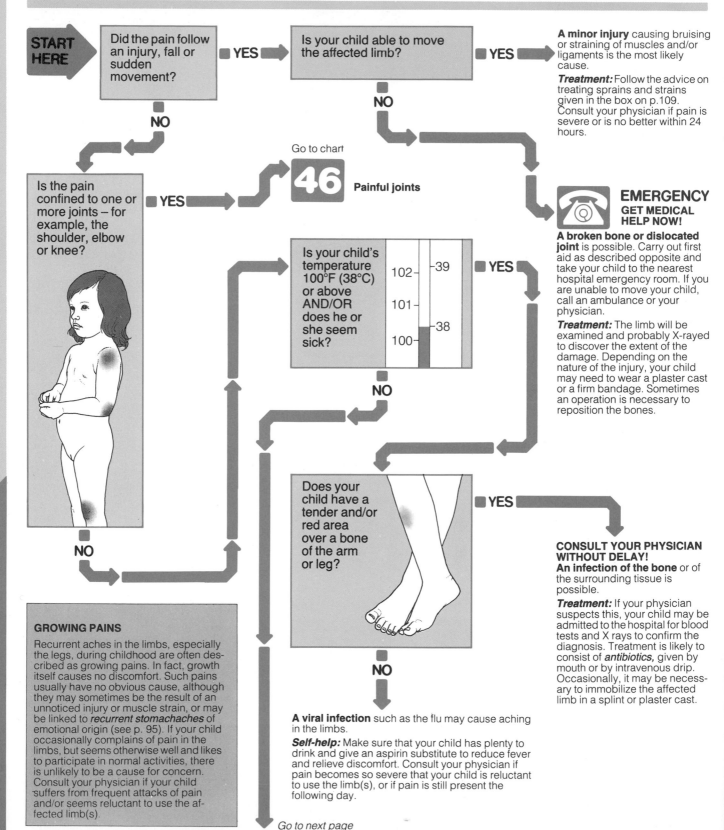

START HERE

Did the pain follow an injury, fall or sudden movement? — **YES** →

Is your child able to move the affected limb? — **YES** →

A minor injury causing bruising or straining of muscles and/or ligaments is the most likely cause.

Treatment: Follow the advice on treating sprains and strains given in the box on p.109. Consult your physician if pain is severe or is no better within 24 hours.

NO ↓ (from "Did the pain follow an injury...")

NO ↓ (from "Is your child able to move the affected limb?")

Go to chart **46** **Painful joints**

Is the pain confined to one or more joints – for example, the shoulder, elbow or knee? — **YES** → Go to chart 46

Is your child's temperature 100°F (38°C) or above AND/OR does he or she seem sick?

102 — 39
101 —
100 — 38

— **YES** →

EMERGENCY GET MEDICAL HELP NOW!

A broken bone or dislocated joint is possible. Carry out first aid as described opposite and take your child to the nearest hospital emergency room. If you are unable to move your child, call an ambulance or your physician.

Treatment: The limb will be examined and probably X-rayed to discover the extent of the damage. Depending on the nature of the injury, your child may need to wear a plaster cast or a firm bandage. Sometimes an operation is necessary to reposition the bones.

NO ↓ (temperature)

NO ↓ (is the pain confined to one or more joints)

Does your child have a tender and/or red area over a bone of the arm or leg? — **YES** →

CONSULT YOUR PHYSICIAN WITHOUT DELAY!
An infection of the bone or of the surrounding tissue is possible.

Treatment: If your physician suspects this, your child may be admitted to the hospital for blood tests and X rays to confirm the diagnosis. Treatment is likely to consist of *antibiotics,* given by mouth or by intravenous drip. Occasionally, it may be necessary to immobilize the affected limb in a splint or plaster cast.

NO ↓

A viral infection such as the flu may cause aching in the limbs.

Self-help: Make sure that your child has plenty to drink and give an aspirin substitute to reduce fever and relieve discomfort. Consult your physician if pain becomes so severe that your child is reluctant to use the limb(s), or if pain is still present the following day.

GROWING PAINS

Recurrent aches in the limbs, especially the legs, during childhood are often described as growing pains. In fact, growth itself causes no discomfort. Such pains usually have no obvious cause, although they may sometimes be the result of an unnoticed injury or muscle strain, or may be linked to *recurrent stomachaches* of emotional origin (see p. 95). If your child occasionally complains of pain in the limbs, but seems otherwise well and likes to participate in normal activities, there is unlikely to be a cause for concern. Consult your physician if your child suffers from frequent attacks of pain and/or seems reluctant to use the affected limb(s).

Go to next page

Continued from previous page

Has your child suffered from this type of pain on several occasions in the past?

YES

NO

Minor straining of the muscles or ligaments as a result of vigorous play is the most likely cause of pain in the arm or leg with no other symptoms. No special treatment is needed. Consult your physician if your child is reluctant to use the affected limb(s), if pain is present the following day, or if your child seems sick.

Recurrent limb pains are common in childhood and are generally no cause for concern (see *Growing pains,* opposite). Consult your physician if your child becomes reluctant to use the affected limb(s), if pain is still present the following day, or if your child seems sick.

FIRST AID FOR SUSPECTED BROKEN BONES AND DISLOCATED JOINTS

You may suspect that your child has broken a bone or dislocated a joint if he or she is unable to move the affected part, or if it looks misshapen.

General points
- If there is any bleeding from the wound, treat this first (see p.19).
- Do not try to manipulate the bone or joint back into position yourself; this should only be carried out by a physician.
- While waiting for medical help, keep the child warm and be as calm as possible.
- Give nothing to eat or drink; a general anesthetic may be needed to reset the bone.
- If medical help is readily available, get assistance and then move the child as little as possible.
- If medical help may be some time arriving, or if you have to move the child, immobilize the limb in the most comfortable position by use of bandages and splints as described below.
- As soon as you have carried out first aid, summon medical help; or if your child can be moved (as in the case of an arm injury), take him or her to the emergency room of the local hospital.

Splints
A splint is a support used to immobilize an injured part of the body (usually an arm or a leg) to reduce pain and the likelihood of further damage. Always secure a splint in at least 2 places not too close to the injury – preferably on either side of it. Use wide lengths of material or bandages (not rope or string), and be careful not to tie these too tightly (you should be able to insert one finger between the bandage and limb). In an emergency you can make an improvised splint with a broom handle or rolled-up newspaper (see below). A pillow taped around an injured arm also makes a very effective splint.

Improvising splints
A household object such as a rolled-up newspaper (left) can serve as a splint in an emergency. Make sure that you tie it securely in at least 2 places (below left) and make sure it is not too tight (below). You can provide additional support for an injured leg by securing it to the sound one with a well-padded splint in between (bottom).

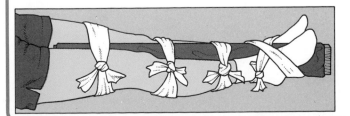

Arm injury
Gently place the injured arm in the bent position across the chest. Some padding should be placed between the arm and the chest (below left). Support the weight of the arm together with the padding in a sling along its length (below right). If the arm cannot be bent, use bandages to secure the arm to the side of the body. A splint (see below left) may provide increased support.

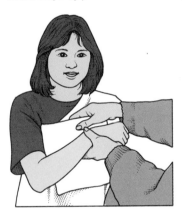

Shoulder, collarbone or elbow injury
Support the weight of the arm in a sling in the most comfortable position for the child.

Leg injury
Secure the injured leg to the sound one. If possible, place a well-padded splint (see left) between them.

Knee injury
Support the joint in the most comfortable position for the child. If the knee is bent, apply a bandage extending well above and below the knee to support it in the bent position (below). If the knee is unable to bend, support the leg along its length from underneath using a board (or something similar) as a splint. Place padding between the knee and the splint, and around the heel.

Bandaging a knee injury
When an injured knee is most comfortable in the bent position, bandage it firmly but not too tightly to provide support. Take care to extend the bandage well above and below the injured knee (below).

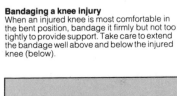

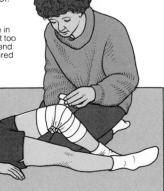

46 Painful joints

Pain in the joints – in particular, in those of the arm or leg – is almost always the result of injury or straining the muscles and ligaments surrounding a joint. Serious disorders causing pain in one or more joints are, fortunately, rare. However, such disorders need to be ruled out by your physician if pain is accompanied by generalized signs of being sick, or if your child suffers from persistent or recurrent pain.

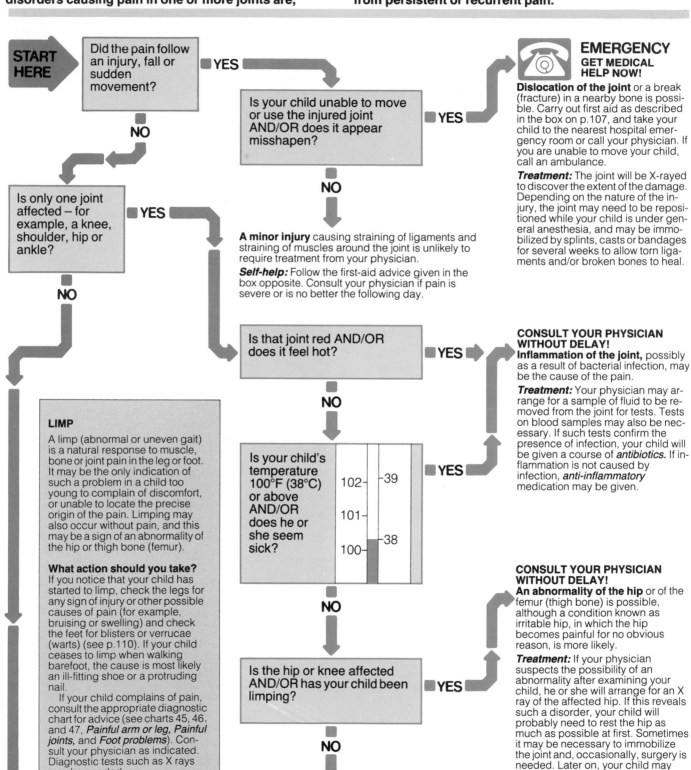

START HERE

Did the pain follow an injury, fall or sudden movement?

NO

Is only one joint affected – for example, a knee, shoulder, hip or ankle?

NO

YES

Is your child unable to move or use the injured joint AND/OR does it appear misshapen?

NO

A minor injury causing straining of ligaments and straining of muscles around the joint is unlikely to require treatment from your physician.

Self-help: Follow the first-aid advice given in the box opposite. Consult your physician if pain is severe or is no better the following day.

Is that joint red AND/OR does it feel hot?

NO

Is your child's temperature 100°F (38°C) or above AND/OR does he or she seem sick?

102– –39
101–
100– –38

NO

Is the hip or knee affected AND/OR has your child been limping?

NO

A minor sprain or strain as a result of an unnoticed injury or awkward movement is the most likely cause of joint pain in an otherwise well child.

Self-help: Encourage your child to rest the affected joint for a day or so. Consult your physician if pain persists or if your child becomes sick.

EMERGENCY
GET MEDICAL HELP NOW!
Dislocation of the joint or a break (fracture) in a nearby bone is possible. Carry out first aid as described in the box on p.107, and take your child to the nearest hospital emergency room or call your physician. If you are unable to move your child, call an ambulance.

Treatment: The joint will be X-rayed to discover the extent of the damage. Depending on the nature of the injury, the joint may need to be repositioned while your child is under general anesthesia, and may be immobilized by splints, casts or bandages for several weeks to allow torn ligaments and/or broken bones to heal.

CONSULT YOUR PHYSICIAN WITHOUT DELAY!
Inflammation of the joint, possibly as a result of bacterial infection, may be the cause of the pain.

Treatment: Your physician may arrange for a sample of fluid to be removed from the joint for tests. Tests on blood samples may also be necessary. If such tests confirm the presence of infection, your child will be given a course of **antibiotics.** If inflammation is not caused by infection, **anti-inflammatory** medication may be given.

CONSULT YOUR PHYSICIAN WITHOUT DELAY!
An abnormality of the hip or of the femur (thigh bone) is possible, although a condition known as irritable hip, in which the hip becomes painful for no obvious reason, is more likely.

Treatment: If your physician suspects the possibility of an abnormality after examining your child, he or she will arrange for an X ray of the affected hip. If this reveals such a disorder, your child will probably need to rest the hip as much as possible at first. Sometimes it may be necessary to immobilize the joint and, occasionally, surgery is needed. Later on, your child may need to do exercises to strengthen the muscles of the leg. If no cause of the pain is found, your physician will probably advise rest for about a week and avoidance of strenuous physical activity for one week more. This usually cures an irritable hip.

YES
YES
YES
YES
YES

LIMP
A limp (abnormal or uneven gait) is a natural response to muscle, bone or joint pain in the leg or foot. It may be the only indication of such a problem in a child too young to complain of discomfort, or unable to locate the precise origin of the pain. Limping may also occur without pain, and this may be a sign of an abnormality of the hip or thigh bone (femur).

What action should you take?
If you notice that your child has started to limp, check the legs for any sign of injury or other possible causes of pain (for example, bruising or swelling) and check the feet for blisters or verrucae (warts) (see p.110). If your child ceases to limp when walking barefoot, the cause is most likely an ill-fitting shoe or a protruding nail.
If your child complains of pain, consult the appropriate diagnostic chart for advice (see charts 45, 46, and 47, *Painful arm or leg, Painful joints,* and *Foot problems*). Consult your physician as indicated. Diagnostic tests such as X rays may be needed.

Go to next page

Continued from previous page

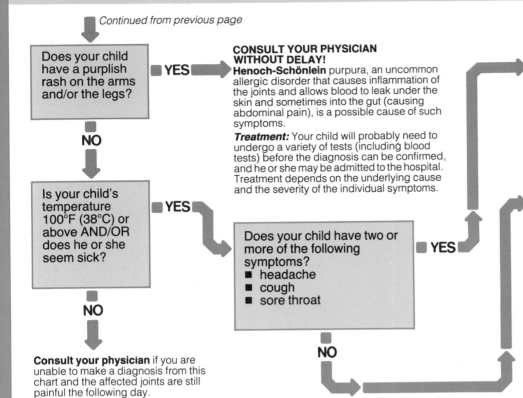

Does your child have a purplish rash on the arms and/or the legs?

YES →

NO ↓

Is your child's temperature 100°F (38°C) or above AND/OR does he or she seem sick?

YES →

NO ↓

Consult your physician if you are unable to make a diagnosis from this chart and the affected joints are still painful the following day.

CONSULT YOUR PHYSICIAN WITHOUT DELAY!
Henoch-Schönlein purpura, an uncommon allergic disorder that causes inflammation of the joints and allows blood to leak under the skin and sometimes into the gut (causing abdominal pain), is a possible cause of such symptoms.
Treatment: Your child will probably need to undergo a variety of tests (including blood tests) before the diagnosis can be confirmed, and he or she may be admitted to the hospital. Treatment depends on the underlying cause and the severity of the individual symptoms.

Does your child have two or more of the following symptoms?
- headache
- cough
- sore throat

YES →

NO ↓

A viral infection such as the flu is the most likely cause of such symptoms.
Self-help: Make sure that your child has plenty to drink and give an aspirin substitute to reduce fever and relieve discomfort. Consult your physician if the pain in the joints becomes so severe that your child is reluctant to use them, or if pain is still present the following day.

CONSULT YOUR PHYSICIAN WITHOUT DELAY!
Juvenile polyarthritis (inflammation of the joints of unknown cause) is a possible explanation for joint pain in a child who seems sick.

Treatment: To make a diagnosis, your physician may need to take samples of blood for analysis and may arrange for your child to have X rays. If the diagnosis is confirmed, your child will probably be given ***anti-inflammatory*** medication. Regular exercise of the affected joints under the guidance of an occupational or physical therapist is likely to be necessary, and your child may need to wear light splints at night for a few months.

FIRST AID FOR SPRAINS AND STRAINS

A joint is said to be sprained when it is wrenched or twisted beyond its normal range of movement – in a fall, for example – tearing some or all of the ligaments that support it. Ankles are especially prone to this type of injury. The main symptoms, which may be indistinguishable from those of a minor strain, are pain, swelling and bruising. If your child is unable to move or put weight on the injured part, if it looks misshapen, or if pain affects parts of the limb other than the joints, a broken bone or dislocated joint is possible and you should carry out first aid as described on p. 107. In other cases, try the following first-aid treatment:

1 For the first 24 hours after the injury, cool the injured part (below left).

2 Support an injured joint or limb with a firm, but not tight, bandage (below right). An arm or wrist may be more comfortable in a sling.

3 Encourage your child to rest the injured part for a day or so. If it is a foot, leg or ankle that is injured, keep it raised whenever possible.

When to call your physician
If your child has a badly sprained ankle that is still painful the day after the injury, go to your physician, local hospital emergency room or urgent care center to have the joint firmly bandaged to prevent movement while the injury is healing. In this case, make sure that your child rests the joint for at least a week.

Cooling an injury
Applying cold to any injury that has caused pain, swelling and/or bruising will help reduce swelling and relieve pain. This is best done by use of an ice bag or a cloth bag filled with ice, but you can improvise using a cloth pad soaked in cold water or an unopened packet of frozen vegetables. After the first 24 hours, you should apply warmth to the affected part to speed healing.

Bruises
Bruising occurs when damage to a blood vessel near the surface of the skin causes blood to leak into the surrounding tissues. This produces the characteristic purplish-blue color of a bruise. Small bruises need no special treatment, but you can reduce the pain and severity of a large bruise by applying cold to the area immediately after the injury (see above).

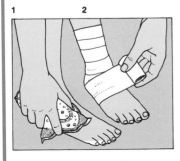

1 2

BACK PROBLEMS IN CHILDHOOD

In children, problems affecting the back are almost always related to injury resulting from awkward movements in sport or play, or from falls or unusual strain. Such injuries may cause pulled muscles, strained ligaments and bruising, leading to pain and stiffness. These symptoms usually disappear within a day or so without special treatment.

Serious back injuries
If your child suffers a major injury to the back – for example, a fall from a great height – **seek emergency help.** Do not attempt to move the child unless he or she is unconscious (see p. 21) – this could lead to further damage. In addition, if your child suffers from any of the following symptoms in the days following an apparently minor back injury, call your physician at once:

- Difficulty moving any limb
- Loss of bladder or bowel control
- Numbness or tingling in any limb

Persistent back pain
If your child has persistent back pain or stiffness for more than a day or two, whether or not he or she has suffered an injury, consult your physician.

Curvature of the spine
Some children are born with a sideways curvature of the spine (scoliosis) and this is usually noticed and treated in the first few years of life. However, some normal children develop such a curvature later on in childhood. This is particularly likely to occur in adolescence and affects girls more frequently than boys. It is important that curvature of the spine be assessed as soon as possible so that, if necessary, treatment by exercises, use of braces on the spine and/or surgery can be undertaken to correct the problem. If you notice that your child's spine has started to curve sideways, see your physician. Your physician will check the spine and, if necessary, send your child to a specialist for further assessment.

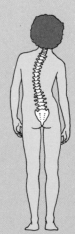

47 Foot problems

It is not unusual for a baby to be born with a foot or ankle that has been bent as a result of pressure within the uterus. The foot can be pressed gently into position and will correct itself over the following weeks. More serious malformations, such as club foot, will be noted by the physician at the first complete examination after birth and, if necessary, treatment will then be arranged. Consult this chart if your child develops any problem affecting one or both feet. Such problems may include pain, swelling, infection, injury, irritation or unusual appearance of the feet, such as flat feet or bent toes. Your physician will be able to offer advice.

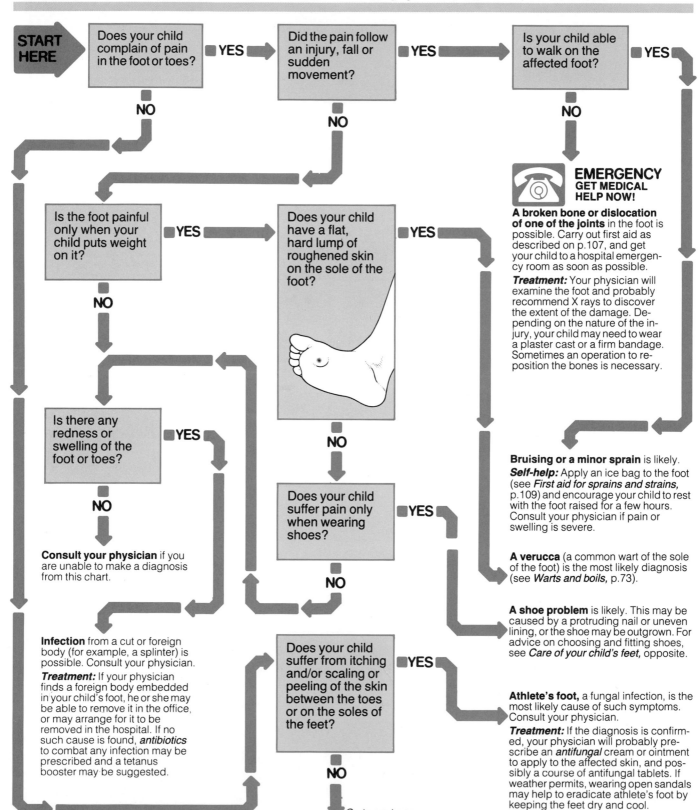

START HERE

Does your child complain of pain in the foot or toes? **YES** → Did the pain follow an injury, fall or sudden movement? **YES** → Is your child able to walk on the affected foot? **YES** →

NO ↓ **NO** ↓ **NO** ↓

EMERGENCY GET MEDICAL HELP NOW!

A broken bone or dislocation of one of the joints in the foot is possible. Carry out first aid as described on p.107, and get your child to a hospital emergency room as soon as possible.

Treatment: Your physician will examine the foot and probably recommend X rays to discover the extent of the damage. Depending on the nature of the injury, your child may need to wear a plaster cast or a firm bandage. Sometimes an operation to reposition the bones is necessary.

Is the foot painful only when your child puts weight on it? **YES** → Does your child have a flat, hard lump of roughened skin on the sole of the foot? **YES** →

NO ↓

NO ↓

Is there any redness or swelling of the foot or toes? **YES** →

NO ↓

Bruising or a minor sprain is likely.
Self-help: Apply an ice bag to the foot (see *First aid for sprains and strains,* p.109) and encourage your child to rest with the foot raised for a few hours. Consult your physician if pain or swelling is severe.

Does your child suffer pain only when wearing shoes? **YES** →

NO ↓

A verucca (a common wart of the sole of the foot) is the most likely diagnosis (see *Warts and boils,* p.73).

Consult your physician if you are unable to make a diagnosis from this chart.

A shoe problem is likely. This may be caused by a protruding nail or uneven lining, or the shoe may be outgrown. For advice on choosing and fitting shoes, see *Care of your child's feet,* opposite.

Infection from a cut or foreign body (for example, a splinter) is possible. Consult your physician.
Treatment: If your physician finds a foreign body embedded in your child's foot, he or she may be able to remove it in the office, or may arrange for it to be removed in the hospital. If no such cause is found, *antibiotics* to combat any infection may be prescribed and a tetanus booster may be suggested.

Does your child suffer from itching and/or scaling or peeling of the skin between the toes or on the soles of the feet? **YES** →

Athlete's foot, a fungal infection, is the most likely cause of such symptoms. Consult your physician.
Treatment: If the diagnosis is confirmed, your physician will probably prescribe an *antifungal* cream or ointment to apply to the affected skin, and possibly a course of antifungal tablets. If weather permits, wearing open sandals may help to eradicate athlete's foot by keeping the feet dry and cool.

NO ↓

Go to next page

Continued from previous page

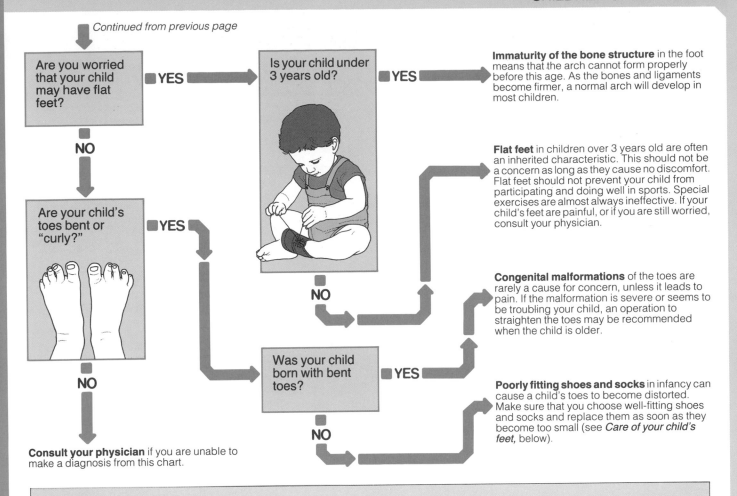

Are you worried that your child may have flat feet? → **YES** →	**Is your child under 3 years old?** → **YES** →	**Immaturity of the bone structure** in the foot means that the arch cannot form properly before this age. As the bones and ligaments become firmer, a normal arch will develop in most children.

NO ↓

NO ↓

Flat feet in children over 3 years old are often an inherited characteristic. This should not be a concern as long as they cause no discomfort. Flat feet should not prevent your child from participating and doing well in sports. Special exercises are almost always ineffective. If your child's feet are painful, or if you are still worried, consult your physician.

Are your child's toes bent or "curly?" → **YES** →

NO ↓

Was your child born with bent toes? → **YES** →

NO ↓

Congenital malformations of the toes are rarely a cause for concern, unless it leads to pain. If the malformation is severe or seems to be troubling your child, an operation to straighten the toes may be recommended when the child is older.

Poorly fitting shoes and socks in infancy can cause a child's toes to become distorted. Make sure that you choose well-fitting shoes and socks and replace them as soon as they become too small (see *Care of your child's feet,* below).

Consult your physician if you are unable to make a diagnosis from this chart.

CARE OF YOUR CHILD'S FEET

The bones in the foot are not fully formed until about 18 years of age (see right). Throughout childhood, and especially in the first 5 years of life, the bones and joints are soft and easily distorted by pressure from ill-fitting shoes and socks.

Baby feet
Young babies who are not yet walking should be left barefoot for as long as possible. If you need to cover your baby's feet to keep them warm, put on socks, soft bootees, or all-in-one suits that allow plenty of room for the toes to wriggle and stretch. Discard these as soon as the feet fill them.

When your child starts to walk, delay buying shoes until your child is steady on his or her feet and needs shoes for protection when walking outside. Allow your child to walk barefoot inside the house whenever possible.

Choosing and fitting your child's shoes
Well-fitting shoes in childhood are essential for healthy feet and toes in adult life. The main points to remember when choosing shoes for your child are listed below.

- Have your child's feet measured at regular intervals throughout childhood, at least every 3 months. More frequent measuring may be necessary at times of rapid growth.
- Where possible, go to a shop where the salespeople are trained to fit children's shoes.
- Choose shoes that are available in a variety of width fittings and that have adjustable fastenings over the instep.
- When you buy new shoes, make sure that there is about ¾ in. (2 cm) between the longest toe and the end of the shoe.
- Choose a style that has a straight inside edge and allows adequate room across the toes. Fashion shoes, especially those with raised heels, should be kept for special occasions only.
- If you can afford them, leather shoes are best but, even though they are expensive, do not be tempted to delay replacing them when they are outgrown. It is better to buy cheaper shoes that you can afford to replace more often.

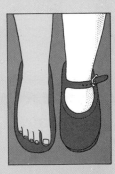

1 year

5 years

18 years

- Remember that tight socks may also damage young feet, and you should take care to replace socks when they become too small.
- Shoes that are painful as soon as your child puts them on or after an hour or so are probably a poor fit and are likely to be damaging your child's feet.

Fitting shoes
A salesperson will accurately measure the length and width (top left) of your child's foot and check that the shoes fit well, with about ¾ in. (2 cm), or a finger's width, to spare between the toes and the end of the shoes-(top and bottom right).

Everyday care
When you wash your child's feet, be careful to dry them thoroughly, especially between the toes to reduce the likelihood of infections such as athlete's foot. Trim the toenails regularly (see *Nail care,* p.71).

48 Genital problems in boys

Consult this chart if your son develops any pain or swelling within the scrotum (the supportive bag that encloses the testes) or in the penis. In all cases you should consult your physician. Severe pain in the genital area is a matter of urgency. Medical attention should be sought immediately.

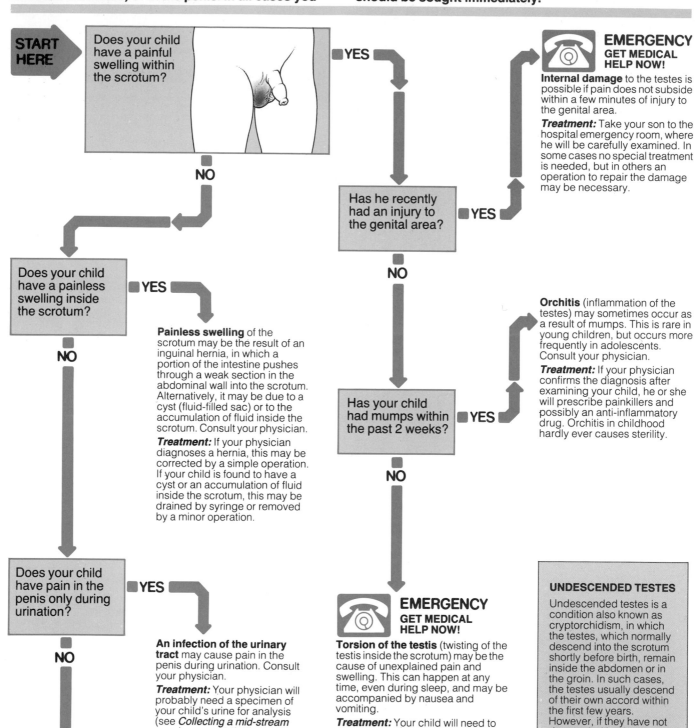

START HERE

Does your child have a painful swelling within the scrotum?

YES →

NO ↓

Does your child have a painless swelling inside the scrotum?

YES →

NO ↓

Painless swelling of the scrotum may be the result of an inguinal hernia, in which a portion of the intestine pushes through a weak section in the abdominal wall into the scrotum. Alternatively, it may be due to a cyst (fluid-filled sac) or to the accumulation of fluid inside the scrotum. Consult your physician.

Treatment: If your physician diagnoses a hernia, this may be corrected by a simple operation. If your child is found to have a cyst or an accumulation of fluid inside the scrotum, this may be drained by syringe or removed by a minor operation.

Does your child have pain in the penis only during urination?

YES →

NO ↓

An infection of the urinary tract may cause pain in the penis during urination. Consult your physician.

Treatment: Your physician will probably need a specimen of your child's urine for analysis (see *Collecting a mid-stream specimen,* p. 103). If your child is found to have a urinary tract infection, he may be prescribed a course of *antibiotics*. You will probably be advised to ensure that your child drinks plenty of fluids during this treatment.

Go to next page

Has he recently had an injury to the genital area?

YES →

NO ↓

Has your child had mumps within the past 2 weeks?

YES →

NO ↓

EMERGENCY GET MEDICAL HELP NOW!

Torsion of the testis (twisting of the testis inside the scrotum) may be the cause of unexplained pain and swelling. This can happen at any time, even during sleep, and may be accompanied by nausea and vomiting.

Treatment: Your child will need to be examined. If the diagnosis is confirmed, a physician may try to untwist the testis by gently manipulating it. If this is not successful, surgery may be necessary. The results of such surgery are better the sooner the twist is corrected.

EMERGENCY GET MEDICAL HELP NOW!

Internal damage to the testes is possible if pain does not subside within a few minutes of injury to the genital area.

Treatment: Take your son to the hospital emergency room, where he will be carefully examined. In some cases no special treatment is needed, but in others an operation to repair the damage may be necessary.

Orchitis (inflammation of the testes) may sometimes occur as a result of mumps. This is rare in young children, but occurs more frequently in adolescents. Consult your physician.

Treatment: If your physician confirms the diagnosis after examining your child, he or she will prescribe painkillers and possibly an anti-inflammatory drug. Orchitis in childhood hardly ever causes sterility.

UNDESCENDED TESTES

Undescended testes is a condition also known as cryptorchidism, in which the testes, which normally descend into the scrotum shortly before birth, remain inside the abdomen or in the groin. In such cases, the testes usually descend of their own accord within the first few years. However, if they have not descended by the time a boy is 1 to 2 years old, an operation to lower the testes into the scrotum may be necessary. Your child's future fertility and sex life should not be affected.

*Continued from
previous page*

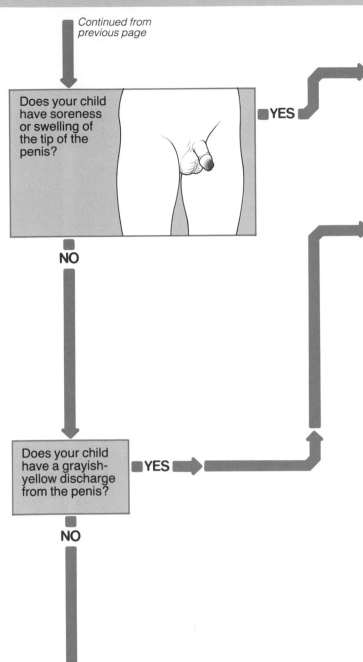

Does your child
have soreness
or swelling of
the tip of the
penis?

YES

Balanitis (inflammation of the tip of the penis) may be caused by
irritation from friction with damp underclothing or overzealous or
inadequate washing. Consult your physician.

Treatment: If balanitis is diagnosed, your physician will probably
prescribe a soothing cream to apply to the penis, and may advise
you to add a mild antiseptic to your child's bath water. While the skin
is inflamed, your son should avoid using soap to wash the penis.

NO

A foreign body in the urethra (see the box below left) is a common
cause of discharge in a young child. Consult your physician.

Does your child
have a grayish-
yellow discharge
from the penis?

YES

NO

Consult your physician if you are unable to make a diagnosis from this
chart.

OVERTIGHT FORESKIN

The foreskin (the fold of skin that covers the tip of the penis)
cannot normally be drawn back during the first few years of life,
and you should not try to draw it back when washing your baby.
Usually the foreskin becomes looser and more easily retracted
as the child grows older. However, in a small proportion of cases,
the foreskin remains tight and may cause pain, particularly
during an erection. This condition is known as phimosis and is
normally treated by *circumcision* (below).

CIRCUMCISION

This is a surgical operation to remove the foreskin – the fold of
skin that covers the tip of the penis. Occasionally, the operation
is carried out for medical reasons – for example, if the foreskin is
overtight (see above). However, most circumcisions in infancy
are performed for social and religious reasons.

Circumcision does not necessarily improve hygiene; adequate
cleanliness can be maintained by ensuring that, once your son is
old enough, he is taught to wash all secretions from beneath the
foreskin. Like any operation, circumcision carries a small risk
and, for this reason, most physicians now advise against the
operation unless it is medically necessary or desired for religious
reasons.

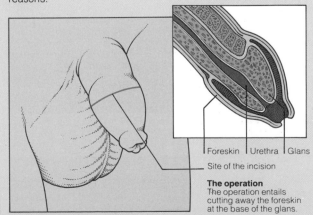

Foreskin Urethra Glans

Site of the incision

The operation
The operation entails
cutting away the foreskin
at the base of the glans.

FOREIGN BODY IN THE URETHRA

Occasionally, a curious young child may push a small object into the
urethral opening. If this is not promptly expelled during urination, it
may lead to infection, which produces a grayish-yellow discharge
from the penis. If you notice that your child has such a discharge,
consult your physician. If there is a foreign body in the urethra, it may
need to be removed by a minor operation under local anesthetic.
Some children may require general anesthesia.

49 Genital problems in girls

The most common genital problem in young girls is itching and inflammation of the vulva – the external genital area. This may be caused by infection or by irritation from soaps or other substances, and may lead to pain during urination. You may also be worried because your child has an unusual vaginal discharge. Consult this diagnostic chart if you or your daughter notice any such problems.

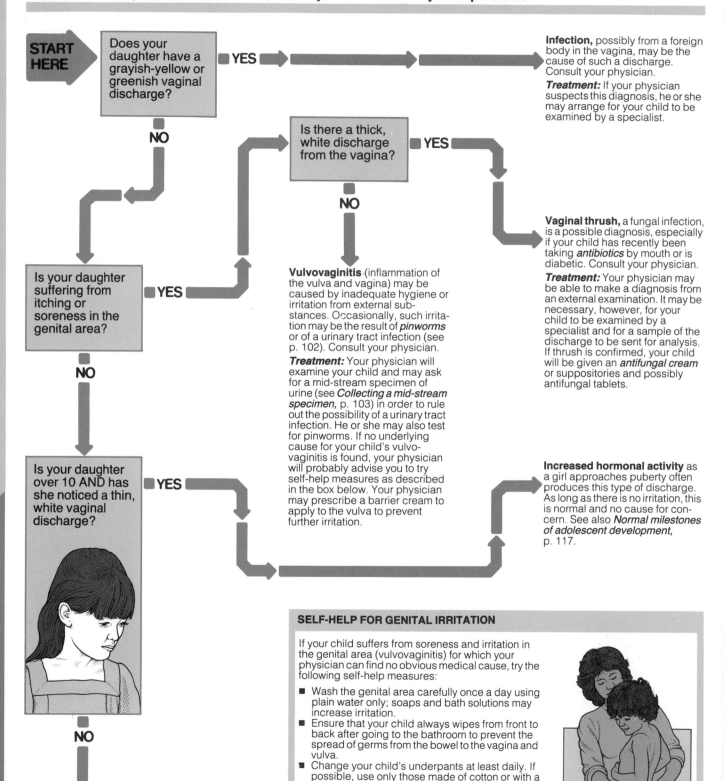

START HERE

Does your daughter have a grayish-yellow or greenish vaginal discharge?

YES → **Infection,** possibly from a foreign body in the vagina, may be the cause of such a discharge. Consult your physician.
Treatment: If your physician suspects this diagnosis, he or she may arrange for your child to be examined by a specialist.

NO ↓

Is there a thick, white discharge from the vagina?

YES → **Vaginal thrush,** a fungal infection, is a possible diagnosis, especially if your child has recently been taking *antibiotics* by mouth or is diabetic. Consult your physician.
Treatment: Your physician may be able to make a diagnosis from an external examination. It may be necessary, however, for your child to be examined by a specialist and for a sample of the discharge to be sent for analysis. If thrush is confirmed, your child will be given an *antifungal cream* or suppositories and possibly antifungal tablets.

NO ↓

Is your daughter suffering from itching or soreness in the genital area?

YES → **Vulvovaginitis** (inflammation of the vulva and vagina) may be caused by inadequate hygiene or irritation from external substances. Occasionally, such irritation may be the result of *pinworms* or of a urinary tract infection (see p. 102). Consult your physician.
Treatment: Your physician will examine your child and may ask for a mid-stream specimen of urine (see *Collecting a mid-stream specimen*, p. 103) in order to rule out the possibility of a urinary tract infection. He or she may also test for pinworms. If no underlying cause for your child's vulvovaginitis is found, your physician will probably advise you to try self-help measures as described in the box below. Your physician may prescribe a barrier cream to apply to the vulva to prevent further irritation.

NO ↓

Is your daughter over 10 AND has she noticed a thin, white vaginal discharge?

YES → **Increased hormonal activity** as a girl approaches puberty often produces this type of discharge. As long as there is no irritation, this is normal and no cause for concern. See also *Normal milestones of adolescent development,* p. 117.

NO ↓

Consult your physician if you are unable to make a diagnosis from this chart.

SELF-HELP FOR GENITAL IRRITATION

If your child suffers from soreness and irritation in the genital area (vulvovaginitis) for which your physician can find no obvious medical cause, try the following self-help measures:

- Wash the genital area carefully once a day using plain water only; soaps and bath solutions may increase irritation.
- Ensure that your child always wipes from front to back after going to the bathroom to prevent the spread of germs from the bowel to the vagina and vulva.
- Change your child's underpants at least daily. If possible, use only those made of cotton or with a cotton lining. Be especially careful to rinse all traces of detergent from your child's underpants when you wash them.

3 Adolescents

50 Delayed puberty

Puberty is the stage of development during which a child starts to undergo the physical changes that mark his or her transition into adulthood. Both sexes show a marked increase in height and weight and the apocrine sweat glands become active. In girls, physical changes include the development of breasts and pubic and underarm hair, as well as the onset of menstruation (monthly periods). Boys start to develop facial and other body hair, the voice deepens, the Adam's apple becomes apparent and the genitals become larger. The age at which a child reaches puberty is primarily a matter of inheritance. A girl whose mother started her periods late is also likely to be a late developer. A boy who has been taller than average throughout childhood is likely to reach puberty sooner than shorter, lighter boys. In the overwhelming majority of cases, later-than-average onset of puberty is no cause for medical concern. Occasionally, however, delay in sexual development may be linked to an underlying condition that may influence hormone secretion. Consult this diagnostic chart if you are worried because your child seems abnormally late in reaching puberty.

GIRLS

START HERE

Has your daughter had her first period? → YES

The start of menstruation is a clear sign that the hormonal activity that governs sexual development is operating normally. It is extremely unlikely that there is any cause for medical concern, even if, for example, your daughter's breasts seem small or growth of pubic hair seems sparse. It is also common for periods to be irregular at first and they may cease for several months at a time. This is no cause for concern unless your child shows other signs of ill health.

NO ↓

Has your daughter shown either of the following signs of puberty?
■ appearance of pubic hair
■ breast and/or nipple enlargement
→ YES

Such early signs of hormonal activity usually precede the first period and are usually a sign that a girl is developing normally. Consult your physician only if your daughter has not had a period by the time she is 14.

NO ↓

Is your daughter less than 14 years old? → YES

Later-than-average development is generally no cause for concern in this age range. Many girls do not show marked signs of sexual development until their early teens. Consult your physician if your daughter has not had her first period by the time she is 14, or if she is growing more slowly than expected according to the charts on pp. 124–125.

NO ↓

Delay in the onset of puberty is usually the result of a normal, inherited characteristic. However, it may also be caused by poor general health, certain forms of drug treatment and, in rare cases, hormonal or chromosomal (genetic) abnormalities. Consult your physician.

Treatment: Your physician will examine your daughter and may carry out an internal (vaginal) examination. He or she may also take a blood sample to assess the level of hormones and chromosomal characteristics. In most cases, your physician will be able to reassure you that all is well. Occasionally, it may be necessary to refer the child to a specialist for diagnosis and treatment with hormones.

BOYS

START HERE

Is your son under 12 years old? → YES

Few of the changes of puberty are obvious at this age in the majority of boys, and there is certainly no cause for concern if your boy is still childlike at this age. He may seem to be lagging behind in development if any of his male friends are unusually early developers, or in comparison with girls of the same age, who reach puberty sooner than boys.

NO ↓

Has your son shown either of the following physical signs of the onset of puberty?
■ enlargement of the genitals
■ growth of pubic and/or other body hair
→ YES

The appearance of either one of these signs of an increase in hormonal activity is a sure indication that your child has entered puberty, even if other changes are not yet obvious. The different milestones do not always occur in the precise order described in the table opposite, and any variation has no effect on an adolescent's long-term development.

NO ↓

Is your son under 14 years old? → YES

Late development within a broad age range is seldom any cause for concern. It is likely that late onset of puberty is a family characteristic and/or that your child was smaller than average throughout childhood. Less common causes of late development include prolonged periods of illness in childhood and certain forms of drug treatment. Consult your physician only if your son shows no signs of puberty by the time he is 14 or if he is growing abnormally slowly according to the charts on pp. 124–125.

NO ↓

Delay in the onset of puberty after the age of 14 is unusual and may be the result of underlying hormone deficiency or chromosomal (genetic) abnormality. Consult your physician.

Treatment: Your physician will examine your son and may arrange for blood tests so that hormone levels can be measured and chromosomal characteristics checked. If such tests reveal that your son is deficient in any hormone, supplements of that hormone will be prescribed. Such treatment ensures that puberty progresses normally.

NORMAL MILESTONES OF ADOLESCENT DEVELOPMENT

GIRLS

Aspect of development	Age at which change usually begins	Age at which rapid change usually ceases	Description of the changes	
Increase in height and weight	10–11	14–15	In childhood, growth continues at an average rate of 2 in. (5 cm) a year. One of the earliest signs of puberty is an increase in this rate up to a maximum of about 3 in. (8 cm) a year. The growth spurt may last for up to 4 years, but is most rapid in the first two years (see the growth charts on pp.124–125). There is a parallel increase in weight; the pelvis broadens and fat is deposited around the hips and thighs.	
Breast development	10–12	13–15	The first stage of breast development is usually the enlargement of the nipple and areola (the colored area surrounding the nipple). This is known as "budding." A year or so later the breasts themselves start to enlarge and the nipples and areola darken. Breast development normally ceases by the age of 15.	
Growth of pubic and underarm hair	pubic 10–11 underarm 12–13	pubic 14–15 underarm 15–16	Pubic hair normally first starts to appear as a light down around the external genital area. The hair gradually darkens and coarsens over the next 2 to 3 years and spreads to cover the pubic mound. Underarm hair appears 1 to 2 years after the emergence of pubic hair. The precise extent, color and thickness of body hair growth depends on inheritance and racial type.	
Development of apocrine sweat glands	12–13	15–16	Apocrine sweat glands produce a different type of sweat from that produced by the eccrine glands that are active all over the body from babyhood. Apocrine glands become active under the arms, in the groin and around the nipples during adolescence and produce a type of sweat that may lead to body odor if not regularly washed away.	
Onset of menstruation	First period (menarche) 11–14	Establishment of regular cycle 15–16	In the United States the average age for the occurrence of the menarche (first period) is 12 or 13. However, for some girls it is normal to start menstruating as early as 10 or as late as 17. It usually happens about 2 years after the start of the growth spurt and is unlikely to occur until a girl weighs at least 99 lb (45 kg). A girl may notice a thick, white, vaginal discharge in the year preceding the menarche. In the first few years following the menarche, periods are likely to be irregular and may cease altogether for several months.	

BOYS

Aspect of development	Age at which change usually begins	Age at which rapid change usually ceases	Description of the changes	
Increase in height and weight	12 – 13	17 – 18	In childhood, growth continues at an average rate of 2 in. (5 cm) a year. One of the earliest signs of puberty is an increase in this rate up to a maximum of about 3 in. (8 cm) a year. The growth spurt may last for up to 4 years, but is most rapid in the first two years (see the growth charts on pp.124–125). There is a parallel increase in weight; the pelvis broadens and fat is deposited around the hips and thighs.	
Genital development and ejaculation	11 – 13	15 – 17	Hormonal activity at the start of puberty stimulates the development of the male sex glands, the testes, leading to a noticeable increase in their size. The skin of the scrotum darkens and the penis lengthens and broadens. The ability to ejaculate seminal fluid usually develops within 2 years of such genital development.	
Growth of body and facial hair	11 – 15	15 – 19	The growth of hair in the genital (pubic) area normally starts first and is followed a year or so later by the growth of hair on the face, under the arms and, depending on inherited characteristics, in other areas of the body such as the legs, chest and abdomen.	
Development of apocrine sweat glands	13 – 15	17 – 18	Apocrine sweat glands produce a different type of sweat from that produced by the eccrine glands that are found all over the body from babyhood. Apocrine glands start to develop under the arms, in the groin and around the nipples during adolescence and produce a type of sweat that may lead to body odor if not regularly washed away.	
Deepening of the voice	13 – 15	16 – 17	The voice box (larynx) starts to enlarge and may develop into a noticeable "Adam's apple." The voice deepens ("breaks") within a year or so of such enlargement.	

EMOTIONAL DEVELOPMENT

The physical changes of puberty are accompanied by psychological changes that are also triggered by the secretion of sex hormones. In both boys and girls these hormones stimulate interest in sexuality. Rising levels of the male hormone testosterone are thought to play a part in the increased aggression and adventurousness typical of teenage boys. The increased output of hormones by the adrenal glands also influences behavior by increasing natural assertiveness, which helps to explain why teenagers have a tendency to be rebellious and argumentative.

Children whose physical development is delayed are also likely to be late maturers emotionally. This can sometimes cause social and psychological difficulties for the child, who must come to terms with being smaller, less physically developed and less assertive than most of his or her contemporaries.

51 Adolescent behavior problems

Adolescence, the transitional period between childhood and adulthood, is a time when difficult behavior and conflict with parents and other forms of authority are most likely to arise. The reasons for this may be partly physiological – the child is experiencing new and perhaps confusing feelings as a result of the hormonal activity that starts at puberty. However, there are also social and psychological factors present, including the need to develop both practical and emotional independence from the parents and to establish a separate identity. Few families with adolescent children escape arguments and misunderstandings – usually about dress, language or general conduct – but, providing that the parents are willing to allow sufficient flexibility while retaining a recognizable and affectionate family framework, family relationships are unlikely to suffer permanent damage. Most adolescent behavior problems can be successfully resolved within the family without the need for outside help. However, if you feel that any behavior problem is getting outside your control, to the extent that you fear that your adolescent may be endangering his or her health or risking conflict with the law, it is a good idea to discuss the problem with your physician. Although medical treatment is only rarely appropriate, your physician may put you in touch with relevant support services.

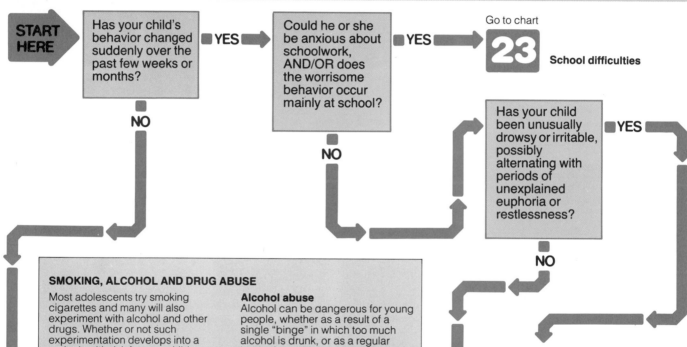

START HERE

Has your child's behavior changed suddenly over the past few weeks or months?

YES → Could he or she be anxious about schoolwork, AND/OR does the worrisome behavior occur mainly at school?

YES → Go to chart **23** School difficulties

NO

NO

Has your child been unusually drowsy or irritable, possibly alternating with periods of unexplained euphoria or restlessness?

YES

NO

SMOKING, ALCOHOL AND DRUG ABUSE

Most adolescents try smoking cigarettes and many will also experiment with alcohol and other drugs. Whether or not such experimentation develops into a major health risk for your child depends on a number of factors, including whether you smoke or drink regularly yourself, how prevalent the use of such substances is among your child's friends, and whether or not your child has an underlying emotional difficulty that may lead him or her to seek to escape through the use of drugs.

Cigarette smoking
Although smoking is unlikely to damage your child's health in the short term, it is one of the most serious risks to health in adult life. The habit is easily established in adolescence. It is therefore essential that parents make every effort to discourage smoking through their own example and by ensuring that their child is fully aware of the risks at an early age. Ominous warnings of lung cancer have little impact on teen behavior. Teens do respond, however, to the implication that smoking is a smelly, unattractive habit, which will lead to early wrinkles, bad breath and impaired athletic performance.

Alcohol abuse
Alcohol can be dangerous for young people, whether as a result of a single "binge" in which too much alcohol is drunk, or as a regular habit. If you drink, it is unreasonable to try to ban your teenager from drinking at all. However, you can ensure that he or she learns to drink sensibly by limiting alcoholic drinks to special occasions or small amounts at some mealtimes. Drinking to excess should always be clearly condemned.

Drug and solvent abuse
This is the problem that often causes parents the most worry. Arm yourself and your child with the facts about the dangers of drug-taking well before you think there may be any risk of your child being tempted to try any of these substances. Advice that is based on sound information is likely to be treated with greater respect than reactions based on instinctive fear of the problem. And an atmosphere in which a child feels free to talk about the subject may encourage your child to confide in you if he or she feels under pressure from friends to try drugs. Always consult your physician if you fear your child is taking drugs of any kind.

Drug abuse, drinking alcohol or inhaling solvents ("glue sniffing") are all possible explanations for this type of behavior, especially if your child always seems short of money and has any additional symptoms such as slurred speech, excessive sweating or abnormally large or small pupils.

Self-help: This is a worrisome problem that should always be tackled as soon as you suspect there may be any cause for concern. Talk to your child and try to find out whether or not your suspicions are correct. If your child admits to drinking or taking drugs of any kind, you will obviously try to convince him or her of the dangers of this type of behavior. If you are unable to do this because of difficulties in communication or because you do not feel sufficiently well-informed, consult your physician, who may be able to talk to your child more easily than you and will be able to offer sound advice. If your child denies drug-taking, it is also worthwhile seeking medical advice because this type of behavior may also indicate an underlying emotional problem (see also *Smoking, alcohol and drug abuse,* left).

1 *Go to next page column 1*

2 *Go to next page column 2*

1 Continued from previous page column 1

2 Continued from previous page column 2

Has your child seemed unusually low or "blue" for some time, eating little, sleeping badly and isolating himself or herself from family and friends?

YES →

NO ↓

Could your child have any cause for worry – for example, conflict between parents or other family members or difficulties in a relationship with a girlfriend or boyfriend?

YES →

NO ↓

Does your child's worrisome behavior concern his or her eating habits?

YES →

NO ↓

Are you concerned because your child seems to have few friends and spends much of his or her spare time alone?

YES →

NO ↓

Are you worried by hostility, rebelliousness and/or disregard for your feelings in your child?

YES →

NO ↓

Consult your physician if the problem that worries you is not covered in this chart.

Periods of depression are common during adolescence and normally pass within a week or so. But prolonged depression is not normal and may be rooted in some underlying anxiety or emotional difficulty. Consult your physician.

Treatment: If your physician feels there is any cause for concern after talking to your child, he or she may recommend that the child see a child psychiatrist. Further treatment will depend on the cause of the depression, but may include discussions involving the whole family and, in some cases, treatment with medication (see also *Child guidance,* p. 67).

Faddishness about food is common, particularly among adolescent girls who may either experiment with fad diets or eat excessively. This is unlikely to be a cause for concern unless your child has become either excessively thin or overweight (see *Food fads,* p. 96).

See also chart

53 **Adolescent weight problems**

Are your most frequent disagreements about clothes, personal appearance and/or language?

YES →

NO ↓

Rebelliousness is a normal part of an adolescent's development into an independent individual, and parents must learn to accept that they cannot expect the same level of obedience from an adolescent as they can from a younger child.

Self-help: Trying to enforce too many rules of behavior may only deepen and prolong any conflict, so try to limit the number of ground rules you insist on to those that are important for your child's own health and safety, for the well-being of the rest of the family or to conform to legal and socially acceptable behavior. Allow your child to make decisions and take responsibility for matters affecting his or her own life so as to reduce potential areas of conflict and encourage independence.

Anxiety about a specific problem can cause an adolescent to behave out-of-character. Unusual behavior may include aggressiveness, sullenness, rudeness or, at the other end of the spectrum, child-ishness or overdependence on the parents.

Self-help: As with most adolescent behavior problems, you should start by discussing the matter directly with your child. You may be able to discover the cause of the problem and at the same time allay any fears or take practical steps to resolve a problem yourself. However, if you are unable to help your child or if you have difficulty discovering the reason for your child's changed behavior, consult your physician, who will be able to offer specific advice.

Natural shyness or solitariness may be a normal part of your child's personality and this will not suddenly change during adolescence. However, if you suspect that there may be an underlying cause for your child's withdrawn behavior – for example, self-consciousness about a physical problem such as severe acne or being overweight – you should try to deal with it.

Self-help: If your child seems shy, try to ensure that he or she has plenty of opportunity to participate in activities that he or she enjoys, perhaps with the rest of the family or where your child has the chance to meet other young people who share similar interests. If your child has a skin or weight problem, consult chart 53, *Adolescent weight problems* or chart 52, *Adolescent skin problems.*

Looking and sounding like their contemporaries is important to most adolescents. It gives them a separate identity from their parents and the security of feeling that they belong to a group. Although extremes of dress or bad language can be distressing for parents, such behavior is rarely a cause for concern, providing that it does not lead, for example, to conflict in school. Every generation has its own hair and dress pattern; your adolescent is simply conforming to his or her friends' dress pattern. Accept this as a norm unless other behavioral problems, such as drug use, accompany the dress pattern.

Self-help: It is best to ignore such behavior if possible, only insisting that your child conform when it may cause offense to others. Most young people eventually learn to compromise between expressing themselves extremely in dress and language and the need in some circumstances to conform.

52 Adolescent skin problems

The onset of adolescence often produces marked changes in the skin. Infantile eczema, which often affects younger children, may clear up altogether during adolescence. But another form of eczema may occur for the first time as a result of contact with certain metals or cosmetics, causing an itchy red rash. In addition, certain skin problems caused by infection or infestation may become more common as a result of close contact with other teenagers. However, the most noticeable skin changes during adolescence are caused by rising levels of sex hormones that encourage the sebaceous glands in the skin to produce increasing amounts of sebum – an oily substance that helps to lubricate and protect the skin. Not only does increased sebaceous activity give the skin an oily appearance, but it encourages the development of acne, the principal skin condition affecting adolescents. There are several types of acne and the condition may occur with varying degrees of severity. Consult this diagnostic chart if you are uncertain what, if any, treatment to advise for your adolescent's acne or oily skin. For other skin problems, see chart 25, Spots and rashes.

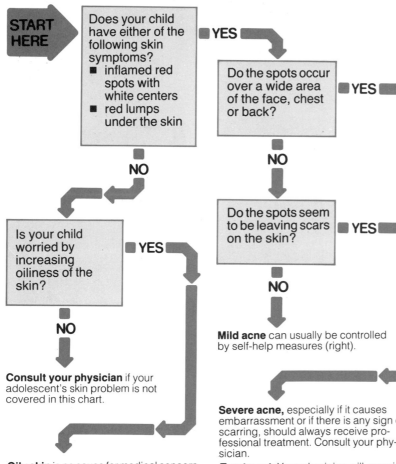

START HERE

Does your child have either of the following skin symptoms?
- inflamed red spots with white centers
- red lumps under the skin

YES

Do the spots occur over a wide area of the face, chest or back?

YES

NO

NO

Is your child worried by increasing oiliness of the skin?

YES

Do the spots seem to be leaving scars on the skin?

YES

NO

NO

Mild acne can usually be controlled by self-help measures (right).

Consult your physician if your adolescent's skin problem is not covered in this chart.

Severe acne, especially if it causes embarrassment or if there is any sign of scarring, should always receive professional treatment. Consult your physician.

Oily skin is no cause for medical concern if it does not lead to acne. However, it may be embarrassing for your child.
Self-help: Regular washing with mild soap and water is normally all that is needed to keep oily skin under control. An astringent "skin-freshening" lotion may also be helpful.

Treatment: Your physician will examine your child's skin and will probably recommend some of the self-help treatments described in the box at right. Depending on the severity with which your child is affected, your physician may refer your child to a skin specialist (dermatologist) and/or prescribe *antibiotics* or other forms of treatment.

ACNE

Acne is the name used to describe a group of related skin symptoms that mainly affects the face, chest and upper back. It is caused by blockage and infection of hair follicles in the skin and occurs principally during adolescence, when hormonal activity increases the production of sebum (natural skin oil), which makes the skin more susceptible to this disorder.

Symptoms
There are several main types of acne as follows:

Blackheads: See below left.

Pustules: Inflamed, raised spots that develop white centers. They are caused by bacterial activity in sebum that has collected in a hair follicle.

Cysts: Tender, inflamed lumps under the skin that are caused by scar tissue forming around an inflamed area under the skin. Cystic acne spots may leave permanent scars.

Self-help
Mild acne can usually be controlled using preparations that are available over-the-counter at your pharmacy.

Antibacterial skin-washing creams, lotions and soaps: These may help mild acne by reducing bacterial activity on the skin.

Sulfur or benzoyl peroxide preparations: These can help moderately severe acne, but should be used cautiously because they can make the skin sore.
Abrasives and keratolytics: These remove the top layer of skin, help to clear the blocked hair follicles that encourage acne and are good for getting rid of blackheads. However, these products should not be used too often or too vigorously. They may not be suitable if the skin is severely inflamed. In addition to these treatments, many people find that exposure to sunlight helps to reduce acne.

Professional treatment
When self-help measures are ineffective, or if acne is severe enough to cause embarrassment or scarring, your physician may prescribe one or more of the following treatments:
Keratolytics: These may be stronger than the over-the-counter preparations described but act in a similar way.
Antibiotics: These are given by mouth in low doses over an extended period. They help to counter bacterial activity in the skin and often produce a marked improvement in severe cases of acne.
Other drugs: Various drugs, including hormones and vitamin A derivatives, are sometimes prescribed for adults with severe acne, but your physician may be reluctant to prescribe them for those in their early teens.

BLACKHEADS

Blackheads (comedones) are tiny, black spots that principally occur around the nose and chin. They are caused by dead skin cells and sebum collecting in a hair follicle and becoming discolored by exposure to air. Blackheads may occur together with the more disfiguring forms of acne or on their own. If your adolescent is affected only by blackheads, treatment is unlikely to be necessary. However, if widespread blackheads are causing embarrassment, which is quite common for adolescents, they can be removed individually using a blackhead remover or by use of abrasives or keratolytic preparations (see *Acne,* right). Squeezing of blackheads by hand should be discouraged; this may lead to infection and abcess formation in the affected areas.

53 Adolescent weight problems

The rapid increase in height and the development of adult body proportions that occur in adolescence can lead a teenager to appear either too thin or too fat. Adolescence is also a time when young people are likely to be particularly sensitive about their appearance and worry unnecessarily about their figures. Girls are more likely than boys to be concerned about minor changes in weight. They are also much more likely to be affected by anorexia nervosa (see below), the most serious weight-related disorder of adolescence. However, although boys less commonly become seriously

underweight, they are often overweight. In such cases, helpful and sympathetic advice from parents is just as important as for girls. The best way to determine whether or not your child's changing body shape indicates unhealthy weight gain or loss is to check that both weight and height are increasing at a parallel rate as indicated in the weight charts on pp. 124-125. Minor deviations from the standard growth curves are unlikely to be a cause for concern, but consult this chart if your child is significantly over 7 lb (3 kg) heavier or lighter than expected for his or her age and height.

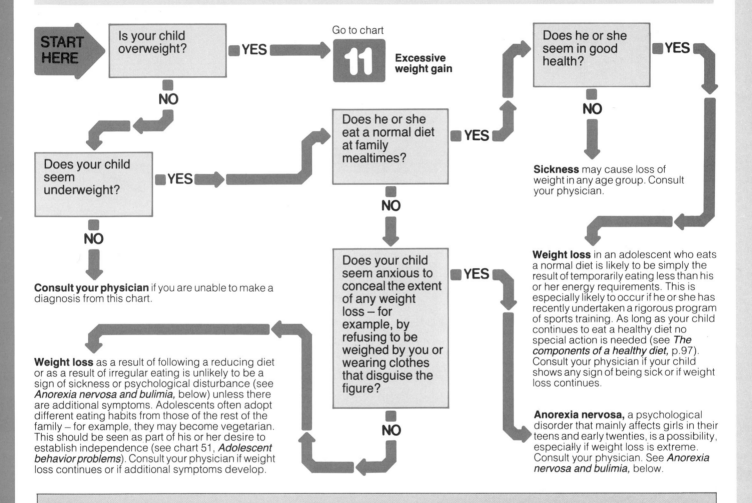

START HERE

Is your child overweight? **YES** → Go to chart **11** **Excessive weight gain**

NO

Does your child seem underweight? **YES**

NO

Consult your physician if you are unable to make a diagnosis from this chart.

Does he or she eat a normal diet at family mealtimes? **YES**

NO

Does he or she seem in good health? **YES**

NO

Sickness may cause loss of weight in any age group. Consult your physician.

Does your child seem anxious to conceal the extent of any weight loss – for example, by refusing to be weighed by you or wearing clothes that disguise the figure? **YES**

NO

Weight loss as a result of following a reducing diet or as a result of irregular eating is unlikely to be a sign of sickness or psychological disturbance (see *Anorexia nervosa and bulimia,* below) unless there are additional symptoms. Adolescents often adopt different eating habits from those of the rest of the family – for example, they may become vegetarian. This should be seen as part of his or her desire to establish independence (see chart 51, *Adolescent behavior problems*). Consult your physician if weight loss continues or if additional symptoms develop.

Weight loss in an adolescent who eats a normal diet is likely to be simply the result of temporarily eating less than his or her energy requirements. This is especially likely to occur if he or she has recently undertaken a rigorous program of sports training. As long as your child continues to eat a healthy diet no special action is needed (see *The components of a healthy diet,* p.97). Consult your physician if your child shows any sign of being sick or if weight loss continues.

Anorexia nervosa, a psychological disorder that mainly affects girls in their teens and early twenties, is a possibility, especially if weight loss is extreme. Consult your physician. See *Anorexia nervosa and bulimia,* below.

ANOREXIA NERVOSA AND BULIMIA

Anorexia nervosa is a psychological disturbance in which a person (most commonly a teenage girl or young woman) refuses food because of an irrational fear of putting on weight. An anorectic convinces herself that she is too fat and that she has not lost enough weight even though she has. Many girls go through a temporary phase of excessive dieting, but of these only a few develop anorexia nervosa. The bulimia purge syndrome is a variant of anorexia nervosa. In the case of bulimia, a person eats or overeats and then induces vomiting and/or diarrhea (with the use of laxatives).

The signs of anorexia

The illness usually starts with normal dieting, but an anorectic eats less and less each day and, even if her figure becomes skeletal, she still sees herself as plump and is terrified of putting on weight. She may be reluctant to undress or weigh herself in front of others in order to conceal her weight loss. To avoid family pressure to eat sensibly she may hide food and throw it away. Or she may make herself vomit after

meals. As weight loss progresses there may be hormonal disturbances that result in cessation of menstrual periods. She may also become depressed and withdrawn.

What action should you take?

If your adolescent has an unrealistic image of herself as being too fat and seems to be dieting excessively, although already very thin, you should discuss the matter with your physician. If, after examining your child, your physician thinks that she may be suffering from anorexia nervosa, he or she will probably arrange for treatment by a specialist in psychological disorders. In severe cases it may be necessary to admit your child to the hospital where food intake can be closely supervised.

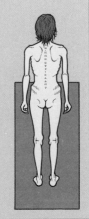

Growth charts

These growth charts and those on pp. 124-125 are based on the standard growth charts used by physicians in the United States. You can use these charts to keep your own record of your child's growth as measured by your pediatrician.

The growth charts on this and the facing page are for recording the progress of babies of both sexes up to the age of one year. The charts on pp. 124-125 are for boys and girls from 1 to 18 years.

Standard growth curves
On each chart you will find 3 solid lines already drawn. These lines are the standard growth curves for small, average and large children of "normal" development. The standard curves enable you to compare your child's progress with the expected growth of children of similar size at birth. Remember that there is a wide range of variation among children. Girls may mimic their mothers in growth patterns, and boys their

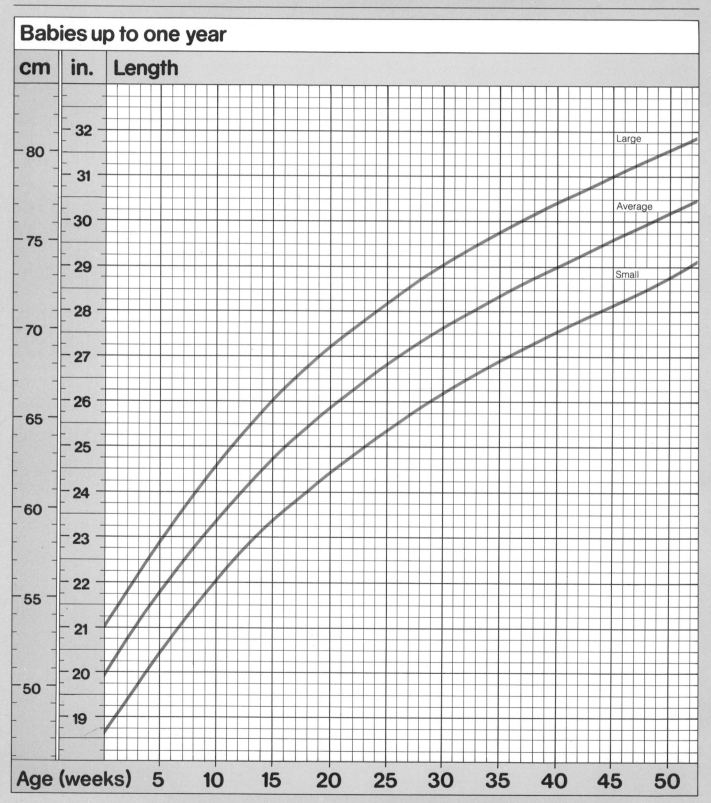

Babies up to one year

| cm | in. | Length |

Age (weeks) 5 10 15 20 25 30 35 40 45 50

fathers. If you have any concerns about your child's growth, discuss them with your pediatrician.

Recording your child's growth
When your pediatrician weighs and measures your child during his or her well-baby visits, mark the results on the appropriate chart. You may even want to take the charts, along with your immunization record, to the office with you. Use a ruler to help you read horizontally across from the scale on the left of the chart to the point where it meets the vertical line up from your child's age at the bottom of the chart. Mark the point where the two lines cross. By linking this mark with the previous result you will soon build a curve showing your child's growth.

Also consult diagnostic chart 1, *Slow weight gain;* chart 10, *Slow growth;* chart 11, *Excessive weight gain;* or chart 53, *Adolescent weight problems,* as appropriate.

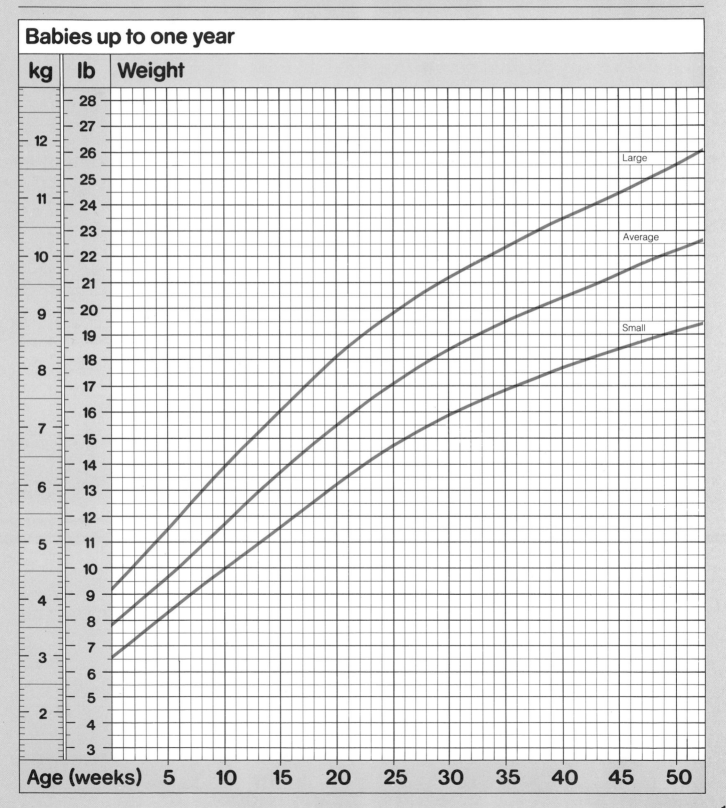

Babies up to one year

| kg | lb | Weight |

Age (weeks)   5   10   15   20   25   30   35   40   45   50

Growth charts

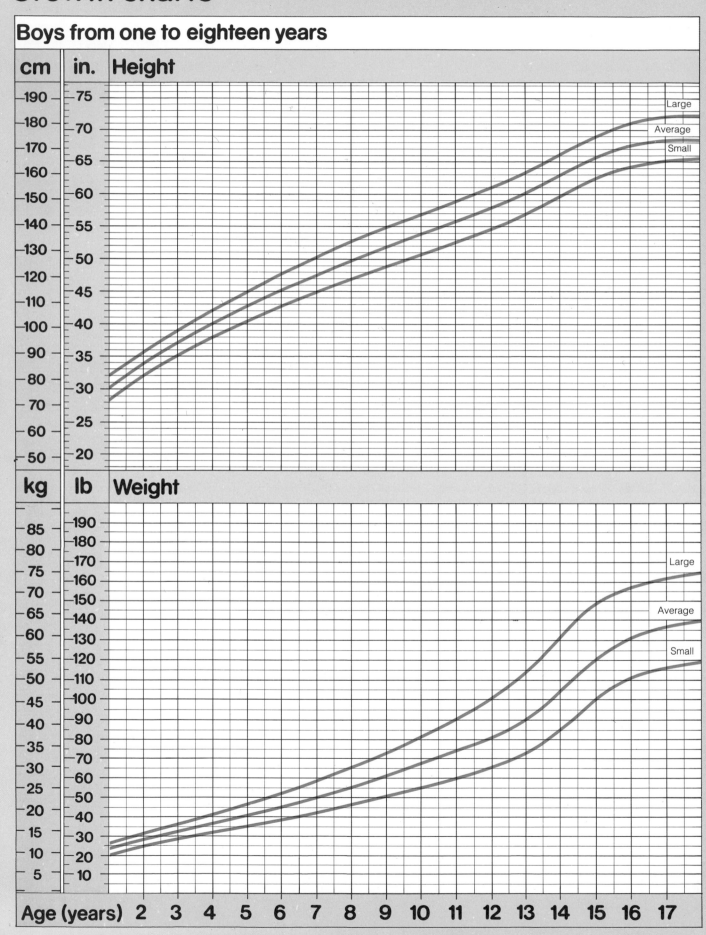

Boys from one to eighteen years

cm	in.	**Height**

Large
Average
Small

kg	lb	**Weight**

Large
Average
Small

Age (years) 2 3 4 5 6 7 8 9 10 11 12 13 14 15 16 17

Girls from one to eighteen years

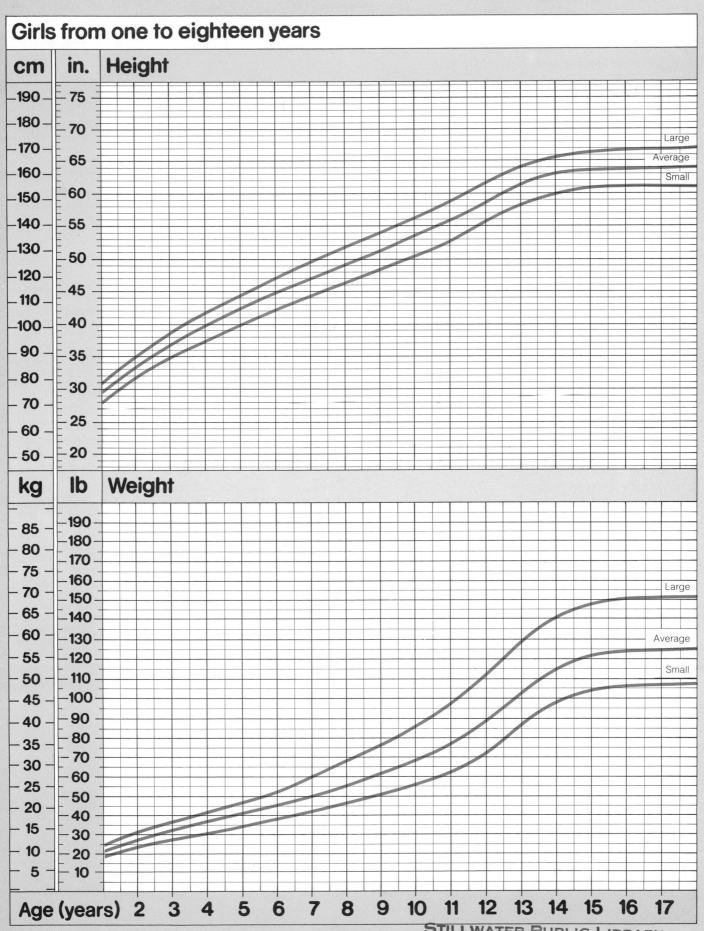

		Height
cm	in.	

Height curves labeled: Large, Average, Small

		Weight
kg	lb	

Weight curves labeled: Large, Average, Small

Age (years) 2 3 4 5 6 7 8 9 10 11 12 13 14 15 16 17

Index

Each of the symptom charts in this book is designed to help you discover the possible reason for your child's complaint. The book contains thousands of physiological references, and this index must of necessity be selective. For a full guide to the basic symptoms analyzed in the 53 charts and how to find the chart you need, see pp. 22-26. References within the following index are to page numbers of topics from the entire book, not just from the charts. Titles of information boxes within the charts and significant subtopics discussed in these boxes are italicized to emphasize their importance. Titles of the charts themselves and information contained within the introductory section preceding the charts are in **bold** typeface.

INDEX